LIFE'S THREE GREATEST QUESTIONS

LIFE'S THREE GREATEST QUESTIONS

DOES GOD EXIST?

IS CHRISTIANITY THE "TRUE" RELIGION?

IS THE CHURCH OF JESUS CHRIST OF LATTER-DAY SAINTS ["MORMON"] THE TRUE FORM OF CHRISTIANITY?

BY

THOMAS E. JOHNSON

BONNEVILLE BOOKS ™
Springville, Utah

This work is not officially endorsed or supported by The Church of Jesus Christ of Latter-day Saints, nor is it meant to add or detract from the Church's official doctrines. The author takes full and complete responsibility for his own opinions expressed in this work, but not for those authors whom he has quoted.

ISBN: 1-55517-740-9
e.1

Published by Bonneville Books
Imprint of Cedar Fort, Inc.
www.cedarfort.com

Distributed by:

Cover design by Nicole Cunningham

Printed in the United States of America
10 9 8 7 6 5 4 3 2 1

Printed on acid-free paper

Library of Congress Control Number: 2003114287

To: My father and mother—Elden and Jean Johnson

My brothers and sister—Lance, Robin, Holly and Chris

My wife—Norma Christensen

My children—Mindy, Elisabeth, Eve, Susanna and Heidi

My grandchildren—Sage, Autumn, Aidan, and those to come

My friends—who have shared life's experiences with me

My teachers—who have guided me

All seekers of truth everywhere

TABLE OF CONTENTS

PREFACE

All men and women are faced with the question of whether God exists. Whether they are born and living in a society with one or many religions, or simply living in a "state of nature" observing the rhythms of nature, they are confronted with and forced to consider the existence of a "Higher Being," Creator, or supernatural power—which we can term "God"—and the nature and attributes of that Being. If a person concludes that he or she does believe in God, he or she is still confronted with the question of which of all the many religions professing a belief in God or a "Way" or a "Path" that exist in the world is "true"—or whether they are all equally or partially true or false. Finally, if he or she concludes that Christianity is the "true" religion, he or she must still determine whether there is one "true" sect, variety, or form of Christianity. These are not easy questions, but for the earnest seeker of truth these questions cannot be ignored and justify a lifelong pursuit.

If a person is not sure of the answers to these questions, he or she will be plagued with doubt; his or her confidence in his or her judgments, values, and direction will be minimal, and his or her actions will be timid and weak. Indeed, many believe it is impossible for a person to obtain the fullness of happiness in this life and salvation in the next existence without getting the right answers to these questions. Ironically, for many people they will be unable to acquire satisfactory answers to the first two questions until they have also received an answer to the third question. For others, they will have already answered questions one and two before they encounter the doctrines of The Church of Jesus Christ of Latter-day Saints.

In part, this book is a collection of information that I found was influential to me in my own search for answers to these great questions. I have written it primarily for my family and friends, but will be pleased if it finds a wider audience. It is offered for your consideration and evaluation. My effort was to present information about the beliefs of various religions directly from their own authoritative writings insofar as I have been able to understand them. My intention has been comparison, not criticism. I do believe that a comparison of beliefs and doctrines can bring conviction where there has been doubt. My respect for all men and women everywhere causes me to believe that they are able to discern truth when they understand it. Whether they will obey it is another question. May your pursuit of truth be fruitful.

I express my appreciation to Lyle Mortimer, Lee Nelson, and Chad Daybell at Cedar Fort, Inc., to my editors Natalie Roach and Kyle Waterman, to my indexer Melody Englund, and to Nicole Cunningham for the cover design.

I welcome any comments on, or corrections to, this work. Please send them to the publisher, who will forward them to me, or to JohnsonFamily7@msn.com.

Thomas E. Johnson, 2003

PART I

DOES GOD EXIST?

THE IMPORTANCE OF THE KNOWLEDGE OF GOD

There are many things that we can learn and come to know during our life. All people spend time learning various things. These may include how to read, how to play baseball, how to grow vegetables or crops, how to dance, how to apply the laws of mathematics or chemistry, how to operate an automobile or a computer, and thousands of other things that require our time and attention in order to meet the needs of daily survival or provide recreation and enjoyment for our existence.

But, the question arises—is there some knowledge that is more important than other knowledge? Clearly, different people have different opinions about what knowledge is the most important to pursue—at least it appears so based on how they spend their time. The value of different knowledge or the priority of some knowledge over other knowledge could be greater or lesser at different times or circumstances in our life, but if there was some knowledge which was overarching—which would give the greatest direction, order, meaning, and satisfaction to our life—shouldn't we pursue it with all of our energy?

Some of the fundamental questions that all persons are confronted with in their lives are: Where did I come from—do I have an existence separate from my body and did I exist before my birth in this world? Why am I here—do I or any other person have a purpose for being here? Where am I going—is death the end of this person called "me"?[1]

In order to answer these questions one is naturally led to the question that has occupied the minds of all mankind throughout history—Is there a God or gods? If so, what is he (she or they) like? Do I have a relationship to him (her or them)?

In 1952 Encyclopedia Britannica published a set of 54 volumes entitled *Great Books of the Western World.* The work was revised and expanded to 60 volumes in 1990. The collection compiled 517 of the most important books of Western civilization from 130 authors in all the fields of political science, physical science, social science, economics, literature, poetry, history, religion, philosophy, mathematics, and psychology. Then, in an incredible undertaking, the authors spent seven years abstracting and indexing from those works the 102 "Great Ideas" of these authors—the ideas that have occupied and commanded the attention of the greatest thinkers Western civilization has been able to produce. In the chapter on "Theology" the authors state:

> *It has seldom been disputed that the questions with which theology deals are of critical significance for all the rest of human knowledge.*[2]

In the chapter on "God" the authors said the following:

> *With the exception of certain mathematicians and physicists, almost all the authors of the great books are represented in this chapter. In sheer quantity of references, as well as in variety, it is the largest chapter. The reason is obvious.* ***More consequences for thought and action follow from the affirmation or denial of God than from answering any other basic question****. They follow for those who regard the question as answerable only by faith or only by reason, and even for those who insist upon suspending judgment entirely.*
>
> *In addition to the primary question of God's existence, there are all the problems of the divine nature and of the relation of the world and man to the gods or God. The solutions of these problems cannot help influencing man's conception of the world in which he lives, the position that he occupies in it, and the life to which he is called.*
>
> *The whole tenor of human life is certainly affected by*

> *whether men regard themselves as the supreme beings in the universe or acknowledge a superior—a superhuman being whom they conceive as an object of fear or love, a force to be defied or a Lord to be obeyed. Among those who acknowledge a divinity, it matters greatly whether the divine is represented merely by the concept of God—the object of philosophical speculation—or by the living God whom men worship in all the acts of piety which comprise the rituals of religion [emphasis added].*[3]

The points made in the foregoing quotations are thought-provoking. Is it true that our belief, lack of belief or, perhaps, indifference to the knowledge of God has the most profound consequences in our life of any idea or concept? Upon reflection, we may discover that everything we do in our life is to some extent based upon our attitude on this subject. Whether we believe there is no God, whether we believe there is a personal God who is aware of and interested in us, whether we believe there is a God who has prescribed "commandments" for punishment or blessing, whether we believe some day we will face a "judgment" in regard to the actions of our life—all of these things and many more growing out of our beliefs routinely direct the lives of literally billions of people upon the earth each day. Jesus said, "And this is life eternal, that they might know thee the only true God, and Jesus Christ, whom thou has sent"[4] and that "eternal life" is the "greatest of all the gifts of God."[5] In Christian thinking this knowledge of God, which leads to eternal life, is the greatest knowledge we can acquire in this life.

REASONS FOR BELIEVING IN GOD

There are many who believe that God does not exist or that we cannot know if he exists. Some are greatly troubled over the obvious existence of evil in the world, including suffering by the innocent and seemingly meaningless natural disasters and tragedies. They question why a caring God, if he has super-human power, would allow this. Others accept that there may be a God of "nature" who works through natural law but who is indifferent to the needs of mankind. Others see only a multiplicity of religions, with some overlapping but many conflicting doctrines and practices, causing them to conclude that no God could be the author of such confusion and that religion and God are the invention of man. Sigmund Freud argued that God was merely the projection by mankind of their own childhood father.[6] Karl Marx, following the opinion of Friedrich Nietzsche,[7] described religion as the "opium of the people" because he believed it lulled them into lazy acceptance of poverty and bad social conditions in this life in expectation of better conditions in the next life.[8] (Of course, we may observe that just because he believed that religion had a bad effect on people does not prove there is no God). Blaise Pascal, a devout believer in God, admitted, "Men never do evil so completely and cheerfully as when they do it from religious conviction."[9]

On the other hand, billions of people on the earth hold a belief in the existence of God. All of the adherents of the major world religions, Judaism, Christianity, Islam, Hinduism, Sikhism, Shintoism, Mahayana Buddhism, and Confucianism, perhaps with the exceptions of Hinayana Buddhism, Taoism, and Jainism, share a belief in God. It is undeniable that countless acts of courage, kindness, and goodness to relieve human suffering, including those of St. Francis of Assissi, Mother Theresa, and millions of ordinary people, have been done because of religious belief.

When we explore the reasons given by those who believe in God, we find that they fall into numerous categories. In this sense belief in God is always "personal"—the reasons fully satisfactory to one person may not be sufficient for another person, and vice-versa. Some of those reasons are as follows:

THE WONDERS OF NATURE

Many people are simply struck by the wonders of nature. As Arthur Conan Doyle says through Sherlock Holmes:

> *'What a lovely thing a rose is . . . . There is nothing in which deduction is so necessary as in religion,' said he, leaning with his back against the shutters. 'It can be built up as an exact science by the reasoner. Our highest assurance of the*

goodness of the Providence seems to rest in the flowers. All other things, our powers, our desires, our food are really necessary for our existence in the first instance. But this rose is an extra. Its smell and its color are an embellishment of life, not a condition of it. It is only goodness which gives extras, and so I say again that we have much to hope from the flowers.'[10]

Those who see the majesty of the heavens—the planets, moons, sun, and stars set in their places and operating to bring about the conditions necessary for the life of man—are often constrained to confess the existence of a Higher Power or Creator. *The Bible* declares that God created the heavens and the earth, animals, insects, fishes, birds, man and woman.[11] God says that he created vegetation "that is pleasant to the sight and good for food."[12] He told the prophet Isaiah, "I have made the earth and created man upon it,"[13] and Isaiah declared, "The whole earth is full of the glory of God."[14] The Greek philosopher Epictetus states simply:

"Good Heaven! Any one thing in the creation is sufficient to demonstrate a Providence to a humble and grateful mind. The mere possibility of producing milk from grass, cheese from milk and wool from skins; who formed and planned it? Ought we not, whether we dig or plough or eat, to sing this hymn to God."[15]

Henry David Thoreau, the author of the unique chronicle of his life in nature, *Walden*, said in his Journal, "Nature is full of genius, full of the divinity; so that not a snowflake escapes its fashioning hand."[16] In his essay on "Spiritual Laws" Ralph Waldo Emerson exudes:

O my brothers, God exists. There is a soul at the centre of nature, and over the will of every man, so that none of us can wrong the universe. It has so infused its strong enchantment into nature, that we prosper when we accept its advice; and when we struggle to wound its creatures, our hands are glued to our sides, or they beat our own breasts. The whole course of things goes to teach us faith.[17]

The Psalmist of the Old Testament wrote,

"The heavens declare the glory of God; and the firmament showeth his handywork."[18]

In the New Testament Paul declares to the Romans:

Because that which may be known of God is manifest in them [the unrighteous]; for God hath showed it unto them. For the invisible things of him from the creation of the world are clearly seen, being understood by the things that are made, even his eternal power and Godhead; so they are left without excuse [in the judgment day].[19]

When Paul taught the people of Lystra he told them that God:

[M]ade heaven and earth, and the sea, and all things that are therein . . . Nevertheless he left himself not without witness, in that he did good, and gave us rain from heaven, and fruitful seasons, filling our hearts with food and gladness.[20]

Following a spring rain Martin Luther said:

Praise God. He is giving us one hundred thousand gulden worth. It is raining corn, wheat, barley, wine, cabbage, onions, grass, and milk.[21]

To those who questioned Job's faith he replied, in part:

But ask now the beasts, and they shall teach thee; and the fowls of the air, and they shall tell thee. Or speak to the earth and it shall teach thee; and the fishes of the sea shall declare unto thee. Who knoweth not in all these things the hand of the Lord hath wrought this?[22]

In a lengthy passage God asks Job to reflect upon the creations of the earth and the natural laws to understand the power of God[23] and says, "Hearken unto this, O Job: stand still, and consider the wondrous works of God."[24]

In *The Book of Mormon*, the prophet Alma declared to the unbeliever Korihor, "[A]ll things denote there is a God; yea, even the earth, and all things that are upon the face of it, yea, and its motion, yea, and also all the planets which move in their regular form do witness that there is a Supreme Creator."[25] Joseph Smith said:

> *Think for a moment of the greatness of the Being who created the Universe; and ask, could He be so inconsistent with his own character as to leave man without a law or rule by which to regulate his conduct, after placing him here, where, according to the formation of his nature he must in a short period sink into the dust? Is there nothing further; is there no existence beyond this vail of death which is so suddenly to be cast over all of us? If there is, why not that Being who had power to place us here, inform us something of the hereafter? If we had power to place ourselves in this present existence, why not have power to know what shall follow when that dark vail is cast over our bodies? If in this life we receive our all; if when we crumble back to dust we are no more, from what source did we emanate, and what is the purpose of our existence? If this life were all, we should be led to query whether there was really any substance in existence, and we might with propriety say, 'Let us eat, drink and be merry for tomorrow we die!' But if this life is all, then why this constant toiling, why this continual warfare, and why this unceasing trouble? But this life is not all, the voice of reason, the language of inspiration, and the Spirit of the living God, our Creator, teaches us, as we hold the record of truth in our hands [The Bible], that this is not the case, that this is not so; for the heavens declare the glory of a God, and the firmament showeth his handiwork; and a moment's reflection is sufficient to teach every man of common intelligence, that all these are not the mere productions of chance, nor could they be supported by any power less than an Almighty hand; and He that can mark the power of Omnipotence, inscribed upon the heavens, can also see God's own handwriting in the sacred volume; and he who reads it oftenest will like it best, and he who is acquainted with it, will know the hand wherever he can see it; and when once discovered, it will not only receive an acknowledgment, but an obedience to all its heavenly precepts.*[26]

Let us consider a number of the facts pertaining to the universe we live in:

The Heavens and the Earth [27] —The earth upon which we live is at just the right distance from the sun to sustain life at an average temperature of 59 degrees. Venus has a temperature of 900 degrees. To our other side, Mars has a temperature of minus 80 degrees. The next planet, Jupiter, is at minus 200 degrees. Gravity permits the earth to retain its air and atmosphere, including water. Rain water is the universal solvent, breaking down chemicals and minerals which are distributed to plant life all over the face of the earth. Water has the amazing property of expanding when it freezes, thereby floating on top of lakes and oceans and preventing the rest of the water from freezing to the bottom, thus preserving fish life. The surface tension of water permits "capillarity"— the ability of trees to raise such water to great heights to their branches and leaves in defiance of gravity. There is an amazing water cycle powered by the sun that re-circulates the water from the oceans to the mountaintops and back again through rain and rivers, in the course of which salt is removed and the water is purified. The atmosphere protects us from radiation and meteors and holds in the heat. There are heating and cooling winds necessary for the transportation of fresh water inland for plant life. The earth is offset on its axis by 23 degrees from vertical, making possible seasons and the moderation of unbearable heat or cold for prolonged periods. Our earth rotates on its axis once each day providing heating and cooling, creating the winds and providing needful rest for animals and man. The combination of heat, water and sun provides for the germination of plant life and the basis for the food chain for higher animals and man. We have just a single moon, which is at a proper distance to create tides that prevent stagnation of the oceans but not tidal waves that would destroy life on land. We have a fertile soil for plants, much different than the rocky, barren or liquid surfaces of other planets in our solar system.

Plant and Animal Life—There are over one million species of plant and animal life. Each is endowed with the ability to grow and reproduce. God has provided insects for pollinating the plants, and wind, water, and fire as means of dispersing and renewing the seeds and plant life. Plants and animals provide oxygen, food, medicine, and clothing for humans. Many of our scientific advances come from understanding and imitating the animals, including sonar from bats and dolphins and spider webs that are stronger and lighter than equivalent steel. The salmon's sense of smell to return to its place of birth and the aerodynamics of a bird's flight are astonishing. The poet Joyce Kilmer expressed her feelings, "I think I shall never see a poem as lovely as a tree. Poems are made by fools like me but only God can make a tree."[28] Indeed, we cannot create a single plant without using seed from an existing plant.

The most marvelous of the natural creations is man. Sophocles, the Greek playwright, exclaims, "Numberless are the world's wonders, but none more wonderful than man."[29] To review just a few of the wonders of man:

Science often copies the body. The entire computer revolution is based on an imitation of the on-off electrical charges on the neurons of the brain and the binary code. Our brains are capable of storing the equivalent of 20 million books, which would be equivalent to learning something new every second for 3 million years. Our heart is the most efficient pump in the world, pumping 2,000 gallons a day, or 55 million gallons in a lifetime through 60,000 miles of blood vessels. Our skeletal system is amazingly light for its strength. We have a marvelous cooling system of evaporation through the pores and circulation of the blood. The entire construction of robots is based on levers, hinges, pivots, ball and socket joints, and self lubricating joints copied from the body. The hand alone has 25 joints and 58 movements. According to Leonardo Da Vinci the hand is the most versatile instrument on earth. In the process of human reproduction, from two tiny cells, by the third week of pregnancy the spine is being formed; by the ninth week the heart beats; eventually it grows to 60 trillion cells. These cells, all originating from the original two are as diverse as dental enamel and as delicate as the cornea of the eye. Each is pre-programmed to grow to the correct size, form and function. Humans are capable of thinking, reasoning and speaking to a far more advanced degree than any animal counterpart. Humans have the ability to learn from experience and to "feel"—only humans weep from emotion.[30]

The more we study creation, the more persuasive it is that there was an incredibly intelligent creator—a great witness to those who have "eyes to see" and "ears to hear." The statement of the Creator to Moses was, "All things are created and made to bear record of me . . . things which are in the heavens above, and things which are on the earth, and things which are in the earth, and things which are under the earth, both above and beneath: all things bear record of me."[31] We cannot help be astonished at the complexity and design of the entire world—the absolute impossibility of its continuation for a single day without the operation of thousands of natural laws. In regard, particularly, to the creation of man, *The Book of Mormon* King Benjamin taught that God "created" us and also "preserved us day to day, by lending us breath."[32] The modern philosopher, Mortimer J. Adler has said:

> *Philosophical reflection can appraise all the scientific evidence and the facts of common experience that have a bearing on the special status of man in the order of nature. It can establish, beyond a reasonable doubt, the conclusion that man differs from all other animals, by virtue of having intellectual powers and powers of action not possessed by them to any degree. It can explain why a human being and nothing else on earth, is properly regarded as a 'person.' To this extent, philosophy makes contact with the Western religious belief that man and man alone is made in the image of God, who is also a person, not a thing.*[33]

Even Charles Darwin, the proponent of evolution, believed that creation began with God. He said:

> *Thus, from the war of nature, from famine and death, the most exalted object which we are capable of conceiving, namely, the production of the higher animals, directly follows. There is grandeur in this view of life, with its several powers, having been originally breathed by the Creator into a few forms or into one, and that whilst this planet has gone cycling on according to the fixed law of gravity, from so simple a beginning endless forms most beautiful and most wonderful have been and are being evolved.*[34]

RATIONAL LOGIC

Two of the greatest Greek philosophers, Plato and Aristotle, concluded that the existence of God can be affirmed from natural reason. Plato, through the words of the Athenian Stranger, explains to Cleinieas that inanimate matter is moved by a soul, which exists throughout the universe.[35] Aristotle reasoned that there must be a "Prime Mover" that initiated all motion we can observe on the earth and in the heavens.[36]

Anselm argued that God was "that being which nothing greater than can be conceived."[37] This is sometimes called the ontological or "a priori" proof of God's existence. In fact it is based on definition. If God is defined in the way that Anselm defines him, a being that actually exists will be greater than a being that exists only in our minds, so, argued Anselm, God must exist. Others, however, have replied that just because such a being can be imagined does not prove that such a being in fact exists.

The great Catholic theologian, Thomas Acquinas, wrote *Summa Theologica*, a comprehensive analysis of God and the Christian religion. In the early part of his exposition he asks "Whether the Existence of God is Self-Evident?"[38] He then says that the existence of God is not self-evident but needs to be demonstrated to us by "effects." He continues, "Hence the existence of God, in so far as it is not self-evident to us, can be demonstrated from those of His effects which are known to us."[39] Next he asks, "Whether God exists?"[40] In his answer, based in part on the arguments of Aristotle, he states, "The existence of God can be proved in five ways." He says (1) there are many things in our world that are in motion, that all things in motion were put into motion by a mover, and the initial or prime mover before any other mover existed was God; (2) our experience in the world teaches us that effects arise from causes and that the world is full of many existing conditions which were caused by previous actions; tracing such causes and effects back to the beginning results in a realization that there must have been an initial cause for all subsequent effects and that cause was God; (3) things that do not exist cannot create things that do exist; since many things in the universe now exist, it is necessary to conclude that a Creator must exist; (4) we can observe in nature and life an order of gradation, from the simple to that which is more complex, from that which is good to that which is better—the ultimate in goodness, being, power and knowledge we must understand as God; and (5) there is an order in the governance of the world which is observable; nature moves toward an end as an "arrow directed by the archer"—the author of this design is God.

While it must be conceded that many have disputed the validity of Acquinas' proofs and have found more force in some than others, few have claimed to be able to disprove all of them. For example, Descartes, the famous author of "I think, therefore I am," agreed with Acquinas.[41] John Locke agreed with Acquinas' third argument—"non-entity cannot produce any real being"—since we exist, someone created us. Sir Isaac Newton agreed that the order of the universe shows the existence of a designer. In his book, *Mathematical Principles of Natural Philosophy*—one of the three greatest scientific books in the history of modern Europe according to Will Durant—Newton said:

> *This most beautiful system of the sun, planets, and comets, could only proceed from the counsel and dominion of an intelligent and powerful Being . . . This Being governs all things, not as the soul of the world, but as Lord over all . . . . All that diversity of natural things which we find suited to different times and places could arise from nothing but the will of a Being necessarily existing.*[42]

Professor Dummelow identified an additional argument—the "a fortiori" argument—from the quotation in Psalms 94:9: "He that planned the ear, shall he not hear? he that formed the eye, shall he not see?"[43]

The Roman Catholic Church has officially accepted that the existence of God can be proven from natural reason:

> *Starting from movement, becoming, contingency and the world's order and beauty, one can come to a knowledge of God as the origin and end of the universe.*[44]

Our Holy Mother, the Church, holds and teaches that God, the first principle and last end of all things, can be known with certainty from the created world by the natural light of human reason.[45]

The famous Jewish philosopher, Moses Maimonides, claimed God's existence could be proved by reason but not his attributes.[46]

The two Muslim philosophers, Al-Kindi in the 9th century and Al-Ghazali in the 11th century, argued that everything that exists had a cause for its existence, the universe began to exist and the cause of the universe's existence is God. This is known as the "Kalam" argument.[47]

SCRIPTURE

Despite Acquinas' later efforts to prove the existence of God from natural reason, he starts his treatise with the following:

It was necessary for man's salvation that there should be a knowledge revealed by God, besides the philosophical sciences built up by human reason . . . . Hence it was necessary for the salvation of man that certain truths which exceed human reason should be made known to him by divine revelation.

Even as regards those truths about God which human reason can discover, it was necessary that man should be taught by a divine revelation, because the truth about God such as reason could discover could only be known by a few, and that after a long time, and with the admixture of many errors. But man's whole salvation, which is in God, depends upon the knowledge of the truth. Therefore, in order that the salvation of men might be brought about more fitly and more surely, it was necessary that they should be taught divine truths by divine revelation.[48]

In *The Bible* we find Zophar asking Job:

Canst thou by searching find out God? Canst thou find out the Almighty unto perfection? It is as high as heaven; what canst thou do? Deeper than hell; what canst thou know? The measure thereof is longer than the earth, and broader than the sea.[49]

Mortimer Adler, in his book, *How to Think About God*, analyzed the rational arguments for God's existence, including Acquinas' arguments, and concluded that the existence of God could be established by natural reason,

[B]ut beyond this, philosophy cannot go. Belief in the immortality of the human soul, in its separate existence apart from the body after the death of the organism, in its having a personal life hereafter, and its reunion with a resurrected body at the end of the world—all this lies beyond reason's power to establish, even by a preponderance of the evidence, much less beyond reasonable doubt.[50]

The Roman Catholic Church also states:

By natural reason man can know God with certainty on the basis of his works. But there is another order of knowledge, which man cannot possibly arrive at by his own power, the order of divine Revelation.[51]

In Reformed Protestant Christianity, the authors of *The Westminster Confession of Faith* of 1646 said:

Although the light of nature, and the works of creation and providence, do so far manifest the goodness, wisdom and power of God, as to leave men inexcusable; yet are they not sufficient to give that knowledge of God, and of his will, which is necessary unto salvation; therefore, it pleased the Lord at sundry times and divers manners to reveal himself, and to declare his will unto his Church; and afterwards, for the better preserving and propagating of the truth, and for the more sure establishment and comfort of the Church against the corruption of the flesh and the malice of Satan and of the world, to commit the same wholly unto writing; which maketh the holy Scripture to be most necessary; those former ways of God's revealing his will unto his people being now ceased.[52]

In all of those religions that use written scriptures we find they declare the existence of God or gods. *The Bible*, *The Torah*, *The Koran*, the *Vedas* and *Upanishads*, the *Guru Granath*—each of these purport to declare truth that goes beyond mere human reasoning. The revelations given in such scriptures are accepted by their believers as more authoritative than the conflicting opinions of men. Of course, there are conflicts between, and in the interpretation of such scriptures (which we will take up hereafter in Parts II and III), but they all affirm that God does exist, that he has revealed himself, and that we can know Him through those scriptures.

EYEWITNESS TESTIMONY

In *The Bible*, John says in an ungrammatical statement, "No man hath seen God at any time; the only begotten Son, which is in the bosom of the Father, he hath declared him."[53] However, we find John apparently contradicting himself just a few chapters later where he says, "Not that any man hath seen the Father, save he which is of God, he hath seen the Father."[54] In addition, there are references in the New Testament to the "invisible" God.[55] We may counter that God is only "invisible" to the unrighteous, or that ordinary persons who do not have the special calling of a prophet are required to live by faith without seeing God, so he remains "invisible" to them.

There is, however, much more persuasive evidence than arguing over the interpretation of such scriptures. The writers of *The Bible* recorded seeing God at least 12 times. God gave instruction to Adam and Eve in the Garden of Eden.[56] Enoch declared that he "saw the Lord and he stood before my face and he talked with me even as a man."[57] Abraham saw God on at least four different occasions—when he arrived in Canaan,[58] when Abraham was promised children,[59] when he was ninety years old,[60] and when he had a lengthy discussion with God about the destruction of Sodom and Gomorrah.[61] Abraham declared, "And I Abraham talked with the Lord face to face as one man talketh with another."[62] Jacob (Israel) called a certain place "Peniel because I have seen God face to face and my life is preserved."[63] *The Bible* says, "And the Lord entered into the tabernacle and spoke unto Moses face to face as a man speaketh unto his friend."[64] When Moses' brother Aaron and sister Miriam spoke against Moses, God chastised them and told them, "I will speak mouth to mouth with Moses and my similitude he shall behold."[65] According to *The Bible*, Aaron, Nadab, Abihu and 70 of the elders of Israel "saw the God of Israel and there was under his feet as it were a paved work of a sapphire stone."[66] Further, the Lord "appeared" to Solomon twice, once in Gibeon and once when he completed the building of the temple.[67] Isaiah testifies,"In the year of the death of King Uzziah I saw God sitting upon the throne."[68]

In the New Testament, Jesus taught that blessed are the pure in heart for they shall "see" God.[69] At his baptism[70] and the transfiguration on the Mount[71] his apostles heard the Father's voice. Stephen, suffering death by stoning for his belief in Christ, looked into Heaven and saw God—and Jesus Christ standing on the right hand of God.[72] John promised that when God appears we shall "see" him as he is,[73] and Paul says we shall see him "face to face."[74]

In addition to these appearances of God, there are many additional references to his "finger,"[75] his "hand,"[76] his "face,"[77] his "mouth,"[78] his "form,"[79] his "loins"[80] his "lips" and "tongue,"[81] his "eyes and ears,"[82] his "arm"[83] and his "body"[84] in the Old and New Testaments.

In *The Book of Mormon*, the prophets Lehi,[85] Nephi and his brother Jacob,[86] Alma[87] and the brother of Jared[88] all testified that they saw God. In modern time Joseph Smith,[89] Sidney Rigdon,[90] Lorenzo Snow and others[91] testified they saw God.

The Bible and *The Book of Mormon* repeatedly testify that certain men—"prophets"— not only received communication from God in dreams, visions, or by inspiration, but also "saw" God and received instruction from Him, usually to be communicated to others for their blessing or warning. It was these testimonies to their contemporaries and their descendants that established the knowledge of God from the beginning of history. While those who have not had the same experience of seeing God are not required or expected to simply believe, and some dismiss such statements as mere metaphorical language, the words used in the scriptures are clear and the testimony of so many eye-witnesses must be seriously evaluated before concluding that no God exists.

PERSONAL SPIRITUAL EXPERIENCES

There are, of course, throughout the ages, in all religions, those who have had some type of personal spiritual experience that convinced them of the existence of God. Although such persons are often unable to communicate to others the same experience (described by some as trying to describe the taste of salt to someone who has never tasted it), such experiences are often much more powerful and permanent than the doubts and uncertainty engendered by philosophical argument. These include the experiences of Dionysius the Areopagite, St. John of the Cross, St. Teresa of Avila, George Fox, Blaise Pascal, Mohammed and many others. Such "mystical" experiences are often considered unattainable by the ordinary person and the frustration felt by some in not being able to replicate such experiences has left them disillusioned and skeptical.

Jesus taught, "Neither knoweth any man the Father, save the Son, and he to whomsoever the Son will reveal him."[92] Paul taught, "[T]he things of God knoweth no man but [by] the Spirit of God."[93] John Calvin said:

> *If we desire to provide in the best way for our consciences—that they may not be perpetually beset by the instability of doubt or vacillation, and they may not also boggle at the smallest quibbles—we ought to seek our conviction in a higher place than human reasons, judgments, or conjectures, that is in the secret testimony of the Spirit.*[94]

In other words, conviction of the existence of God comes by revelation from Christ through the Holy Spirit communicating to our own spirit. Joseph Smith taught that merely knowing about God intellectually would not be sufficient to meet life's adversities and temptations.

> *An actual knowledge to any person, that the course of life which he pursues is according to the will of God, is essentially necessary to enable him to have that confidence in God*

without which no person may obtain eternal life. It was this that enabled the ancient saints to endure all their afflictions and persecutions, and to take joyfully the spoiling of their goods, knowing (not believing merely) that they had a more enduring substance (Hebrews 10:34) . . . For a man to lay down his all, his character and reputation, his honor, and applause, his good name among men, his houses, his lands, his brothers and sisters, his wife and children, and even his own life also—counting all things but filth and dross for the excellency of the knowledge of Jesus Christ—requires more than mere belief or supposition that he is doing the will of God; but actual knowledge, realizing that when these sufferings are ended, he will enter into eternal rest, and be a partaker of the glory of God.[95]

Joseph Smith asked:

'How do men obtain a knowledge of the glory of God, his perfections and attributes?' and answered, 'By devoting themselves to his service, through prayer and supplication incessantly strengthening their faith in him, until, like Enoch, the brother of Jared and Moses, they obtain a manifestation of God to themselves.'[96]

INTUITION AND CONSCIENCE

John Calvin, one of the founders of "Reformed" Protestant Christianity, maintained:

That there exists in the human mind, and indeed by natural instinct, some sense of Deity, we hold to be beyond dispute, since God himself, to prevent any man from pretending ignorance, has endued men with some idea of his Godhead, the memory of which he constantly renews and occasionally enlarges, that all to a man, being aware that there is a God, and that he is their Maker, may be condemned by their own conscience when they neither worship him nor consecrate their lives to his service.[97]

Blaise Pascal declared, "It is the heart which experiences God, and not the reason. This, then, is faith: God felt by the heart, not by the reason."[98]

Five of the six schools of Hinduism also teach that knowledge of the ultimate reality is beyond reason and can only be known by intuition, revelation, direct perception, or experience.[99]

The philosopher Jean Jacques Rousseau said:

> *Conscience! Conscience! Divine instinct, immortal voice from heaven; sure guide of creature ignorant and finite, indeed, yet intelligent and free, infallible, judge of good and evil, making man like God. In thee consists the excellence of man's nature and the morality of his actions; apart from thee I find nothing in myself to raise me above the beasts—nothing but the sad privilege of wandering from one error to another by the help of an unbridled intellect and reason which knows no principle.*[100]

Immanuel Kant, in his first book, *A Critique of Pure Reason* [1781], denied that God can be known from natural reason, but in his second book, *A Critique of Practical Reason* [1788], he asserted that each person can feel, and can observe in the words and actions of others, a sense of moral duty, a feeling of obligation to do what is "right." This, that some would describe as a conscience, Kant called the "categorical imperative."[101] This feeling emanates from God and is inherent in us because we are created by God. This awareness of our moral duty further establishes that we have free will, since we are aware that we can choose to obey or disregard our moral duty. In addition, we can sense that the injustices of this life must be recompensed at some later time so that we can also intuitively understand that men will live again after death. This leads to the conclusion that there must be a God who can bring about immortality and administer these rewards and punishments.

Similarly, a more modern writer, C.S. Lewis, says:

> *First, that human beings all over the earth have this curious idea that they ought to behave in a certain way, and can't really get rid of it. Secondly, that they don't in fact [always] behave in that way.*[102]

Lewis calls this idea that men have intuitively the "Moral Law." He states further:

Supposing science ever became complete so that it knew every single thing in the whole universe. Don't you see that the questions, 'Why is there a universe? Why does it go on as it does? Has it any meaning?' Would remain just as they were.[103]

According to the Roman Catholic Church:

When he listens to the message of creation and to the voice of conscience, man can arrive at certainty about the existence of God, the cause and the end of everything.[104]

By his reason, man recognizes the voice of God which urges him 'to do what is good and avoid what is evil.' Everyone is obliged to follow this law, which makes itself heard in conscience and is fulfilled in the love of God and of neighbor.[105]

For man has in his heart a law inscribed by God . . . His conscience is man's most secret core and his sanctuary. There he is alone with God whose voice echoes in his depths . . . When he listens to conscience, the prudent man can hear God speaking.[106]

Bertrand Russell criticizes reliance on conscience:

And conscience is a most fallacious guide, since it consists of vague reminiscences of precepts heard in early youth, so that it is never wiser than its possessor's nurse or mother.[107]

The Catholic Church teaches that certain precepts or commandments of God are known intuitively and are binding on the conscience of mankind:

Since they express man's fundamental duties toward God and towards his neighbor, the Ten Commandments reveal, in their primordial content, grave obligations. They are fundamentally immutable, they oblige always and everywhere. No one can dispense from them. The Ten Commandments are engraved by God in the human heart.[108]

Many people would disagree that "conscience" is no more than moral precepts learned from others in our youth. Paul taught the Romans that many men do the things that are right "by nature" without knowing the commandments of God, "their conscience also bearing witness."[109] As missionaries, they preached the Gospel "commending ourselves to every man's conscience in the sight of God."[110] Paul taught Timothy that by the commission of sin a person's conscience is "seared with a hot iron" and is no longer able to judge truth, good or evil.[111] This is especially true in the case of sexual sin.[112] Paul taught Titus:

> *Unto the pure all things are pure: but unto them that are defiled and unbelieving is nothing pure; but even their mind and conscience is defiled.*[113]

The Church of Jesus Christ of Latter-day Saints teaches that the "Spirit of Christ is given to every man"[114] and the "Spirit giveth light to every man."[115] As a result, each person is accountable to God for ignoring or rejecting that light or enlightenment.

PURPOSE

Mel Thompson has observed, "If religion did not actually give people a sense of purpose, it would not survive. And indeed, if it had not met a deep need, it would probably never have appeared in the first place."[116] For example, Paul promises to the believers that "the peace of God, which passeth all understanding, shall keep your hearts and minds . . . ."[117] Perhaps William James, the Harvard professor, analyzed the effects of religious conversion as thoroughly as anyone. He found that such persons (1) lose all their worry and find a feeling of peace and harmony; (2) perceive new truths not previously comprehended about life; and (3) obtain a new view of the world and others as cleaner and more beautiful.[118] This gives their life newly-discovered purpose. While decrying those who become fanatics, including ascetics, he identifies that the usual "fruits" of such conversion include willingness to sacrifice, unselfishness, charity, equanimity, patience, fortitude, and purity.[119] Of course, there are many who have not experienced fulfillment of their deepest needs or found a sense of purpose that a belief in God provides—perhaps because their concept of God is erroneous—but many others have.

PROBABILITY

Even those who believed that God's existence could not be proven have maintained that men should behave as if there is a God. Blaise Pascal, a devout believer in God proposed that non-believers should approach the issue as a "wager." In his *Pensees*, written in 1670, Pascal argued that the rewards of believing and serving God are so superior to the inconveniences and restrictions of doing so that all men should bet their lives that there is a God, and if there is not, they will have lost much less than if they had lived their lives without obedience to his commandments.[120]

William James, tired of those who considered belief in God unworthy of an accomplished philosopher and psychologist, stated his belief in terms of his famous "pragmatic" philosophy:

> *Moral questions immediately present themselves as questions whose solution cannot wait for sensible proof. A moral question is a question not of what sensibly exists, but of what is good, or would be good if it exists. Science can tell us what exists; but to compare the worth, both of what exists and of what does not exist, we must consult not science, but what Pascal calls our heart. Science herself consults her heart when she lays it down that the infinite ascertainment of fact and correction of belief are the supreme goods for man . . . . Science says things are; morality says some things are better than other things; and religion says essentially two things. First he says the best things are the more eternal things . . . . The second affirmation of religion is that we are better off even now if we believe her first affirmation to be true.*
>
> *We cannot escape the issue by remaining skeptical and waiting for more light, because, although we do avoid error in that way if religion be untrue, we lose the good, if it be true, just as certainly as we positively chose to disbelieve . . . . When I look at the religious question as it really puts itself to concrete men, and when I think of all the possibilities*

which both practically and theoretically it involves, this command that we shall put a stopper on our heart, instincts, and courage, and wait—acting of course meanwhile more or less as if religion were not true—till doomsday, or till such time as our intellect and senses working together may have raked in evidence enough—this command, I say seems to me the queerest idol ever manufactured in the philosophic cave.[121]

In another place James says:
We can act as if there were a God; feel as if we were free; consider Nature as if she were full of special designs; lay plans as if we were to be immortal; and we find then that these words do make a genuine difference in our moral life.[122]

Further:

Religion thus makes easy and felicitous what in any case is necessary; and if it can be the only agency that can accomplish this result, its vital importance as a human faculty stands vindicated beyond dispute.[123]

Finally, he declares the "instinctive belief of mankind" is that "God is real since he produces real effects."[124]

Soren Kierkegaard, a proponent of existentialism, argued that even if God's existence cannot be proven, men need to make the "leap of faith" to achieve the true potential of their lives.[125]

Similarly, in *The Book of Mormon*, the prophet Alma testified of the existence of God and taught that those who wished to know if his words were true should conduct an "experiment":

Awake and arouse your faculties, even to experiment upon my words and exercise a particle of faith, yea, even if ye can do no more than desire to believe, let this desire work in you, even until you believe in a manner that ye can give place for a portion of my words.

Now we will compare the word unto a seed. Now, if ye give place, that a seed may be planted in your heart, behold, if it be a true seed, or a good seed, if ye do not cast it out by your unbelief, that ye will resist the Spirit of the Lord, behold, it will begin to swell within your breasts; and when you feel these swelling motions, ye will begin to say within yourselves—It must needs be that this is a good seed, or that the word is good, for it beginneth to enlarge my soul; yea, it beginneth to enlighten my understanding, yea, it beginneth to be delicious to me . . .

And behold, as the tree beginneth to grow, ye will say: let us nourish it with great care, that it may get root, that it may grow up, and bring forth fruit unto us. And now behold, if ye nourish it with much care it will get root, and grow up, and bring forth fruit.

But if ye neglect the tree, and take no thought for its nourishment, behold it will not get any root; and when the heat of the sun cometh and scorcheth it, because it hath no root it withers away, and ye pluck it up and cast it out.

Now, this is not because the seed was not good, neither is it because the fruit thereof would not be desirable; but is because your ground is barren, and ye will not nourish the tree, therefore ye cannot have the fruit thereof . . . .

But if ye will nourish the word, yea, nourish the tree as it beginneth to grow, by your faith with great diligence, and with patience, looking forward to the fruit thereof, it shall take root; and behold it shall be a tree springing up unto ever-lasting life.

And because of your diligence and your faith and your patience with the word in nourishing it, that it may take root in you, behold, by and by ye shall pluck the fruit thereof, which is the most precious, which is sweet above all that is sweet, and which is white above all that is white, yea, and pure above all that is pure; and ye shall feast upon this fruit even until ye are filled, that ye hunger not, neither shall ye thirst.[126]

ATHEISM AND AGNOSTICISM

In regard to atheism, J.R. Dummelow makes the following point:

Atheism is self-condemned by its presumption. To prove a negative is confessedly a difficult task in any field, and the atheist claims to have proved it in the widest field of all—the universe—and in face of the many sided testimony of Nature and Human Nature. To be justified in a flat and categorical denial of the existence of a deity I must be furnished with full knowledge of the universe both as a whole and its details, so as to be competent to declare that nowhere in all the realms of things existing is there any trace of evidence which might even probably tell in favor of Theism. None but a mind practically infinite, omni-present and all-knowing could compass this. And so it might be suggested that the atheist really claims for himself the divine qualities and attributes of which he denies in the existence in a God.[127]

One of the most outspoken critics of religion in modern times was Bertrand Russell. Russell was a very accomplished mathematician and philosopher. However he said, "I do not pretend to be able to prove that there is no God."[128]

Francis Bacon said, "A little philosophy inclineth man's mind to atheism, but depth in philosophy bringeth men's minds about to religion."[129] William Thomas Cummins, while addressing a group of soldiers in the Philippines during World War II, is reported to have said, "There are no atheists in foxholes."[130] An anonymous author has stated, "I feel sorry for the atheist—when he feels grateful, he has no one to thank." Sometimes a person is so vehement and unreasonable about his or her insistence that there is no God that it appears that he or she is not really open to investigating the evidence. Sometimes such an attitude may come from an experience where that person feels let down by God, such as abusive parents, physical disabilities, job loss, or sickness. William James quotes a colleague, "He believes in No-God, and he worships him," and comments that such a temperament is indistinguishable from religious zeal.[131] C.S. Lewis says:

There are all sorts of reasons for believing in God, and here I'll mention only one. It is this. Supposing there was no intelligence behind the universe, no creative mind. In that case nobody designed my brain for the purpose of thinking. It is merely that when the atoms inside my skull happen for physical or chemical reasons to arrange themselves in a certain way, this gives me, as a by-product, the sensation I call thought. But if so, how can I trust my own thinking to be true? It's like upsetting a milk-jug and hoping the way the splash arranges itself will give you a map of London. But if I can't trust my own thinking, of course I can't trust the arguments leading to atheism, and therefore have no reason to be an atheist or anything else. Unless I believe in God, I can't believe in thought: so I can never use thought to disbelieve in God.[132]

There are some, of course, who are more circumspect than claiming to be able to prove that God does not exist. Napoleon said, "Everything proclaims the existence of God but to say whence I came, what I am, or where I am going is above my comprehension."[133] Blaise Pascal divided the people in the world into three groups: Those who know God and love him; those who do not know God but seek him; and those who neither know God nor seek him.[134] He further said:

God has willed to redeem men and to open salvation to those who seek it. He has willed to make Himself quite recognizable by those; and thus, willing to appear openly to those who seek Him with all their heart, and to be hidden from those who flee from Him with all their heart. He so regulates the knowledge of Himself, visible to those who seek Him, and not to those who seek Him not.[135]

Similarly, Joseph Smith, the first prophet of The Church of Jesus Christ of Latter-day Saints, instructed:

Let us here observe, that after any portion of the human family are made acquainted with the important fact there is a God who has created and does uphold all things, the extent of their knowledge will depend upon their diligence and faithfulness in seeking after him.[136]

Joseph Smith also taught that a certain seriousness is necessary to search out these truths:

> *A fanciful and flowery and heated imagination beware of; because the things of God are of deep import; and time, and experience, and careful and ponderous and solemn thoughts can only find them out.*[137]

The Book of Mormon prophet Alma counseled each of his three sons to "Be sober."[138]

The current Catholic Catechism says:

> *Agnosticism can sometimes include a certain search for God, but it can equally express indifferentism, a flight from the ultimate question of existence, and a sluggish moral conscience. Agnosticism is too often equivalent to practical atheism.*[139]

> *The ignorance can often be imputed to personal responsibility. This is the case when a man 'takes little trouble to find out what is true and good, or when conscience is by degrees almost blinded through the habit of committing sin.'*[140]

If someone claims merely that he or she does not know whether God exists, we may then, by furnishing them reasons for belief and giving them opportunities to confirm the reasons, expect that they will not continue in this category if they are sincerely seeking to know. When they go further, however, and assert that they cannot know, we may suspect that they are unwilling to make the effort required in order to know (the third of Pascal's groups). Furthermore, if they allege that no one can know, they speak on behalf of others without authority and in direct contradiction of those that say they do know.

THE NATURE AND ATTRIBUTES OF GOD

In considering whether God exists it is natural to try to understand God's nature, attributes, and character. As Dr. Mortimer Adler put it, "If God, or if the Supreme Being really exists, what is the existence of God, or of the Supreme Being like?"[141] Our willingness to accept the existence of God is directly related to what our concept of God is and what his attributes are. Dr. Adler sharpens the issue by pointing out:

> *There is no rational necessity to think of the supreme being as morally good, as just and merciful, or as benevolently disposed toward the world of men.*[142]

Whether we regard God as indifferent or loving, stern or compassionate, judgmental or merciful, powerful or impotent deeply affects our attitude toward God and how we conduct our lives. If we believe that he is all-powerful and all-knowing, we may have more confidence that God understands our problems and has the power to help, including the ability to overcome all evil. If we believe God is a spirit that fills the immensity of space and inhabits every plant and animal (the "pantheism" of Benedict Spinoza or Plotinus), that he exists but is indifferent to us personally, i.e., hears no prayers and performs no miracles (the "deism" of Lucretius and Denis Diderot), that he existed but now is "dead" (Friedrich Nietzsche), or is our Father and takes a personal interest in our lives, in each case we will try to understand ourselves, our purpose, and our future based on our relation to our concept of God.

The Moslem, for example, as well as the Christian and Jew, genuinely believes that God will reward those who do his will and in the judgment day he or she will be recompensed for all his or her efforts to understand God's will and obey him. The Christian missionary Paul taught, "[F]or he that cometh to God must believe that he is, and that he is a rewarder of them that diligently seek him."[143]

Next, we want to review and compare the concept of God, his nature and attributes as taught by the leading religions of the world.

1. ISLAM

According to Islam, "Allah has no physical attributes. He has no name, shape, no mother, no appetites."[144] "Allah is immaterial and hence invisible."[145] *The Koran* declares:

> *He is God; there is no god but He. He is the Knower of the unseen and the visible; He is the All-Merciful, the All-Compassionate. He is God; Holy, the All-Peace, the Guardian of Faith, the All-Preserver, the All-Mighty, the All-Compeller, the All-Sublime, Glory be to God, above that they associate! He is God the Creator, the Maker, the Shaper, to Him belongs the Names Most Beautiful. All that is in the heavens and the earth magnifies Him; He is the All-Mighty, the All-Wise.*[146]

2. JUDAISM

Leo Trepp, a Jewish rabbi says:

> *The relationship between God and Jew has always been intensely personal. God is a person, but at the same time, the Jew has understood that God has absolutely no human features, that his essence cannot be fathomed. He has willed that we understand him as a person, while remaining ineffable.*[147]

Sephardic Orthodox Jews chant on the eve of the Sabbath:

> *Praise God existent through eternity! . . . A spirit, holy, bodiless is He. No semblance or no image can portray.Himself, First Cause, without beginning lived . . . .*[148]

Rabbi Simeon ben Zemah Duran, writing about 1400 A.D. said:

> *Do not say . . . God, blessed be He, has no organs, and because He has no organs—since on high there is no such thing as body or matter—He therefore cannot have the faculties exercised by those organs, namely, seeing and hearing. So too, do not say that there is forgetfulness before Him because he has no organ with the power of remembrance, as humans have.*[149]

In the Old Testament, the prophet Jeremiah taught:

But let him that glorieth glory in this, that he understandeth and knoweth me, that I am the Lord which exercise loving-kindness, judgment, and righteous in the earth: for in these things I delight, saith the Lord.[150]

Jews recite the "Liturgy of God's Attributes" at Yom Kippur based on Exodus 34:6-7. God is compassionate, full of grace, patient, truthful, kind, and forgiving.

Despite the foregoing, there are instances in the Old Testament where God appears to be quite vengeful, for example, commanding the killing of men, women, and children.[151]

3. HINDUISM

Hinduism was at first polytheistic. In the *Rg Veda* we have hymns to Surya (the sun), Agni (fire), Dyaus (sky), Marats (storms), Vaya (wind), Apas (waters), Usas (dawn), Prthivi (earth), and Indra (thunderstorms).[152] Later, belief became monotheistic. According to Will Durant:

As the number of the gods increased, the question arose as to which of them had created the world. This primal role was assigned now to Agni, now to Indra, now to Soma, now to Prajapati.[153]

The later Vedas expressly acknowledged that earlier Indians had worshipped many different gods but declared, "God is one but men call him by many names."[154] Finally, the six Hindu schools emerged—Nyaya or logical realism, the Vais(h)esika or realistic pluralism, the Samkhya or evolutionary dualism, the Yoga or disciplined meditation, the Purva Mimamsa or earlier interpretative investigations of the Vedas relating to conduct, and the Uttara Mimamsa, or later investigations of the Vedas relating to knowledge.[155] The scholars Sarvepalli Radhakrishnan and Charles Moore refer to these six schools, plus the "heterodox" schools of Carvaka and two sects of Jainism as:

[E]vidence enough of the diversity of views in Indian philosophy. The variety of the Indian perspective is unquestionable. Accordingly, it is very difficult to cite any specific doctrines

or methods as characteristic of Indian philosophy as a whole and applicable to all the multitudinous systems and subsystems developed through nearly four millenniums of Indian philosophical speculation.[156]

Nevertheless, they summarize the Hindu views about God for the six major Hindu sects as follows:

[T]he Samkya [school] says nothing about the possible existence of God, although it is emphatic in its doctrine of the theoretical undemonstrability of his existence; the Vaisesika and the Yoga, especially the latter, admit the existence of God, but do not consider him to be the creator of the universe; the Mimamsa speaks of God but denies his importance and efficacy in the moral ordering of the world. To emphasize the point further, reference should be made also to the early Buddhist systems, which reject God, and to the Caravakas, who deny God without qualification.[157]

They add that the Nyaya school's physical and metaphysical views are essentially the same as the Vaisesika,[158] and that the Vedanta school and Buddhism became "monist"—believing in an impersonal, unknowable God.[159] Will Durant states:

This is one value of the Vedas to us, that through them we can see religion in the making, and can follow the birth, growth, and death of gods and beliefs from animism to philosophic pantheism, and from the superstition of the Atharva Veda to the sublime monism of the Upanishads.[160]

Huston Smith states that the supreme reality of this later Hinduism—after the rise and decline of Buddhism in India—is the incomprehensible "Eternal Spirit" Brahman—the Creator, Vishnu—the Preserver, and Shiva—the Destroyer, with the chief attributes of "being, awareness, and bliss"[161] These are the "trimurti" or "three forms" of God.[162] Smith, says, however, there is a deep division within the leading interpreters of Hinduism whether God is personal as Ramanju (Ramanuja) of the Vedanta school asserted, or impersonal as Shankara (Samkara) of the same school contended.[163] Such impersonal belief systems are sometimes called "theosophical."

Jainism, one of the "heterodox' sects of Hinduism because it does not accept the authority of the Vedas, is monistic.

4. BUDDHISM

Buddhism, founded by Siddhartha Gautama (563-483 A.D.) in India, was an off-shoot of Hinduism, a "Protestant" attempt to reform certain aspects of Hinduism.[164] For example, in an effort to avoid endless wrangling about the existence and nature of the various gods of Hinduism, Gautama taught that it was useless to try to know God—men should concentrate on correct living in the present life as the best preparation for the future. (This is similar to the general attitude of Judaism)[165] His teachings emphasized that the way to avoid suffering, including release from the cycle of reincarnation, is by achieving "nirvana." This was accomplished by understanding the "Four Noble Truths" and following the "Eightfold Path." Unlike Hinduism, Gautama taught that it was possible to attain enlightenment in one lifetime.[166] After his death, however, the Buddhist schools split. The Mahayana school that became predominant in Mongolia, Tibet, China, Korea, and Japan "deified" Buddha as a god or "savior" and taught:

> *Common people believe that Buddha was born a prince and learned the way to Enlightenment as a mendicant; actually, Buddha has always existed in the world which is without beginning or end.*[167]

Mahayana Buddhism now teaches that "the Eternal Buddha has no set form, but can manifest himself in any form,"[168] that Buddha's "body fills every corner of the universe,"[169] that he knows the "thoughts and feelings of all men,"[170] and that Buddha loves "everyone as if each were his only child."[171] Will Durant says, "Buddha himself founded a religion without a god; after his death Buddhism developed a complex theology, including gods, saints, and hell."[172] Huston Smith said,

> *The religion that began, according to the evidence of the earliest records, as a revolt against rites, speculation, grace, and the supernatural, ends with all of these back in the picture and its founder, who was an atheist in respect to belief*

in a personal God, transmogrified into God himself."[173]

The Hinayana or "Theravada" school of Buddhism that became predominant in Sri Lanka, Burma, Thailand, and Cambodia regard Buddha as a "saint" and teach that believers should renounce the world and seek enlightenment as monks.[174]

5. SIKHISM

For the Sikh, God is the ultimate and eternal "guru" (Saguru). "Although essentially beyond description, God is described as one who is merciful, eternal, all-powerful, determining all that takes place, whether good or evil. God is present everywhere, in the worm as in the elephant."[175]

6. TAOISM, CONFUCIANISM, AND MOHISM

Taoism, founded by Lao Tzu, believed in an "impersonal ordering principle" of the universe that man could learn to comprehend by following the "Way" of the Tao.[176] K'ung Ch'iu, commonly known as "Confucius," also encouraged his disciples to follow the "Way"[177] and believed in a universal spiritual substance called "chi'i" that mingled with each person's blood.[178] He recognized the "spirits of the mountains and rivers"[179] and encouraged prayers to "Heaven" and the "ancestral spirits and gods."[180] The disciples of Mo Tzu ("Mohists") believe that the universe is ruled by Shang Ti, the Sovereign on High, a personal God who "loved men dearly."[181]

7. SHINTOISM

The indigenous Japanese religion, Shintoism, is described by William Bunce as follows:

> *As a religion it is concerned with a variety of deities known as 'kami,' which vary in nature from the spirits of trees, foxes, and mountains to deified ancestors, heroes, emperors, and a pantheon of heavenly deities, chief among whom is the Sun Goddess. The worship of these kami centers in the observance of ceremonies and festivals which are closely related to community and national traditions.*[182]

Mirrors, swords, stones, tablets, images, trees, mountains, caves, waterfalls, pigeons, and animals such as the snake and fox are among the most common objects of worship.[183]

Will Durant says:

Shinto, the Way of the Gods, took three forms: the domestic cult of family ancestors, the communal cult of clan ancestors, and the state cult of the imperial ancestors and the founding gods . . . Shinto required no creed, no elaborate ritual, no moral code; it had no special priesthood, and no consoling doctrine of immortality and heaven . . . .[184]

8. CHRISTIANITY

In 325 A.D. the Creed of Nicaea was adopted as an early Christian statement about God and is accepted by the Roman Catholic, Eastern Orthodox and many other Christian churches:

We believe in one God, the Father, Almighty maker of all things visible and invisible; And in one Lord Jesus Christ, the Son of God, begotten of the Father, only-begotten, that is, from the substance [ousia] of the Father; God from God, Light from Light, Very God from Very God, begotten not made, of one substance [homousia, consubstantial] with the Father, through whom all things were made, both in heaven and on earth . . . And in the Holy Spirit.[185]

The Roman Catholic Church has used the "Apostles Creed" as the outline for its latest catechism:

I believe in God, the Father almighty, creator of heaven and earth. I believe in Jesus Christ, his only Son, our Lord. I believe in the Holy Spirit . . . .[186]

The Eastern Orthodox Church teaches:

We believe in one God, true almighty and infinite, the Father, the Son, and the Holy Spirit, the Father unbegotten; the Son begotten of the Father before the ages, and consubstantial with Him; and the Holy Spirit proceeding from the Father, and consubstantial with the Father and the Son.[187]

The concept of three gods in one (the "Trinity") was the subject of numerous debates in the early Christian church and will be discussed in greater detail in Part III, Section 10. In response to those who objected to this description of God as being incomprehensible, the Catholic Church Father Augustine said, "If you understood him, it would not be God."[188] In the Middle Ages in Western civilization, the most widely quoted Christian definition of God was that "God is a sea of infinite substance."[189] In 1534 the author Rabelais had Panurge refer to the common conception of God:

> *May the intellectual sphere whose center is everywhere, and its circumference nowhere, whom we call God, keep you in his Almighty protection.*[190]

Another more modern but comprehensive Christian definition of God is that of John Henry Newman, the Anglican prelate who became a Catholic cardinal:

> *God is First Cause, absolute, necessary, one, unique, unlimited, infinitely perfect, spirit, simple, immutable, actual, immense, boundless, omnipresent, eternal, intelligent, omniscient, omnipotent, self-reliant, holy, good, just, possesses will, lives and is a person.*[191]

In his book, *A Concise Guide to the Catholic Church*, the Franciscan monk Felician Foy lists the attributes of God as:

> *[A]lmighty, eternal, holy, immortal, immense, immutable, incomprehensible, ineffable, infinite, invisible, just, loving, merciful, most high, most wise, omnipotent, omniscient, omnipresent, patient, perfect, provident, supreme and true.*[192]

The current Catechism of the Catholic Church teaches:

> *Scripture constantly recalls this rejection of 'idols,' [of] silver and gold, the work of men's hands. They have mouths, but do not speak; eyes, but do not see . . . God, however, is the 'living God' who gives life and intervenes in history.*[193]

> *In no way is God in man's image. He is neither man nor woman. God is pure spirit in which there is no place for the difference between the sexes.*[194]

In Protestant Christianity, *The Westminster Confession of Faith* (1646) of the "Reformed" churches declared:

There is but one only living and true God, who is infinite in being and perfection, a most pure spirit, invisible, without body, parts and passions, immutable, immense, eternal, incomprehensible, almighty, most wise, most holy, most free, most absolute, working all things according to the counsel of his own immutable and most glorious will, for his own glory; most loving, gracious, merciful, long-suffering, abundant in goodness and truth, forgiving iniquity, transgression, and sin; the rewarder of them that diligently seek him; and withal most just and terrible in his judgments; hating all sin, and who will by no means clear the guilty.[195]

The Thirty-Nine Articles of the Church of England of 1563 and the American Revision of 1801 were somewhat shorter:

There is but one living and true God, everlasting, without body, parts and passions; of infinite power, wisdom, and goodness; the Maker, and Preserver of all things both visible and invisible. And in unity of this Godhead there be three Persons, of one substance, power and eternity: the Father, the Son and the Holy Ghost.[196]

CREATED IN THE "IMAGE" OF GOD

The atheist Robert Ingersoll condemned the popular concept of God, "Think of that! Without body parts or passions! I defy any man in the world to write a better description of nothing!"[197] Although the book of Genesis teaches that man is made in the "image of God," Rabbi Joseph ben Joseph Nahmias says:

By 'image,' no physical likeness is intended. The term 'image' refers to the intelligence and understanding . . . . And it is by this image that man is distinguished from the beasts and the fowl.[198]

Rabbi Morris Kertzer says, "it is a cardinal tenet of our faith that God is purely spiritual; He admits of no human attributes."[199] Thomas Acquinas also argued that creation in the "image of God" meant only that man has reason and intelligence.[200]

Joseph Smith, the first prophet of The Church of Jesus Christ of Latter-day Saints disagreed—he said, "It is the first principle of the Gospel to know for a certainty the character of God and to know that we may converse with him as one man converses with another . . . ."[201] He taught, "That which is without body, parts and passions is nothing,"[202] that an "immaterial substance" is a contradiction in terms,[203] and that

> *The Father has a body of flesh and bones as tangible as man's; the Son also; but the Holy Ghost has not a body of flesh and bones but is a personage of Spirit. Were it not so, the Holy Ghost could not dwell in us.*[204]

In reference to God he further said:

> *I say, if you were to see him today, you would see him like a man in form—like yourselves in the person, image, and very form as a man.*[205]

These teachings were based on his testimony that in answer to his prayers, God, the Father, and the Son, Jesus Christ, appeared to him.[206] In response to those who quoted John 4:24 that "God is a Spirit: and they that worship him must worship him in spirit and truth," he replied that the scriptural text had been corrupted and should have been translated, "For unto such [true worshipers] God hath promised his Spirit [the Holy Ghost]. And they who worship him, must worship in spirit and in truth." *The Bible* itself refers to God planting a garden and walking in it in the cool of the day,[207] as coming down to see what man is doing on the earth,[208] and as shutting the door of the ark behind Noah.[209] To those, like Thomas Acquinas who thought that man's creation in the "image of God' was purely a figure of speech, Joseph pointed out that the author of the same book of Genesis uses the same language when recording that Seth, the son of Adam, was in the "likeness" and "image" of Adam, just as the scripture says that Adam was in the "likeness" and "image" of God.[210] Further, James, the apostle of Jesus Christ taught that man was in the "similitude" of God.[211] Thomas Acquinas admitted that there were some respected doctors of the early Christian Church as well as Aristotle who believed God was corporeal.[212] One scholar, Isaac de

Beausobre, commenting on the belief of the early Christians that God has a body observes:

> *[W]hatever be the error of believing God to be corporeal, religion suffers nothing by it. Adoration, the love of God, and obedience to his sovereign will, remain entire. He is not the less the most holy, the most high, the almighty, and the immortal. Were Tertullian, Melito, etc., who believed God to be corporeal, on that account, the less good Christians?*[213]

Daniel Peterson and Stephen Ricks ask:

> *[D]oes anthropomorphism really disqualify those who believe in it from being Christian? It would be odd if it did, for most Christians of the very earliest period were almost certainly anthropomorphists. As a recent article in the Harvard Theological Review contends, '[O]rdinary Christians for at least the first three centuries of the current era commonly (and perhaps generally) believed God to be corporeal,' or embodied. 'The belief was abandoned (and then only gradually) as Neoplatonism became more and more entrenched as the dominant world view of Christian thinkers.'*[214]

John Milton, the English author of "Paradise Lost"—"the greatest poem in the English language" according to the historian Will Durant—recorded his religious beliefs in his book, *De Doctrina Christiana*. Milton believed:

> *If the Scriptures tell us that God rested, or feared or repented, or was angry or grieved, these statements are to be taken at their face value, and not diluted as metaphors. Even the corporeal parts and qualities ascribed to God are to be accepted as physically true.*[215]

Voltaire wrote:

> *What did the Jews understand by 'let us make man in our own image'? What all antiquity understands—'Moulded in the form of the masterful gods' [Ovid, Metamorphoses, i. 83] Images are made only out of bodies. No nation has conceived of a god without a body, and it is impossible to picture him in*

any other way. We could of course say: 'God is not anything that we know'; but then one can have no idea what he is. Like all other peoples the Jews always believed god to be corporeal. All the first fathers of the church also believed god to be corporeal, until they embraced Plato's ideas.[216]

One of the greatest ironies of Christendom is that in the Sistine Chapel—within the Vatican Headquarters of the Catholic Church—Michelangelo painted on the ceiling great events from *The Bible*, including the creation of man. There he portrayed God in the likeness and form of a man reaching forth with his finger to touch the finger of Adam.

Joseph Smith taught that in order for us to exercise faith in God we must have the idea that God actually exists and a correct idea of his character, perfections and attributes.[217] He summarizes those attributes of God taught in *The Bible* as perfect knowledge (omniscience),[218] power,[219] justice,[220] judgment,[221] mercy,[222] truth,[223] and love.[224] He then explains why each of these attributes is necessary in order to believe in God:

For inasmuch as God possesses the attribute knowledge, he can make all things known to his saints necessary for their salvation; and as he possesses the attribute power, he is able to deliver them from the power of all enemies; and seeing, also that justice is an attribute of the Deity, he will deal with them upon the principles of righteousness and equity, and a just reward will be granted unto them for all their afflictions and sufferings for the truth's sake. And as judgment is an attribute of the Deity also, his saints have the most unshaken confidence that they will, in due time, obtain a perfect deliverance out of the hands of all their enemies, and a complete victory over all those who have sought their hurt and destruction. And as mercy is also an attribute of the Deity, his saints can have confidence that it will be exercised towards them, and through the exercise of that attribute towards them, comfort and consolation will be administered unto them abundantly, amid all their afflictions and tribulations. And, lastly, realizing that truth is an attribute of the Deity, the mind is led to rejoice amid all its trials and temptations, in

> *hope of that glory which is to be brought at the revelation [Second Coming] of Jesus Christ, and in view of that crown which is to be placed upon the heads of the saints in the day when the Lord shall distribute rewards unto them, and in prospect of that eternal weight of glory which the Lord has promised to bestow upon them, when he shall bring them in the midst of his throne to dwell in his presence eternally.*[225]

Finally he states one of the attributes of God, as taught in *The Bible*, is that God is unchanging, which attribute is necessary in order for us to have confidence that God's other attributes will not change over time.[226]

GOD AS OUR "FATHER"

Judaism and Christianity are apparently unique among the major religions of the world in believing in God as our "Father." (Although Islam purports to accept the Old Testament, God is not referred to as "Father" anywhere among the 99 names of God in *The Koran*). In the Old Testament we find Moses and Aaron praying to the "God of the spirits of all flesh"[227] and teaching the Israelites they are "children of the Lord their God."[228] David, in the Psalms, even declares, "Ye are gods . . . children of the most high God."[229] The prophet Malachi asks, "Have we not all one father? Hath not one God created us?"[230]

In the Jewish *Talmud* we find, "Hail unto you Israel: Who cleanses you, and before Whom do you cleanse yourselves? It is your Father in Heaven."[231] At the conclusion of all public worship meetings, Jews recite a special Kaddish including the plea, "May the prayers and supplications of all Israel be subject unto their father in heaven."[232] The morning Jewish prayer is, "The Lord is our God. He is our Father."[233] At Rosh Hashanah, the beginning of the Jewish new year, Jews appeal to "our Father, our King" for a year of blessing and peace.[234]

In the New Testament, Jesus Christ taught men to pray to God as "Our Father which art in heaven,"[235] and exhorted them to be perfect as their "Father in Heaven" [is perfect].[236] Jesus referred to "your Father" and "your Father which is in heaven" fourteen times during his Sermon on the Mount.[237] In one of his most beautiful parables—the prodigal son—he taught about the joy the Father feels when his wayward children return to him.[238] Paul, trying to teach the Athenians of Greece about the "unknown God," declared we are his "offspring"[239] and, later, in his epistle to the Hebrews, he asks:

> *Furthermore we have had fathers of our flesh which corrected us, and we gave them reverence; shall we not much rather be in subjection unto the Father of spirits and live?*[240]

To the Romans he said, "The Spirit itself beareth witness with our spirit, that we are the children of God."[241] Paul also declares to the Ephesians, "There is . . . one God and Father of all . . . ."[242] John Wesley, the founder of Methodist Christianity said, "For a man cannot have a childlike confidence in God till he knows he is a child of God."[243] J.R. Dummelow, in his book, *A Commentary on the Holy Bible*, says, "Without any doubt the leading religious doctrine of Jesus was the Fatherhood of God."[244]

It may be observed here that, despite the fact the Roman Catholic Church teaches that the spirit of each man and woman is created individually and immediately by God,[245] it also teaches that man "becomes" a son of God by "adoption" or rebirth at the time of baptism[246] and is then "entitled to say the prayer of the children of God: 'Our Father.'"[247] The Church of Jesus Christ of Latter-day Saints accepts the previously cited scriptures literally, that mankind were created as spirit children of God, the Father, long before our birth on this earth,[248] and that we are also adopted as children of Christ when we are baptized and keep his commandments.[249]

* * *

Having discussed the various concepts of God, his attributes and the reasons for believing in the existence of God, we next consider how we can know religious truth and some of the major doctrines of the various religions in the world.

PART II

IS CHRISTIANITY THE "TRUE" RELIGION?

Some people believe God exists but are uncomfortable in affirming the truth of any one religion. Many people are skeptical that any religion is "true" or that one religion is any truer than another. Sometimes they may assert that a religion is "true" for one person (subjective truth), but not for all persons (objective truth). Sometimes merely making a person aware of the differences between different religions is all that is needed for their beliefs to solidify. In this Part we will explore the meaning of "truth" and the differences between Christianity and other religions.

WHAT IS TRUTH?

Jesus declared to Pontius Pilate, "[F]or this cause came I unto the world, that I should bear witness of the truth. Everyone that is of the truth heareth my voice." Pilate then asked him, "What is truth?"[250] John does not record whether Jesus gave an answer. Commonly, we may think of someone who tells the truth or tells lies. Telling the truth is simply saying what we believe to be true. As long as we are not saying something that we do not believe to be true we are not "lying." This is the subjective standard of truth. The philosopher Charles Sanders Peirce stated, "Every man is fully satisfied that there is such a thing as truth, or he would not ask any questions."[251] However, our subjective belief may be totally in conflict with reality. When our belief conforms to reality we may say we know the truth—this is the objective standard of truth. Jesus Christ told Joseph Smith, "[T]ruth is knowledge of things as they are, and as they were, and as they are to come."[252]

No one likes to be deceived. As William James pointed out, as quoted in Part I, sometimes people will go to great lengths to suspend judgment despite evidence of the truth just to avoid having to admit at some point with new facts or evidence that they were mistaken. In religious matters they may feel that they cannot adequately distinguish between truth and mere superstition. Mortimer Adler, in his excellent book, *Truth in Religion,* has said:

> *To believe in the guise of religious faith, what is, on scientific or philosophic grounds, factually untrue is to be superstitious. Superstition is a counterfeit of religion and a perversion of it.*[253]

He says that Aristotle divided truth into two categories. The first involves the truthfulness of "descriptive" statements. For example, the car is blue, Los Angeles is in the Western United States, or statements relating to the existence of things, including the existence of God. In such cases, our belief or opinion is "true" if it conforms to reality. In regard to normative or "prescriptive" statements—where someone is stating what we "ought to" or "should" do—the current philosophy of the world is that such statements of "values," "tastes," preferences or priorities are not subject to the same standard of judging truth, and that no one can claim that his or her values are superior to any other person's values. Many people, frustrated with being unable to sort through the many and conflicting religions, have come to feel that religion is just a person's "values"—not subject to any objective standard of truth. Dr. Adler says that Aristotle faced this problem two thousand years ago and taught that "value" statements can and must be evaluated for truthfulness by another standard, i.e., whether the statement is in conformity with "right desire." "Right desire" consists in desiring the things that are really good for us, as contrasted with the things that merely appear to be good for us and turn out to be really bad for us.[254] Socrates said:

> *No man voluntarily pursues evil, or that which he thinks to be evil. To prefer evil to good is not in human nature; and when a man is compelled to choose one of two evils no one will choose the greater when he may have the less. This, however, does not prevent men from desiring what they supposed to be goods although they are really evils. Since they are mistaken*

in their judgment and suppose the evils to be goods, they really desire goods.[255]

The essence of religion is that God, as the creator and father of our spirits and more knowledgeable than any man, is able to teach us what is really good for us, i.e., principles that will bring us the greatest happiness. Only when we desire what God desires for us will our desires be "right" and our values be "true."

Thomas Acquinas taught another view of truth, i.e., when a created thing is in accord with the creator's plan or intention. Thus, a "house is said to be true that fulfills the likeness of the form in the architect's mind."[256] In this sense we may say that religion is true if its doctrines, ordinances and organization are in accord with God's plan, intention or will.

In regard to the difference between subjective truth and objective truth, William James has emphasized that what feels good is not necessarily good. Writing in 1902 he said:

What immediately feels most 'good' is not always most 'true,' when measured by the verdict of the rest of experience. The difference between Philip drunk and Philip sober is the classic instance in corroboration. If merely 'feeling good' could decide, drunkenness would be the supremely valid human experience.[257]

In more modern times, some might substitute drugs for alcohol in the foregoing example, but James concludes that "however acutely satisfying at the moment," its value and good for our life are not borne out over time. The same could be said for all the sensual pleasures from gluttony to sex. We need a different standard for testing truth. James finds little guidance in the many "mystical" experiences he analyzes. He reviews the lives of many mystics in Hinduism, Buddhism, Islam, and Christianity. He concludes:

The fact is that the mystical feeling of enlargement, union, and emancipation has no specific intellectual content whatever of its own. It is capable of forming matrimonial alliances with material furnished by the most diverse philosophies and theologies, provided only they can find a

> *place in their framework for its peculiar emotional mood. We have no right, therefore, to invoke its prestige as distinctively in favor of any special belief. . . .*[258]

He recognizes that for the person who has such experiences, "when well developed, usually are, and have the right to be, absolutely authoritative over the individuals to whom they come,"[259] but "for those who stand outside of them, no authority emanates from them which would make it a duty to accept their revelations uncritically."[260] In other words, he accepts the reality of personal spiritual experience but finds that, unless they can be replicated, they cannot provide satisfactory conviction to others. Similarly, Christianity teaches that there are false spirits that try to mislead and deceive men. In 1831 Jesus Christ warned Joseph Smith:

> *Behold, verily I say unto you, that there are many spirits which are false spirits, which have gone forth in the earth, deceiving the world. And also Satan has sought to deceive you, that he might overthrow you.*[261]

In other words, spiritual experiences may come from God or from the devil—the important thing is to be able to distinguish between them. This gift of "discernment" is part of the gift of the Holy Ghost and of the true priesthood that we will discuss further in Part III.

James generally advocates a "utilitarian" or "pragmatic" approach to testing truth (if a principle "works" it must be true). He apparently adopts Jesus' teaching that we should look at the "fruits" of a doctrine or a principle.[262] However, he also admits that if a doctrine or principle is true, its blessings or "fruits" may not be clear until the next life.[263] Indeed, almost all religions teach that we have to forego certain apparent pleasures in this life for rewards in the next life.

Interestingly, Bertrand Russell, the modern critic of religion, was adamant that the only test for a religion should be its truth:

> *[T]here is a certain tendency in our practical age to consider that it does not much matter whether religious teaching is true or not, since the important question is whether it is*

useful. One question cannot, however, be decided without the other. If we believe the Christian religion, our notions of what is good will be different from what they will be if we do not believe it. Therefore, to Christians, the effects of Christianity may seem good, while to unbelievers they may seem bad. Moreover, the attitude that one ought to believe such and such a proposition, independently of the question whether there is any evidence in its favor, is an attitude which produces hostility to evidence and causes us to close our minds to every fact that does not suit our prejudices.

A certain kind of scientific candor is a very important quality, and it is one which can hardly exist in a man who imagines that there are things which it is his duty to believe. We cannot, therefore, really decide whether religion does good without investigating the question whether religion is true. [264]

He complained that some people argue that we should promote the belief in God or in a particular religion because if people believe these things, "they will act better than if they do not." But, Russell says:

As soon as it is held that any belief, no matter what, is important for some other reason than it is true, a whole host of evils is ready to spring up. Discouragement of inquiry, which I spoke of before, is the first of these, but others are pretty sure to follow. Positions of authority will be open only to the orthodox. Historical records must be falsified if they throw doubt on received opinions. Sooner or later unorthodoxy will come to be considered a crime to be dealt with by the stake, the purge, or the concentration camp. I can respect the men who argue that religion is true and therefore ought to be believed, but I can only feel profound moral reprobation for those who say that religion ought to be believed because it is useful, and that to ask whether it is true is a waste of time.[265]

It must be admitted that there are many instances of people invoking the most popular religion to obtain or maintain political power. As can be seen from the foregoing quotations from Bertrand Russell, sometimes confusion arises regarding the relationship between faith, truth, and knowledge. Sometimes, people such as Bertrand Russell regard faith as dogmatic belief in things that are contrary to all known evidence. However, believers do not become believers or expect others to become believers without any evidence at all. All true faith is based in part on some evidence satisfactory to that believer. Likewise, if a person achieves a conviction that a certain person is a prophet, sage, or has spiritual insight, they may also accept the immortality of the soul because that prophet, sage, or teacher teaches such immortality, although they have never died and actually experienced it.

Even that which the skeptic would classify as "knowledge" rather than "mere belief or faith" is subject to on-going review and revision. Particularly, science, the "god" of some, has always and constantly revised its body of knowledge, so that at any given time it may be more accurate to regard such body of knowledge as no more than the current doctrines in which the scientists have faith. The individual search for truth is a process of discovering objective truth in all its facets. In fact, the objective evidence supporting belief in something that an individual has not himself experienced may be more pervasive and persuasive than the individual is willing to admit. It is better to view "faith" and "knowledge" in a continuum, with some things better supported by more reliable evidence than others. Paul, the greatest missionary of Christianity says, "[F]aith is the substance [assurance] of things hoped for [that are true], the evidence of things not seen.[266] It is impossible to have "faith" in anything that is in fact not true—that would only be superstition, and all "true" faith is based on some evidence.

THE UNITY OF TRUTH

For some, such as adherents of Jainism, the knowledge of truth is only probable or partial. That means that our knowledge always comes from some particular standpoint (naya). Reality expresses itself in multiple forms (anekantavada). An example is the six blind men who touch different parts of the elephant's body and think they have the complete truth and understanding of the elephant, but, in reality, only have a part. But, this idea has been criticized by the other six Hindu sects who believe that ultimate reality is one, whether any one individual can perceive it in its completeness or comprehend it at that time or not. Furthermore, logically contradictory statements cannot both be true—such would merely be an admission that the declarant does not understand the complete truth.[267]

William James accepts religious diversity and pluralism—he finds no need to try to reconcile different manifestations of God. He says:

> *Ought it to be assumed that in all men the mixture of religion with other elements should be identical. Ought it, indeed, to be assumed that the lives of all men should show identical religious elements? In other words, is the existence of so many religious types and sects and creeds regrettable? To these questions I answer 'No' emphatically. And my reason is that I do not see how it is possible that creatures in such different positions and with such different powers as human individuals are, should have exactly the same functions and duties.*[268]

Dr. Adler says that pluralism—the existence of numerous opinions, approaches, and attitudes—is completely acceptable in the realms of poetry, painting, art, fiction writing, music, cuisine, dress, and manners. In these fields, where creativity is to be encouraged, freedom of expression enriches our lives and provides choices for different tastes (subjective truth). However, in other fields, such as history, mathematics, science, philosophy, and religion, we are not promoting the creation of diversity—we are seeking common understanding among people and "truth" to ground our lives and build upon (objective truth).[269] He cites Thomas Acquinas that there is a unity of truth, and science and religion cannot be in conflict if each of them is accurate in its beliefs:

> *There is only one all-embracing sphere of logical or factual truth, in which all the parts, however various or diverse they may be in other respects, must be coherent and compatible with one another.*[270]

Dr. Adler also explains that some propositions in religion are logically contradictory—such as a statement that God exists and another statement that God does not exist. In such cases both statements cannot be true, but one of the two statements is true. In other cases, statements may be merely contrary—such as a statement that there is only one God and the statement that there are many gods. Although these statements conflict with each other and both can't be true, both could be false, for example, if there is no God.[271]

Dr. Adler also emphasizes that we are not talking about the issue of religious liberty, freedom of worship, or religious toleration, which are matters of Church-State relationships and the problem of peaceful co-existence among varying religious beliefs (we will consider this issue in greater depth later in this Part in Sections 14 and 15). Here, we are concerned with our individual pursuit of truth—of seeking to understand if any religious doctrine or precept is "true" in terms of its conformity to reality or its consistency with "right desire." Through this we are seeking to improve our lives and happiness by avoiding error. Jesus taught those that "believed on him" if you "continue in my word . . . ye shall know the truth and the truth shall make you free."[272] This seems to mean that truth frees us from ignorance and error, both of which cause limitation and pain in our lives. It is this comprehensive search for truth that will permit us to attain greater happiness.

Members of The Church of Jesus Christ of Latter-day Saints are taught that "all truth is circumscribed in one great whole." Jesus also taught Joseph Smith, "[A]ll truth is independent in that sphere in which God has placed it . . ."[273] From this we may understand that there are different bodies of truth, such as correct business principles or correct parenting principles, but they are all facets of one body of cohesive truth.

One important reconciliation that must take place in order to see bodies of truth as a unity is the truth of reason and the truth of feeling. This was the debate between Voltaire and Rousseau. All people experience conflicts between what their heads tell them to do and what their hearts tell them to do in particular situations. Sometimes things that "feel right" make no logical sense, yet most people recognize the importance of maintaining some internal consistency in applying principles they believe in their lives—not just doing whatever one feels like at the time. This conflict manifests itself in other aspects of life, for example, conflicts between justice and mercy, conflicts between freedom and equality, and, without over-generalizing, conflicts between the way men see things (logical truth) and the way women see things (emotional truth). Finding a reconciliation, balance, or harmony between these apparently conflicting truths is essential to finding complete truth and understanding the unity of truth. For Christians, this unification occurs in and through the atonement of Jesus Christ.

TRUTH IN RELIGION

When we question if a religion is "true," we usually have in mind completeness and accuracy in all of its doctrines and practices. While recognizing that there will always be some in every religion who claim to accept the doctrines of a religion but do not, in fact, practice them, and that it is unfair to judge any religion by such persons, we are looking for pure truth in the doctrine of the religion. There are some, of course, who believe that no such religion exists. Bertrand Russell says:

> *I think all the great religions of the world—Buddhism, Hinduism, Christianity, Islam, and Communism—both untrue and harmful. It is evident as a matter of logic that, since they disagree, not more than one of them can be true.*[274]

Jonathan Swift satirizes religious contention by telling us of the travels of Lemuel Gulliver to Lilliput where the "little people" of Lilliput have been engaged in a long war with the people of Blefuscu over the "Big-Endian" heresy, which arose over the interpretation of their scriptures as to whether eggs should be broken on the big or little end when cracking them.[275] Similarly, Voltaire commented about religious skepticism in his day, "Their passions make them believe that there is no religion because the only one they are taught is ridiculous."[276]

Yet, many religions claim they are the true religion. Paul told the

Christians in Ephesus, there is "one faith, one baptism, one God and Father of all . . ."[277] Catholics declare that Catholicism is "the one true religion which subsists in the Catholic and apostolic Church." [278] Islam declares that it is the "only true" faith.[279] Jesus Christ told Joseph Smith that The Church of Jesus Christ of Latter-day Saints is "the only true and living church upon the face of the whole earth."[280]

For those who are looking for a religion where there has been no schism, off-shoots, or sects as the test of truth, they will be disappointed. Whether in Christianity, Islam, Judaism, Buddhism, Hinduism, or any of the major world religions, an extra-ordinary number of sects exist. No religion is a monolith.

For example, Buddhism divided into the Mahayana school or northern tradition, which became predominant in Tibet, Mongolia, China, Korea, and Japan, while the Hinayana (or Theravada) southern tradition became predominant in Burma, Sri Lanka, Cambodia, and Thailand. Mahayana split into two major sects in India—the Yogacara (idealism) and the Madhyamika (relativism or nihilism), and into five major sects in China, including Tendai, Zen (Cha'an), and Shingon. According to the Buddhism Missionary Foundation of Japan, there are "84,000 'dharma' (true doctrine) gates" to enlightenment.[281] In Hinayana Buddhism the two main sects are Vaibhasika (direct realism) and Sautrantika (indirect realism).[282]

Christianity has the major divisions of Roman Catholic, Eastern Orthodox (consisting of Greek, Russian, Syrian, Armenian, and Coptic churches), and Protestant, but more than 275 other subsects.[283] Hinduism has six major sects—Gautama's Nyaya, Kanada's Vaisesika, Kapila's Samkhya, Patanjali's Yoga, Jamimini's Purva Mimamsa, and Badarayana's Uttara Mimamsa (also called the Vedanta) and "many subsystems" plus the "heterodox" sects of Carvaka and two sects of Jainism.[284]

In Islam, despite the injunction in *The Koran*, "Do not split up your religion into sects,"[285] shortly after Mohammed's death the first schism occurred splitting Islam into two major sects. Islam's largest sect is the Sunni (North Africa, Egypt, Palestine, and Pakistan), the Shiites are next (Iran) and smaller sects include Wahabbis (Saudi Arabia), Alwaites (Syria), Sufis, Druze, Ikhwan (Muslim Brotherhood), Murites, and Jabrites[286]

Judaism has the Orthodox, consisting of Ashkenazi and Sephardic, the "ultra-orthodox" Hasidic, the Neo-Orthodox, Conservative, Reform and Reconstructionists, as well as smaller sects such as Karaims and the mystical Kaballah.[287] Shintoism, the native religion of Japan, divides into 13 major sects and 63 sub-sects.[288]

Alternatively, some may seek to join the religion of the majority or the most popular religion. By number of adherents, the four major religions of the world are Christianity, Islam, Hinduism and Buddhism. Other religions such as Judaism, Sikhism, Jainism and Shintoism are important minorities. According to the estimates of Dr. David Barrett in his *World Christian Encyclopedia*, updated annually in the International Bulletin of Missionary Research, the religious affiliations in 2003 were as follows:[289]

RELIGION	MEMBERS (MILLIONS)
Christians	2,076
Muslims	1,265
Hindus	849
Buddhists	371
New religionists	105
Ethno-religionists	237
Sikhs	25
Jews	14
Non-religious	786
Atheists	151
Other	10
World population	6,278,289

He also estimates there are 3,608,000 churches in 36,400 denominations. Although one may be tempted to judge truth by the denomination with the most adherents, at least given the teaching of Jesus—*Enter ye in at the strait gate: for wide is the gate, and broad is the way that leadeth to destruction, and many there be which go in thereat. Because strait is the gate and narrow is the way, which leadeth unto life, and few there be that findeth it*[290]—judging the truthfulness of a religion by the number of its adherents could be risky, and is not an intellectually satisfying way to judge the truth. Indeed, we may sense that we are accepting merely the easiest, least restricting or "lowest common denominator" of religions.

In contrast to those who believe no religion is true, some teach that all religions are "true." Professor Raymond Firth says:

> *To me as an anthropologist, each religion, even that which may appear to be intellectually not very sophisticated, contains some explanatory ideas about the world, some rituals as guides to conduct, serving as patterns for human relationships. Therefore I would argue that there is truth in every religion . . .*
>
> *Many of the values of these religious faiths are true values, in the sense that if honestly adopted, they make for a more viable social life—self-sacrifice, thought for others, avoidance of deceit, care for more vulnerable members of society, integrative meaning of rituals, strength in cooperation.*[291]

Similar to the foregoing "humanist" interpretation, some look for the common morality in various religions. For example, almost all of the major religions have some version of the "Golden Rule." Aristotle supposedly taught, "We should behave to our friends as we would wish our friends to behave to us."[292] Confucius taught, "Do not impose on others what you yourself do not desire."[293] Lao Tzu taught, "Do good to him who has done you injury."[294] The Hindu *Mahabharata* teaches that "one should never do to another that which one would regard as injurious to oneself."[295] Buddhism teaches, "[A]s a mother cares for her son, all her days, so toward all living beings a man's mind should be all-embracing."[296] Hillel, the Jewish rabbi, taught, "What is hateful to you do not to your neighbor."[297] Jesus taught, "Therefore, all things whatsoever ye would that men should do to you, do ye even so to them.[298] *The Koran* of Islam teaches, "No man is a true believer unless he desires for his brother that which he desires for himself."[299]

C.S. Lewis, in his book, *The Abolition of Man*, summarizes what he considers to be the doctrines common to "natural religion" as follows:

The Law of General Benificence (for example, do not kill and do unto others as you would have them do unto you); The Law of Special Benificence (for example, love thy spouse); The Duties to Parents, Elders and Ancestors (for example, honor thy father and thy mother); The Duties to Children and Posterity (respect, education); The Law of Justice (being fair to others); The Law of Good Faith and Veracity (including honesty); The Law of Mercy (including kindness); and The Law of Magnanimity (generosity). According to Professor Lewis these precepts are common in all religions.[300]

This overlap of truth in the teachings of various religions helps us be respectful and tolerant of the good in each religion. One explanation for the existence of these truths in various religions is stated by the prophet Alma in *The Book of Mormon*:

> *Why should I desire that I were an angel, that I could speak unto all the ends of the earth?*
>
> *For behold, the Lord doth grant unto all nations, of their own nation and tongue, to teach his word, yea, in wisdom, all that he seeth fit that they should have; therefore, we see that the Lord doth counsel in wisdom, according to that which is just and true.*[301]

According to *The Koran*, "[Allah] raised an apostle in every nation, saying: 'Serve Allah and avoid false gods.'"[302]

Brigham Young taught:

> *Some who call themselves Christians are very tenacious with regard to the Universalists, yet the latter possess many excellent ideas and good truths. Have the Catholics? Yes, a great many very excellent truths. Have the Protestants? Yes, from first to last. Has the infidel? Yes, he has a good deal of truth; and truth is all over the world.*[303]

A variation of the humanist concept is the concept that "all roads lead to heaven." As indicated hereafter, the Hindus teach that all rivers flow to the ocean. Although historically Orthodox Jews believed adamantly that they had the only true religion and that they were the chosen people of God, in more modern times, Rabbi Morris Kertzer says, "Our prayer book tells us: 'The righteous of all nations are worthy of immortality.' We Jews know there are many mountaintops—all of them reach for the stars."[304] Robert Burton was of the opinion, "One religion is as true as another."[305] Of course, this idea is usually offered as a substitute for true analysis of the truth of any particular religion. In fact, a moment's reflection is all that is necessary to understand that some roads may lead to "hell" and that just because a road is hard or easy cannot be the proper test for the truth of a religion. William James is particularly critical of the practices of asceticism in religion as the path of righteousness. Gautama Buddha also was critical of Hindu fakirs and taught the "middle way"—one does not seek pain and suffering because there will be sufficient pain and suffering that will challenge a person's spiritual strength without self-inflicting pain, but neither should a person seek the life of pleasure or ease.

C.S. Lewis, in his book, *Mere Christianity*, tried to distill the essential doctrines of Christianity from the various Christian sects. But he admonished that this "natural Christianity" was not actual Christianity:

> *It is more like a hall out of which doors open into several rooms. If I can bring anyone into that hall I shall have done what I attempted. But it is in the rooms, not in the hall, that there are fires and chairs and meals. The hall is a place to wait in, a place from which to try the various doors, not a place to live in . . . . But you must regard it as waiting, not as camping. You must keep on praying for light: and, of course, even in the hall, you must begin trying to obey the rules which are common to the whole house. And above all you must be asking which door is the true one; not which pleases you best by its paint and paneling. In plain language, the question should never be: 'Do I like that kind of service?' but 'Are these doctrines true; Is holiness here? Does my conscience move me towards this? Is my reluctance to knock at this door due to my pride, or my mere taste, or my personal dislike of this particular doorkeeper.'*[306]

HOW DO WE ACQUIRE TRUTH?

The Catholic Church teaches:

All men are bound to seek the truth, especially in what concerns God and his Church, and to embrace it and hold on to it as they come to know it. This duty derives from the very dignity of the human person.[307]

Some people believe, like Bertrand Russell, that we cannot know if a particular religion is true. Of course, such statements are merely an admission that the person making such a statement has not found for himself or herself any satisfactory way to determine the truth of any religion to which they have thus far been acquainted.

As we saw in Part I, some approach their evaluation of religions from a very logical and rationalistic point of view. While everyone who accepts a religion and, especially those who seek to influence others to accept their beliefs, must be prepared "always to give an answer to every man that asketh you a reason" for his or her belief, as Peter counseled the Christians of his time,[308] the examples cited in Part I make quite clear that all religions (except perhaps Deism) recognize that true conversion requires more than logical and rational analysis. Ralph Waldo Emerson believed that all men can recognize the truth when they see it:

The soul is the perceiver and revealer of truth. We know truth when we see it, let sceptic and scoffer say what they choose . . . We are wiser than we know. If we will not interfere with our thought, but will act entirely, or see how the thing stands in God, we know the particular thing, and everything, and every man. For the Maker of all things and all persons stands behind us, and casts his dread omniscience through us over things.

But beyond this recognition of its own in particular passages of the individual's experience, it also reveals truth . . . For the soul's communication of truth is the highest event in nature . . . We distinguish the announcements of the soul, its manifestation of its own nature by the term Revelation. These are always attended by the emotion of the sublime. For this communication is an influx of the Divine mind into our mind.[309]

However, there are many others who would say that this all-pervading soul of the universe—the "Over-Soul" in which Emerson apparently believed—has not made it sufficiently clear to mankind where the truth lies, as evidenced by the continuing religious diversity, strife, bloodshed and controversy. Joseph Smith taught that there were "many" "among all sects, parties, and denominations, who are only kept from the truth because they know not where to find it."[310]

Of course, one way to approach the problem of finding the true religion is to become a member of, or at least practice the teachings of, all the religions for a sufficient period of time to understand them and to evaluate them. One advantage of that approach is that we would be able to evaluate the "fruits" of living that religion. For example, Jesus taught that if any man would obey his teachings that person would know whether his teachings were from God.[311] Other religions would counter, however, that the same is true of their religion. The real problem is that there are so many religions that this is impossible in the time that we have in life.

What is possible, however, is to study various religions and to compare their doctrines. By such study, coupled with prayer, the truthfulness of certain doctrines can become clearer and the choices left that require further study and, perhaps, practice, can be reduced.

Part of our willingness to act upon truth as we perceive it at any given time is a reflection of our view of God. If we believe that God is a punishing, vindictive God, then we are going to be extremely hesitant to make mistakes and non-committal in most of our actions. On the other hand, if we believe God to be kind and forgiving, that the purpose of this life is to progress in our knowledge and understanding and to substitute new truths whenever we find evidence to justify them, we will proceed with greater confidence and peace in all aspects of our life. Just because we make mistakes or hold incorrect beliefsw will not be eternally condemned. Joseph Smith taught, "It does not prove that a man is not a good man because he errs in doctrine,"[312] but if a person is further enlightened, honesty and integrity impose an obligation to practice the new truth he or she has come to know. Jesus teaches that if we "seek" we shall "find" and if we "knock" it shall be "opened unto us." [313] Jesus promised his disciples that the Holy Spirit would "guide you into all truth."[314] Oliver Wendell Holmes emphasized the importance of continuing effort in this search:

> *I find the great thing in the world is not so much where we stand, as in what direction we are moving. To reach the port of heaven, we must sail sometimes with the wind and sometimes against it—but we must sail and not drift, nor lie at anchor.*[315]

C.S. Lewis also believed that study of a religion's doctrine was essential. In response to a man who had a spiritual experience in the desert he said:

> *You see what happened to that man in the desert may have been real, and was certainly exciting, but nothing comes of it. It leads nowhere. There is nothing to do about it. In fact, that is why a vague religion—all about feeling God in nature, and so on—is so attractive. It is all thrills and no work; like watching the waves from the beach. But you will not get to Newfoundland by studying the Atlantic in that way, and you will not get eternal life by simply feeling the presence of God in flowers or music.*[316]

Oliver Cowdery was told by Jesus Christ that in order to ascertain truth he should "study it out in your mind," and then "you must ask me if it be right," and if your understanding is right, "I will cause that your bosom shall burn within you [by the Holy Spirit]" "[b]ut if it not be right, you shall have no such feelings, but you shall have a stupor of thought that shall cause you to forget the thing which is wrong . . ."[317] Joseph Smith also taught that the passage in the third verse of the 12th chapter of 1 Corinthians which reads, "No man can say that Jesus is the Lord, but by the Holy Ghost," should have been translated, "No man can **know** that Jesus is the Lord, but by the Holy Ghost [emphasis added]."[318] But, Jesus also taught that the Spirit of Truth—the Holy Ghost—is someone "the world cannot receive" because of their sin and unwillingness to repent.[319] Paul wrote to Timothy about those who are "Ever learning, and never able to come to the knowledge of the truth" because they rely on their own wisdom and do not seek enlightenment from God.[320]

COMMON BELIEFS OF THE VARIOUS RELIGIONS

Before contrasting the beliefs of the major religions, it will be helpful to acknowledge and recognize the common beliefs of those religions. As stated above, a common "Golden Rule" of moral living is one important example and the common virtues of "natural religion" described by C.S. Lewis are another. But there are many others. All major religions believe that man is made of body and spirit—that "we" are more than just a body, and that our consciousness or spirit continues beyond death, either to be reborn or to live as a spirit or to be resurrected.

All the major religions believe in some type of judgment, either the Final Judgment of Islam, Judaism and Christianity, or a recurring judgment of rebirth based on the type of life one has lived, as in Hinduism and Buddhism. All the major religions believe in the importance of helping the poor through almsgiving, charitable acts, and financial gifts. All the major religions teach the importance of moral chastity, forbidding adultery and fornication. All the major religions teach some type of prayer or meditation. All the major religions teach that fasting is an appropriate part of worship and purification. All of the major religions, except perhaps Confucianism, teach that men should return good for the evil they receive from others. The three religions of Judaism, Christianity, and Islam teach that there should be a holy day once a week.

Almost all religions share a common belief in many virtues such as honesty, courage, hard work, temperance and self-discipline, justice, patience and long-suffering, kindness and benevolence, humility, tolerance, respect, forgiveness and mercy, wisdom, charity, love, respect for the elderly, continence, diligence, and sacrifice. The Catholic Catechism quotes Paul:

> *Whatever is true, whatever is honorable, whatever is just, whatever is pure, whatever is lovely, whatever is gracious, if there is any excellence, if there is anything worthy of praise, think about these things.*[321]

Joseph Smith, the first prophet of The Church of Jesus Christ of Latter-day Saints listed as the Church's last Article of Faith:

> *We believe in being honest, true, chaste, benevolent, virtuous, and in doing good to all men; indeed, we may say that we follow the admonition of Paul—We believe all things, we hope all things, we have endured many things, and hope to be able to endure all things. If there is anything virtuous, lovely, or of good report or praiseworthy, we seek after these things.*[322]

A recognition that good exists and is being done by the sincere adherents of all the major religions is essential for mutual respect, tolerance, peace, and social progress.

COMPARING THE DOCTRINES

Despite the recognition that there is much common good in all the major religions, if one accepts the concept that ultimate truth is unified, and that inconsistent doctrines cannot all be truthful, and if one has a desire to seek out and know the doctrines of the major religions for the purpose of evaluation no matter how difficult the task might be, it becomes necessary to compare and contrast their doctrines. We will now analyze certain doctrines of the major religions of the world as they compare to Christianity.

1. RELIGION OR ETHICS.

Theism is a belief in the existence of God. In Christianity, Islam, Judaism, Hinduism, and Sikhism acceptance of the God taught in such religions includes duties toward that God as well as duties toward other people. For example, Jesus Christ taught that the first great commandment is that we love God with all our heart, soul, and mind, and the second commandment is that we love our neighbor as ourselves.[323] The Law of Moses had enjoined the Israelites to love God with all their heart, soul, and mind,[324] and to love their neighbor as themselves.[325] In the Ten Commandments of Judaism the first five consist of duties to God and the last five are duties to other people.[326] Believers in these religions recognize the authority and right of God to give "commandments," i.e., to teach truth superior to man's own wisdom that will bless the individuals and communities that keep such commandments. Brigham Young, the second prophet of The Church of Jesus Christ of Latter-day Saints said, "We have something more than morality alone to teach the people. What is it? It is how to redeem the human family."[327]

Moral philosophy, on the other hand, consists of ethical teachings regarding our relationships with other people. Bertrand Russell believed, "Outside human desires there is no moral standard."[328] He argued we should try to improve people by educating them in moral philosophy or ethics. We should recall, however, that George Washington, in his farewell address after his second term of office as president of the United States said:

> *Of all the dispositions and habits which lead to political prosperity, Religion and Morality are indispensable supports. In vain would that man claim the tribute of Patriotism who should labor to subvert these great Pillars of human happiness, these firmest props of the duties of man and citizens . . . . And let us with caution indulge the supposition that morality can be maintained without religion. Whatever may be conceded to the influence of refined education on minds of peculiar structure, reason and experience both forbid us to expect that national morality can prevail in exclusion of religious principle.*[329]

Despite Russell's idealism, we may remark that in actual experience, no one has been able to achieve any widespread or prolonged improvement in the conduct of man without a corresponding belief in God. Russell may argue that even with religion, or in some cases because of it, man's conduct has been deplorable (See Part II, Sections 14 and 15). The response is that both individually, and as nations, religion has improved many men and women. Napoleon said, "Religion introduces into the thought of heaven an idea of equalization which saves the rich from being massacred by the poor."[330]

Moral philosophy excludes any reference to the will of God, commandments of God, or duty to God. Aristotle's Nicomachean

Ethics is an example of moral philosophy. Confucianism and Taoism sometimes refer to offering sacrifices and performing duties to deceased ancestors and the "gods," but there is no exposition of the nature of God and no definition of one's duties to God. According to D.C. Lau, Confucius "taught a moral philosophy with man as the centerpiece."[331] "Confucius taught a way of life in which morality occupies a supreme position . . . . Confucius's view concerning the actual duties of a man was traditional. A man is born into certain relationships and as a result has certain duties."[332] The relationships are: father and son, elder and younger brother, husband and wife.[333] According to *The Analects* of Confucius:

> *The Master instructs under four heads: culture, moral conduct, doing one's best, and being trustworthy in what one says.*[334]

> *The topics the Master did not speak of were prodigies, force, disorder, and gods.*[335]

This duty to family goes quite far:

> *The governor of She said to Confucius, 'In our village there is a man nicknamed 'Straight Body.' When his father stole a sheep, he gave evidence against him.' Confucius answered, 'In our village those who are straight are quite different. Fathers cover up for their sons, and sons cover up for their fathers. Straightness is to be found in such behavior.*[336.]

Buddhism is of the same nature. Although it is difficult to generalize about Buddhism because of the two major divisions, Mahayana and Hinayana, and the numerous sub-sects, it is clear that Siddhartha Gautama, as the founder of Buddhism, did not teach that there was a God or what God was like. His teaching of the way to achieve "enlightenment" neither presumes the existence of God nor teaches that such enlightenment will result in being in the presence of God. Will Durant says, "His conception of religion was purely ethical; he cared everything about conduct, nothing about ritual or worship, metaphysics or theology."[337] While some Buddhist sects now teach that Buddha was a savior and that petitionary prayer to Buddha is appropriate, all Buddhists believe that it is through the knowledge of the nature of suffering and the Eightfold Path that a person can achieve freedom from suffering and enlightenment. The Eightfold Path consists of ethical obligations that one owes to other people: Right View, Right Thought, Right Behavior, Right Livelihood, Right Effort, Right Mindfulness, and Right Concentration[338]—no duty to God is involved.

2. A PERSONAL GOD.

Gordon Kaufman, in his book, *The Theological Imagination: Constructing the Concept of God*, says:

> *There has always been a considerable tension between the two central motifs in the symbol of God-humanness, with its tendency towards anthropomorphism and its emphasis on human fulfillment; and transcendence or absoluteness,with its emphasis on God's radical otherness, God's mystery, God's utter inaccessibility.*[339]

When considering the issue of "theism" versus "deism," or "theism" versus "monism," the essential consideration is whether or not God is a personal god. The theist affirms the existence of a personal God, the deist accepts that there is a God but avers that God is impersonal. Pantheism also affirms the existence of "God" but maintains that everything is God, God is everywhere, in and through all things and the universe itself is God.[340] Monists believe in a single, universal "way," "path" or "cosmic principle," but believe that the existence of God either cannot be known (agnostic), or is irrelevant. Deists are willing to accept that God may be a "person," but they believe God created the universe and established its laws, and through "entelechy," those laws and processes play out through the course of time. Deists have compared the creation of the universe by God to the creation of a watch—once created and wound up it is left to operate without the involvement of the watchmaker.[341] The deists believe, therefore, that it is useless to pray to God or to seek to change events, miracles are non-existent, and all religious ceremonies and rituals are useless. Jean LeRond d'Alembert, Claude Adrien Helvetius, Julien LaMetrie in France and Lord Herbert of Cherbury in England were the best-known Western deists. The doctrine of the

Jewish philosopher, Spinoza—that resulted in his excommunication from Judaism—was his doctrine of pantheism. In pantheism there is really no distinction between the Creator and the created and that belief makes it impossible to distinguish evil from good.[342] In Hinduism, Radhakrishnan and More assert that religious belief evolved from the polytheism of the early Vedas to monotheism to monism—"the doctrine of the impersonal, unknowable One"—in the later Vedas.[343] The original Buddhism of Siddhartha Gautama was essentially agnostic, asserting that it is impossible to know whether God exists or what his nature is. He asserted that there are laws of the universe, however established, that enlightened persons could come to understand that would release them from rebirth and suffering. Later, the Mahayana division of Buddhism taught that Buddha was in fact a God who had always existed in all ages of the world and to whom it was appropriate to pray for help. Confucianism and Taoism do not teach or worship a personal God. Sikhs do believe in a personal God, along with Judaism, Islam and Christianity. In each of these religions, God is a "person" who takes a personal interest in the people of the earth. It is noteworthy that there is no eyewitness account of the appearance of God in Islam, Hinduism, Buddhism, Confucianism, Taoism, Shintoism or Sikhism. Although Shintoists believe in god, indeed many gods, Professor Basil Chamberlain says,

> *[W]e would here draw attention to the fact that Shinto, so often spoken of as a religion, is hardly entitled to that name even in the opinion of those who, acting as its official mouthpiece today, desire to maintain it as a patriotic institution. It has no set of dogmas, no sacred book, no moral code.* [344]

A distinctive aspect of belief in a personal God is petitionary prayer. A beautiful example of such a prayer is that of the Jewish congregation in the morning Amidah Kedushah:

> *Lord our God, hear our voice. Merciful Father, have compassion and pity upon us. Accept our prayers with loving favor, for Thou art God who hearkenest to prayers and supplications. Let us not go from Thy presence without response, O our King, but be gracious unto us and hear and answer our prayer. For Thou hearest the prayer on every lip. Blessed are Thou, Lord who hearest prayer.*[345]

Judaism believes in the fatherhood of God as described in Part I. Christianity clearly teaches the fatherhood of God and the importance of our relationship with him as the Father of our spirit. This love of the Father for his children was manifested most greatly in the atoning mission of his Son, Jesus Christ, who made it possible for mercy to overcome justice through accepting and following the teachings of Jesus Christ. In Hinduism and Buddhism the law of "karma" is inexorable—whatever a person does will result in the application of "justice" in rebirth, in a higher or lower caste—there is no place for mercy. In contemplating the personal God of *The Bible* compared to the impersonal God of the Greek and other philosophers, Blaise Pascal summarized, "The God of Abraham, the God of Isaac, the God of Jacob, not of philosophers and scholars."[346]

3. ONE GOD OR MANY.

Polytheism has existed throughout recorded history. Not only were many people mentioned in *The Bible* polytheistic, but two of the greatest civilizations of history—the Greeks and Romans—believed in multiple gods. The in-fighting, pettiness and "humanity" of those gods brought criticism from many Greeks, Romans, Christians and Jews. Michel Montaigne estimated that the number of Greek and Roman gods and goddesses was 36,000.[347]

Hinduism, certainly in its earlier stages, was polytheistic. In its later stages it adopted a "trinity" of Brahman—the Creator, Vishnu—the Preserver and Shiva—the Destroyer. However, Will Durant says:

> *These are the greater gods of Hinduism, but they are merely five of thirty million deities in the Hindu pantheon; only to catalogue them would take a hundred volumes. Some of them are more properly angels, some are what we should call devils, some are heavenly bodies like the sun, some are mascot like Lakshmi (goddess of good luck), many of them are beasts of the field or fowl of the air.*[348]

In particular, Vishnu, the most-popular of the Hindu gods, has had nine incarnations or "avatars": Matsya, a fish, Kurma, a tortoise, Varah, a boar, Naraasimha, a half man, half lion, Vamen, a dwarf, Parashurama, a human with an axe, Rama, a human, hero of the epic

Ramayana, Krishna, a human and the Buddha.[349]

Confucianism and Taoism refer to multiple gods in their sacred writings. Shintoism, in Japan, worships the gods in nature and is polytheistic.

Judaism was the first known monotheistic religion in recorded history. Jehovah was worshipped as the only true God. The affirmation of all Jews, recited even as their last dying breath, the "Sh'ma Yisrael," taken from the scriptures, is "Hear O Israel: The Lord our God is one Lord."[350]

When Mohammed founded Islam it was in part a reaction to the polytheism of Arabia. He taught that Allah was the only true God and that Jehovah and Allah were the same being.[351]

Christianity has been less clear. Mohammed criticized the Christians for becoming polytheistic because he argued that the Christians worshipped both God the Father and Jesus Christ. Whatever may have been the belief or practice, however, among certain Christians around 600 A.D., the New Testament is very clear that Jesus Christ is the son of God, not God the Father. Jesus himself taught that people should pray to the Father and the Father, on two recorded occasions in the New Testament—at Jesus' baptism and on the Mount of Transfiguration—confirmed to those present by a voice out of heaven that this was his "beloved Son."[352] Paul summarized, "But to us there is one God, the Father, of whom are all things and we in him; and one Lord Jesus Christ, by whom are all things, and we by him."[353] This God is "the Father of our Lord Jesus Christ" and Jesus is the "one mediator between God and men."[354] What complicated matters, however, is that at later stages of Christianity and by the time of Mohammed in 600 A.D., the Christian councils had adopted a definition that God, the Father, Jesus Christ and the Holy Ghost were "homousia"—of the same substance, but with three different manifestations—God, the Father—the Creator, God the Son—the Redeemer, and God the Holy Spirit—the Enlightener. The result was that questions arose as to whether Christianity believed in one God, two Gods or three Gods. This subject will be further discussed in Part III, Section 10, "The Trinity."

4. SAGE, PROPHET OR SAVIOR.

The founders of each religion must be evaluated in terms of what they claimed of themselves, as well as how they were regarded by others. Mohammed taught that he was a "prophet," and that is how his followers regarded him then and today. This meant that he was authorized by and spoke for God—that he had authority from God to teach and that his teachings were "true." ("He that obeys the Apostle obeys Allah himself.")[355] According to The Institute for Islamic Information and Education, "we do not know how many prophets God has sent to humanity," but "[s]ome Muslim scholars have suggested 240 thousand prophets."[356] *The Koran* accepts Adam, Noah, Abraham, Isaac, Jacob, Joseph, Moses, Enoch, Ishmael, David, Solomon, Lot, Elias, Jonah, Elisha, Zacharias and Jesus as prophets. Mohammed is the "true and last prophet of God."[357] (The Bahai religion, which developed as another sect of Shiite Muslims in the 1800's accepts the Jewish prophets, Jesus, Zoroaster, Buddha and Mohammed as prophets and Baha Ullah (1817-92) as the "last" prophet of God.). Mohammed disclaimed power to perform miracles[358] (except the recitation of the words that became *The Koran* as revealed to him by God). He never claimed to be a "savior." Fourteen references in *The Koran* insist that God has no son and Jesus was only a prophet. The following are typical:

> *Those who say: 'The Lord of Mercy has begotten a son' preach a monstrous falsehood, at which the very heavens might crack, the earth break asunder, and the mountains crumble to dust. That they should ascribe a son to the Merciful, when it does not become Him to beget one.*[359]

> *Jesus was no more than a mortal whom We favored and made an example to the Israelites.*[360]

> *Never has Allah begotten a son, nor is there any god besides Him.*[361]

The Koran says that Jesus did not die and was not crucified, as it appeared to Jesus' disciples, for God "lifted him up to his presence."[362]

Siddhartha Gautama never claimed to have had any "revelation" from God, but did claim to have attained certain wisdom that he termed "enlightenment."

Buddha, meaning 'Enlightened,' is among the many titles given to the Master, whose personal name was Siddhartha, and whose clan name was Gautama. He was also called Shakya-muni, or 'Sage of the Shakyas' and Tathagata 'One who Has Won the Truth.'[363]

As such he did not claim to speak for God as a prophet and can be classified as a sage, or wise person. He exhorted his followers to follow the "teachings which I have given you."[364] Will Durant says, "He claimed 'enlightenment,' but not inspiration; he never pretended that a god was speaking through him."[365] There are no miracles in Buddhism—Buddha supposedly said, "By this ye shall know that a man is not my disciple—that he tries to work a miracle."[366] Later, some sects of Buddhism taught that Buddha had always existed and that from time to time he came to earth in an incarnation to try to oppose evil and prevent its triumph. As such he is a "savior" of mankind.[367] One story tells that a hermit saw the child and predicted that he would grow up to be a great king but that if he forsook court life to embrace a religious life he would become a "Buddha, the Savior of the world."[368] The Buddhist Missionary Foundation, in their book, *The Teaching of Buddha*, says:

Buddha does not always appear as a Buddha. Sometimes He appears as an incarnation of evil, sometimes as a woman, a god, a king, or a statesman; sometimes He appears in a brothel or in a gambling house.[369]

However, Radhakrishnan and Moore say:

The Buddha is not so much a savior as an example. The worship of the Buddha is merely an act of commemoration. The popular gods were introduced into Buddhism in its more religious forms to serve as objects for meditation.[370]

The earliest records of his life record no miracles but later teachers attribute miracles to him. The historian Will Durant explains these different conceptions of Buddha as follows:

Within two centuries of Buddha's death eighteen varieties of Buddhistic doctrine had divided the Master's heritage. The Buddhists of south India and Ceylon held fast for a time to the simpler and purer creed of the Founder, which came to be called Hinayana, or the 'Lesser Vehicle': they worshiped Buddha as a great teacher, but not as a god, and their Scriptures were the Pali texts of the more ancient faith. But throughout northern India, Tibet, Mongolia, China and Japan the Buddhism that prevailed was the Mahayana, or the 'Greater Vehicle,' defined and propagated by Kanishika's Council; these (politically) inspired theologians announced the divinity of Buddha, surrounded him with angels and saints, adopted the Yoga asceticism of Patanjali, and issued in Sanskrit a new set of Holy Writ which, though it lent itself readily to metaphysical and scholarly refinements, proclaimed and certified a more popular religion than the austere pessimism of Shakyamuni. The Mahayana was Buddhism softened with Brahmanical deities, practices and myths, and adapted to the needs of the Kushan Tatars and the Mongols of Tibet, over whom Kanishka had extended his rule. A heaven was conceived in which there were many Buddhas, of whom Amida Buddha, the Redeemer, came to be the best beloved by the people; this heaven and a corresponding hell were to be the reward or punishment of good or evil done on earth, and would thereby liberate some of the King's militia for other services. The greatest of the saints, in this new theology, were the Bodhisattvas, or future Buddha's, who voluntarily refrained from achieving the Nirvana (here freedom from rebirth) that was within their merit and power, in order to be reborn into life after life, and to help others on earth to find the Way. As in Mediterranean [sic medieval?] Christianity, these saints became so popular that they almost crowded out the head of the pantheon in worship and art. The veneration of relics, the use of holy water, candles, incense, the rosary, clerical vestments, a liturgical dead language, monks and nuns, monastic tonsure and celibacy, confession, fast days, the canonization of saints, purgatory and masses for the dead flourished in Buddhism as in medieval

Christianity, and seem to have appeared in Buddhism first. Mahayana became to Hinayana or primitive Buddhism what Catholicism was to Stoicism and primitive Christianity. Buddha, like Luther, had made the mistake of supposing that the drama of religious ritual could be replaced with sermons and morality; and the victory of a Buddhism rich in myths, miracles, ceremonies and intermediating saints corresponds to the ancient and current triumph of a colorful and dramatic Catholicism over the austere simplicity of early Christianity and modern Protestantism.[371]

It is hard to identify exactly who would be considered to be the "founder" of Judaism. Moses is credited with being the author of the first five books of the Old Testament (the *Torah* or *Pentateuch*), but Moses records in Genesis the creation of the earth and many other righteous persons who had communion with God before his own time, including Noah and Abraham. The Jews regard these persons as "prophets," "who were granted an immediate vision of the divine and brought God's message to the people, admonishing and rebuking them, comforting them and holding out hope . . ."[372] Professor Dummelow in *A Commentary on the Holy Bible* states:

The popular definition of a prophet is 'one who predicts the future.' This was the conception heathen nations had of their inspired oracles, and it has very largely prevailed in the Christian Church regarding the Old Testament prophets. But such a view is narrow and misleading. The prophet is 'one who speaks for God'—a forth-teller rather than a mere foreteller. This is seen from Exodus 7:1, where Aaron's relation to Moses as his spokesman is compared with the prophet's relation to God. The prophets were men who claimed to have received from Jehovah the truths which they spoke in His name.[373]

The entire Jewish Tanakh (Old Testament) consists of the ministry of various prophets at different times. These prophets were regarded as very important when they were accepted, but many were ignored and even killed. As examples of the prophetic role, Moses, when asked a theological question by the people, responded, "Stand still and I will hear what the Lord will command concerning you. And the Lord spake unto Moses . . ."[374] The prophet Balaam said to Balak, who called him to curse his enemies:

> *If Balak would give me his house full of silver and gold, I cannot go beyond the commandment of the Lord, to do either good or bad of mine own mind; but what the Lord saith, that will I speak.*[375]

The prophet Amos recorded, "Surely the Lord God will do nothing but he revealeth his secret unto his servants the prophets."[376] Later, during the time period approximately 200 B.C to 200 A.D., Jewish rabbis interpreted the Torah in the collection of writings now called *The Mishnah*. After that—from about 200 A.D. to 500 A.D.—other rabbis interpreted *The Mishnah* in the "Gemarah" writings of the Talmud. These interpreters were known as the Tannaim for *The Mishnah* and the Amoraim for the Talmud. The Tannaim and Amoraim were regarded as "sages."[377] None of these sages were regarded as prophets and none of the prophets claimed to be, or was regarded by anyone, as a "savior." Nevertheless, the Jews firmly believed in a "Messiah" who would redeem the people. At the judgment day each Jew will be asked, among other things, "have you been firm in your hope for Messianic redemption."[378] In their Sabbath prayers the Jews pray, "May He hasten the coming of his anointed Messiah in your lifetime and in the life of the whole House of Israel, speedily and soon."[379] After each meal Jews give thanks and pray that they may live to witness the coming of the Messiah,[380] and they seek to enter into the "Yemot ha-Mashiah,"—the Messianic age.[381] But this Messiah does not "atone" for our sins in Jewish belief—sin and repentance is between the individual and God. Despite many symbols in Jewish ceremony of atonement, such as the red heifer, the scapegoat, and laying hands on the bullock offered in sacrifice to transfer the sins of the people to the animal, the prayer of the dying Jew is, "But if now my appointed hour is nigh, then may my death be an atonement for all my sins and transgressions."[382] Rabbi Morris Kertzer says, "Nor can Judaism accept the principle of vicarious atonement—the idea of salvation through Christ. It is our belief that every man is responsible for his own salvation."[383] Indeed, the Jews refer to God as "our Sovereign and Savior,"[384] but, perhaps to make clear the Jews have not adopted Christianity, one of the prayers from the Zohar says:

> *Not in man do I trust, nor do I rely on a son of God, but only in the God of the heavens who is the God of truth, whose Torah is truth and whose prophets are truth and who abounds in doing goodness and truth.*[385]

In Confucianism and Taoism their founders, K'ung Ch'iu and Lao Tzu never claimed to speak for God or to be saviors—they are regarded by their disciples as sages.

Hinduism has no founder that can be identified, and certainly no one that has come down through history as claiming to be either a prophet or a savior. As discussed in Part I, early Hinduism, as expressed in the Vedas, believed in polytheism. In the middle or Epic time period of the Ramayana and Mahabharata, which includes the *Bhagavad Gita*, a single God, Brahman, is accepted along with Vishnu, the Preserver, and Shiva, the Destroyer. The Bhagavad Gita also asserts that Krishna is the incarnation or descent of Vishnu into the human frame as a "savior," which occurs whenever the forces of evil threaten to destroy human values—these are the "avatars."[386] Later, Hindu religious thought evolves to monism—the impersonal, unknowable God. The six sects of orthodox Hinduism have their six authors of the "sutras," establishing their interpretation of the Vedas and a religion or philosophy of life, but none of the writers of such sutras claimed to be prophets or saviors. Similarly, the founder of Jainism, Vardhamana, merely systematized the doctrines of early Hindu writers, Rsabha, Ajitanatha and Aristanemi, mentioned in the Yajur Veda—he did not himself claim any revelation or to be a prophet.[387]

The Sikh religion was founded by the "guru" Nanak who lived between 1469-1538 A.D.[388] After him, there were nine other guru leaders of the religion. None of them claimed to be God. God is the ultimate and eternal "Guru" (Saguru). Sikhs believe God has never appeared or been born on the earth in contrast to the avatars of the Hindu religion.[389]

As for Christianity, Pascal thought that being a prophet was not enough. He says:

> *I see many contradictory religions, and consequently all false save one. Each wants to be believed on its own authority, and threatens unbelievers. I do not therefore believe them. Every one can say this; every one can call himself a prophet. But I see the Christian religion where prophecies are fulfilled; and that is what every one cannot do.*[390]

Jesus Christ proclaimed on several occasions that he was the Son of God. For example, when being questioned before the Jewish Sanhedrin the High Priest asked him, "Art thou the Christ, the Son of the Blessed? And Jesus said, 'I am: and ye shall see the son of man sitting on the right hand of power, and coming in the clouds of heaven.'"[391] He expounded a parable making clear the distinction between the "servants" of God and the "son" of God.[392] And, he taught, "Neither knoweth any man the Father except the Son, and he to whomsoever the Son will reveal him.[393] He said, "I am the way, the truth, and the life: no man cometh unto the Father, but by me."[394] God the Father also confirmed Jesus' claims—at both the baptism of Jesus and on the Mount of Transfiguration—where God the Father referred to Jesus as his "beloved Son."[395] Jesus also declared that he was the "Messiah" the Jews were expecting.[396]

> *Therefore the Jews sought the more to kill him because he not only had broken the Sabbath, but said also that God was his Father, making himself equal with God.*[397]

His birth, life, death and resurrection was prophesied in many passages of the Old Testament before he was ever born. Bruce Richardson lists "at least six indisputable prophecies" about Jesus Christ—Psalms 22:1, 16-18, 34:20, 69:21; Isaiah 7:14, 9: 6-7 and Zechariah 13:6—but says that "some say there are as many as five hundred."[398] Blaise Pascal lists many such prophecies and pointed out that there is no known prophecy of the birth or life of Mohammed before he was born.[399] (*The Koran* claims that Jesus prophesied the advent of Mohammed, but there is no known record of such prophecy.)[400] *The Bible* also teaches that Jesus created the world as the

Father's agent—this occurred, obviously, before Jesus was born in the flesh.[401] The miraculous circumstances of his birth, the many miracles attributed to him—34 specific ones are recorded by the four writers of the gospels of the New Testament according to James Talmage[402] and many more healing miracles are referred to in general that he performed in Galilee and in the temple courts[403]—and his death and miraculous resurrection are the very essence of who he was. Professor Dummelow says:

> *Whereas such teachers as Gautama, Mahomet, and Confucius have claimed faith in their doctrines, not in their persons, Jesus evidently claimed faith in His person, and submission to his authority of an altogether unique kind . . . He was put to death as a blasphemer for claiming to be not merely the Messiah, but the Son of God, and prophesying His future session at God's right hand, and Second Coming to Judgment (Mark 14:62). To His death he attributed a significance unintelligible on the assumption that He was a mere human being. His death, He taught was a 'ransom for man' (10:45), a propitiation for sin, and the establishment of a new covenant between God and man (14:24). Here we find Jesus demanding unlimited faith in His own Person—a faith so intense, and a devotion so consuming none but God can rightly claim it (Luke 14:26, Matthew 10:14, 15, 32, 33, 37, 40, 11:28)*[404]

Jesus taught that as the Son of God he had power in himself to lay down his life and to take it up again.[405] He taught that through their personal sins all men had become estranged from God and that through his atonement he would take upon himself the sins of all men who would repent and follow his commandments. This atonement applied to man from the beginning of the earth to the end of the earth. He also taught that through his resurrection all men would be resurrected and judged. In regard to the belief of his disciples, Peter, when asked by Jesus, "Whom do thou say that I am" replied, "Thou art the Christ, the son of the living God." Jesus then confirmed the correctness of Peter's statement by saying, "Blessed art thou, Simon Barjona: for flesh and blood hath not revealed it unto thee, but my

Father which is in heaven."[406] Whether one believes that Jesus was who he claimed to be or who his disciples regarded him as, Jesus was the only founder of any of the major religions that claimed to be a savior and was so regarded by his disciples. In regard to Jesus Peter testified to the Jewish leaders, "[T]here is none other name under heaven given among men, whereby we must be saved."[407] As stated by J.R. Dummelow, "In the estimation of His followers, Christ's life is the central fact in the history of the world:"[408]

> *A few, generally called Unitarians, are satisfied with regarding Him as the greatest of human prophets, but to the immense majority of Christians, in this as in every preceding age, He is the divine Son of God, who took our nature upon Him to redeem it, and after his suffering upon the Cross, rose from the dead, and ascended into heaven, where, seated upon the throne of the universe, He receives a homage indistinguishable from that paid to the eternal Father.*[409]

Professor Dummelow says further:

> *The synoptists all agree that Jesus was condemned for blasphemy, i.e., for claiming more than mere human powers and attributes. This is inconsistent with the contention of those who maintain that Jesus merely professed to be a mere human teacher, or at most a prophet.*[410]

In judging who Jesus was, Professor Dummelow describes it as the "great dilemma:"

> *We have been led to the conclusion that the Founder of Christianity, who is revered not only by Christians but also by most Freethinkers as the best of men, and the greatest of religious and moral reformers, claimed to be divine. This conclusion is supported by such varied and convergent evidence, that real doubt upon the subject is precluded. We are therefore brought face to face with a very serious dilemma: either the Author of Christianity was divine or He was not good . . . . Either Christ was divine, as He claimed to be, or He was a deceiver.*[411]

In this same vein, C.S. Lewis states:

> *I'm trying to prevent anyone from saying the really silly thing that people often say about Him: 'I'm ready to accept Jesus as a great moral teacher, but I don't accept His claim to be God.' That's the one thing we mustn't say. A man who was merely a man and said the sort of things Jesus said wouldn't be a great moral teacher. He'd either be a lunatic—on a level with the man who says he's a poached egg—or else he'd be the Devil of Hell. You must make your choice. Either this man was, and is, the Son of God: or else a madman or something worse. You can shut Him up for a fool, you can spit at Him and kill Him as a demon; or you can fall at His feet and call him Lord and God. But don't let us come with any patronizing nonsense about his being a great human teacher. He hasn't left that open to us. He didn't intend to.*[412]

The Church of Jesus Christ of Latter-day Saints began by the prayer of Joseph Smith to learn which of all the religions were true. The Father—Elohim, and the Son—Jehovah, known during his mortal life as Jesus Christ, appeared to him. The Church he established was in accordance with the instructions of Jesus Christ. One of the prophets of *The Book of Mormon* writing over 500 years before the birth of Christ states:

> *And we talk of Christ, we rejoice in Christ, we preach of Christ, we prophesy of Christ, and we write according to our prophecies, that our children may know to what source they may look for a remission of their sins.*[413]

The Book of Mormon, accepted as scripture along with *The Bible* by members of The Church of Jesus Christ of Latter-day Saints, records that Christ appeared to the people on the American continent after his resurrection in Jerusalem. The ancient American prophet Mormon, in completing *The Book of Mormon* some 400 years after the death of Christ, wrote that the purpose of the book was "to the convincing of the Jew and Gentile that Jesus is the Christ, the Eternal God, manifesting himself unto all nations."[414]

5. THE NATURE OF MAN.

Judaism, Islam, Christianity, Hinduism, Buddhism, Confucianism and Taoism all teach that man is composed of a physical body and a spirit or soul. Orthodox Jews and The Church of Jesus Christ of Latter-day Saints teach that the spirit or soul existed before birth415 and, together with Christians, believe that it will continue to exist after mortal death. It is this soul that gives the body life and upon death returns to God: "Then shall the dust return to the earth as it was and the spirit shall return to God who gave it."416 In the New Testament, James, in urging the importance of good works, says, "For as the body without the spirit is dead, so faith without works is dead also."417 When Jesus Christ died Luke says that he "gave up the ghost." The Greek philosophers and the Gnostics regarded their body as a "prison,"418 but in the Christian concept, the body is good. The body is a "temple" for the spirit.419 Although some Christians have practiced asceticism, the Lutherans taught that Jesus told his followers they would suffer persecution, but they should not invent their own ascetic practices and mortifications.420 C.S. Lewis states:

> *Christianity is almost the only one of the great religions which thoroughly approves of the body—which believes that matter is good, that God Himself once took on a human body, that some kind of body is going to be given to us even in Heaven and is going to be an essential part of happiness, our beauty, and our energy.*[421]

In regard to the body and the spirit, Joseph Smith taught:

> *The body is supposed to be organized matter, and the spirit, by many, is thought to be immaterial, without substance. With this latter statement we should beg to differ, and state the spirit is a substance; that it is material, but that it is more pure, elastic and refined matter than the body; that it existed before the body, can exist in the body; and will exist separate from the body, when the body will be mouldering in the dust; and will in the resurrection, be united with it.*[422]

Members of The Church of Jesus Christ of Latter-day Saints practice the "Word of Wisdom," refraining from alcohol, tobacco, coffee, tea and illegal drugs to protect the body.[423]

In Hinduism, "matter tends to be regarded as barbarian, soiling everything she touches. Liberation lies ultimately in extricating spirit from its material involvement."[424] The Jains also believe the body is evil.

Buddhism teaches that the body is the source of all suffering and that only when one achieves "nirvana" and can avoid being reborn does suffering end. Siddhartha Gautama taught, "Consider your body: think of its impurity. Knowing that both its pain and its delight are alike causes of suffering, how can you indulge in its desires?"[425] In the Dhammapada we read, "Hunger is the greatest disease, the body the greatest ill."[426] Clothing must be worn to protect the body against extremes of heat and cold and "to conceal the shame of the body."[427] However, in a schizophrenic teaching:

> *At the same time, they do not neglect the care of their bodies, not because they wish to enjoy the physical pleasures of the body, but because the body is temporarily necessary for the attainment of wisdom and their mission of explaining the path to others.*[428]

Consequently, the true Buddhist is "not to take intoxicants of any kind."[429]

Taoism teaches, "The reason I have great trouble is that I have a body. When I no longer have a body what trouble have I?"[430]

Islam also teaches that believers should not drink alcohol.[431]

6. THE PURPOSE OF LIFE.

In Christianity, the purpose of life is to attain happiness. Catholics teach:

> *The Beatitudes [the teachings of Christ in the Sermon on the Mount] respond to the natural desire for happiness. This desire is of divine origin God has placed in the human heart in order to draw man to the One who alone can fulfill it. We all want to live happily; in the whole human race there is not one who does not assent to this proposition . . .*[432]

We achieve this happiness by learning to keep the commandments of God, learning to choose between good and evil and by repenting from the wrong choices that we make. Joseph Smith taught:

> *Happiness is the object and design of our existence; and it will be the end thereof, if we pursue the path that leads to it; and this path is virtue, uprightness, faithfulness, holiness and keeping all of the commandments of God. But we cannot keep all the commandments without first knowing them, and we cannot expect to know all, or more than we now know unless we comply with or keep those we have already received.*[433]

> *Those who have died in Jesus Christ may expect to enter into all that fruition of joy when they come forth [in the resurrection] that they possessed or anticipated here.*[434]

The Christian writer C.S. Lewis talked about the impossibility of finding happiness without God:

> *What Satan put into the heads of our remote ancestors was the idea that they could 'be like gods'—could set up on their own as if they had created themselves—be their own masters—invent some sort of happiness for themselves outside of God, apart from God. And out of that hopeless attempt has come nearly all that we call human history—money, poverty, ambition, war, prostitution, classes, empires, slavery—the long terrible story of man trying to find something other than God which will make him happy. The reason why it can never succeed is this. God made us: invented us as a man invents an engine. A car is made to run on petrol, and it won't run properly on anything else. Now God designed the human machine to run on Himself. He Himself is the fuel our spirits were designed to burn,or the food our spirits were designed to feed on. There isn't any other. That's why it's just no good asking God to make us happy in our own way without bothering about religion.God can't give us a happiness and peace apart from Himself, because it isn't there. There's no such thing.*[435]

Similarly, *The Book of Mormon* prophet Alma taught, "Wickedness never was happiness."[436] When some of Jesus' disciples turned away from him because they realized that he did not intend to overthrow the Romans and establish the physical kingdom of God on the earth, he asked his twelve apostles, "Will ye also go away?" Peter replied, "Lord to whom shall we go?—thou has the words of eternal life"—thereby expressing the view that it would be futile to seek happiness elsewhere.[437]

The purpose of keeping the commandments is to prepare to return to the presence of God in an improved and glorified state. Jesus taught that people generally seek for food, drink and clothing (material things):

> *But seek ye first the kingdom of God, and his righteousness; and all these things shall be added unto you.*[438]

> *For what shall it profiteth a man if he shall gain the whole world and lose his own soul?*[439]

> *And he said unto them [his followers], Take heed and beware of covetousness: for a man's life consisteth not in the abundance of the things which he possesseth.*[440]

He also taught that helping the poor is important to our own happiness:

> *Then said also to him that bade him, When thou makest a supper, call not thy friends, nor thy brethren, neither thy kinsmen, nor thy rich neighbors; lest they also bid thee again, and a recompense be made thee. But when thou makest a feast, call the poor, the maimed, the lame, the blind. And thou shalt be blessed; for they cannot recompense thee; for thou shalt be recompensed at the resurrection of the just.*[441]

This process of learning to choose correctly is of more importance than merely gaining a body. The spirit is to master the appetites and passions of the body.

Jesus said, "The spirit indeed is willing [to keep God's commandments] but the flesh is weak"[442] He also said, "[F]ear not them which kill the body but are not able to kill the soul; but rather fear him [Satan] which is able to destroy both soul and body in hell."[443] Choosing to disobey the commandments of God is "sin." The Roman Catholic Church teaches:

Without the knowledge Revelation gives of God we cannot recognize sin clearly and are tempted to explain it as merely a developmental flaw, a psychological weakness, a mistake, or the necessary consequence of an inadequate social structure, etc. Only in the knowledge of God's plan for man can we grasp that sin is an abuse of the freedom that God gives to created persons so that they are capable of loving him and loving one another.[444]

The ultimate purpose of life is to become like God. For example, Irenaeus, an early Christian writer, says, "[B]ut following the only true and steadfast teacher, the Word of God, our Lord Jesus Christ, who did, through his transcendent love, become what we are, that he might bring us to be even what He is Himself."[445] Although the current Catholic Catechism teaches:

Sin . . . like the first sin . . . is disobedience, a revolt against God through the will to become 'like god,' knowing and determining good and evil.[446]

It also teaches:

The goal of a virtuous life is to become like God.[447]

The Word became flesh to make us 'partakers of the divine nature.' For this is why the Word became man, and the Son of God became the Son of man: so that man, by entering into communion with the Word and thus receiving divine sonship might become a son of God. For the Son of God became man so that we might become God. The only-begotten Son of God, wanting to make us sharers in his divinity, assumed our nature, so that he, made man, might make men gods.[448]

Jesus said, "To him that overcometh will I grant to sit with me in my throne, even as I also overcame, and am set down with my Father in his throne.[449]

The Church of Jesus Christ of Latter-day Saints also teaches that, as spirit children of God, our ultimate purpose is to become like God, our Father. We will receive the "fullness of joy" after our death and resurrection, if we have kept the commandments of God, when we enter into his presence and live with him and his Son eternally in the society of the righteous. [450]

One of the distinctive aspects of Jewish, Christian, and Islamic teaching is that time is linear—that is, the work of God in creating the earth, sending his children to the earth, the final judgment and the assignment to final rewards is a progressive, goal-directed work proceeding through time. "For *The Bible*, history is neither maya nor a circular process of nature; it is the arena of God's purposive activity."[451] In Hinduism, according to Will Durant, quoting Monier-Williams, "There is no final purpose towards which the whole creation moves; there is no 'progress'; there is only endless repetition."[452] John Briggs has stated:

> *If Christianity is an historical religion, it follows that all history is God's history. The succession of the years is not merely an unravellable tangle of events without general meaning. History witnesses to a divine purpose and is moving towards a divine goal, what Charles Kingsley called 'the strategy of God.' Indeed, it was the Jews and the Christians who introduced the idea of time moving towards a goal (linear time) as against the older arbitrary or cyclic views.*[453]

Most importantly, in Christianity, a person's judgment will be based only on one life and there will be no reincarnation or any second chances to get it right. As *The Book of Mormon* prophet Alma taught, "This life is the time for men to prepare to meet God."[454]

Islam and Judaism also teach the purpose of life is to keep God's commandments. Rabbi Joseph ben Judah ibn Aknin taught:

> *Now why are trials brought upon the righteous? In order to make them known in the world as lovers of the Most High whose hearts are steadfast before Him, as it is written, That He might afflict thee to prove thee, to know what was in thy heart, whether thou wouldst keep His commandments, or no (Deuteronomy 8:2).*[455]

Rather than focusing on the next life, Jews believe the emphasis should be on making this life better for oneself and others.[456] Rabbi Machsor Vitry said:

One hour in which to repent and do good works in this world is richer than all the life in the world to come, for in the world to come it is impossible to repent or to do good works.[457]

Buddhism teaches that the purpose of life is to learn to choose good, but the earth and the universe are cyclical. Individual persons may achieve release from suffering by repeated reincarnations, but the universe is not proceeding toward any ultimate different state. "As long as the spirit remains tied to a body its freedom from the particular, the temporal and the changing cannot be complete."[458]

Hinduism agrees with Buddhism, except that Hinduism teaches that it will require multiple reincarnations through the four castes of priest-teacher (brahmin), king or political and military leader (ksatriya), merchant (vaisya) and laborer (sudra) for a person to achieve release,[459] while Buddha taught that it was possible for a person to achieve nirvana in one lifetime and that it was not necessary to be a member of the priestly class (Brahmin) to achieve nirvana. To progress spiritually it is necessary for each person to pass through the "four stages of life"—student, householder, solitary forest dweller and wandering monk.[460]

Confucianism and Taoism offer no views on the purpose of life except that each person is to contribute to the good of society by respecting the social relationships.

7. IMMORTALITY, REWARD AND PUNISHMENT.

Jews believe in the "Olam Haba"—the world to come.[461] The morning prayer is:

May it be Thy will, Lord our God and God of our fathers, that we keep Thy statutes and commandments in this world, and be worthy of inheriting the life of goodness and blessing in the world to come.[462]

Rabbi Judah taught, "The true reward of the good is reserved for the future life."[463] At the funeral of an Orthodox Jew, the mourners circle the coffin seven times and pray:

Have mercy we pray Thee on this Thy son . . .
In new realms of life may he now progress . . .
Be opened before him celestial gates
To enter God's realm where the good have life.
May guardian angels receive him there . . .
His soul led by angels to Machpelah
Go thence to God's garden of future life
Where Israel's saints shall be welcoming
His soul as he rises to destined life.[464]

In regard to resurrection, the Old Testament refers to a resurrection in several different places.[465] When Jews are buried, even outside of Israel, some earth from Israel ("Terra Santa") is sprinkled over their body in the coffin because the "resurrection will commence" in Israel.[466] In the days of mourning following the funeral, the "Tsidduk Hadin" (Justification of the Divine Decree [of Death]) is recited in part as follows:

He will utterly destroy death forever . . .
Thy dead shall live again, The mortal being shall rise up;
Awake and sing joyously, ye that dwell in the dust,
For as the reviving dew on grass shall be thy dew,
When earth shall bring forth her dead.[467]

On visiting a grave, a part of the prayer offered is:

You have passed to the world of goodness, a world of holy spirit. May the Lord hasten your uprising, and when our time comes, may we meet you in the glorious, effulgent celestial world of the spirit.[468]

According to Rabbi Eleazar Hakappar, "They who are born will die, but the dead shall be revived and all living are to be judged, to become aware, to know and to make known that He is God . . . ."[469] Rabbi Simeon ben Zemah Duran referred to both a world of "souls" after death, and the resurrection, which would come later.[470] Rabbi Moses ben Maimon (Maimonides) apparently did not think everyone would be resurrected:

And they [referring to the 'Sages of blessed memory'] also Say that at the Resurrection the Lord, blessed be He, will not revive those who are of a proud disposition.[471]

Rabbi Machsor Vitry seemed to agree:

The ones who will be resurrected will be brought to judgment when the Day of Judgment in the Valley of Jehosephat arrives.[472]

Rabbi Akabya ben Mahalalel said:

Ponder on three things and thou wilt not come into the power of sin: Know whence thou comest, whither thou art going, and before Whom thou art destined to give an accounting. Whence thou comest? From a fetid drop. Whither thou art going? To the place of dust and worms. Before Whom thou art destined to give an accounting? Before the supreme King of kings, the Holy One, blessed be He.[473]

Rabbi Rashi taught:

Man is judged according to the preponderance of his works—if most of these are righteous, he is meritorious; if they are sinful, he is wicked.[474]

Rabbi Joseph ben Judah ibn Aknin said, "All men are destined for a reward in the world to come and for the enjoyment of a feast of the fruits of their good works."[475] According to Leo Trepp, the character of Olam Haba is "beyond human comprehension" and it is "error to regard it as an earthly paradise, transposed into heaven."[476] Further, he says:

This concept of the world to come is a late arrival in Judaism. In the time of the Second Temple the Pharisees emphasized it as an essential of faith, whereas the Saducees denied it.[477] *[Christians may recall the question put to Jesus regarding resurrection as it applied to Levirate marriage.*[478]*]*

Judaism does believe in resurrection. It even speaks of a form of purgatory; this lasts but one year, and relief is given the sufferers on the Sabbath. Judaism does not emphasize this concept, however, for we are to follow the Mitzvot [commandments of God] not for the sake of reward or in fear of punishment, but for love of God . . . . The belief [in the resurrection] has been widely abandoned in non-Orthodox Judaism.[479]

In regard to the "purgatory" mentioned above, Rabbi Trepp elaborates that during the period of mourning following the death of a Jew that parents and children of the deceased recite the "Kaddish" prayer "for eleven months." "Tradition holds that after this period, all except outspoken evildoers are irrevocably admitted to their reward."[480]

Early Hinduism believed in personal immortality and in the world of the gods and the world of the fathers. Good men went to heaven or the world of Vishnu and others to the world presided over by Yama, although Yama was also thought of as the ruler of all the departed spirits.[481] According to Will Durant, Siddhartha Gautama—the founder of Buddhism and steeped in the traditions of Hinduism before he developed his own teachings—rejected personal immortality but accepted reincarnation. Durant comments on Buddhism's teaching that:

Life is change, a neutral stream of becoming and extinction; the 'soul' is a myth which, for the convenience of our weak brains, we unwarrantably posit behind the flow of conscious states . . . But if this is so, how can there be rebirth? If there is no soul, how can it pass into other existences, to be punished for the sins of this embodiment? Here is the weakest point in Buddha's philosophy; he never quite faces the contradiction between his rationalistic psychology and his uncritical acceptance of reincarnation.[482]

Hinduism and Buddhism teach that there is life after death in the form of additional reincarnations (Sikhs also believe in reincarnation[483]). These rebirths occur through six realms: Hell, Hungry Spirits, Animals, Fighting Spirits, Men and Heaven.[484] However, different Hindu and Buddhist schools teach that there is no memory of the previous incarnation so that it is not clear that the same "person" continues to exist. According to Radhakrishnan and Moore:

The goal of life in Hinduism, Buddhism and Jainism is essentially the same. Moksa (liberation) is the ultimate objective for Hinduism and Jainism, and nirvana is the goal in Buddhism. The precise meanings of liberation vary among the different schools, even among those within the framework of Buddhism and Hinduism, but the essential meaning of both moksa and nirvana is emancipation or liberation from turmoil and sufferingand freedom from rebirth.[485]

It will be here observed Christianity rejects reincarnation. The Catechism of the Catholic Church says, "It is appointed for men to die once. There is no 'reincarnation' after death,"[486] and, in response to a person who claimed to have received his ancestor's spirit as a transmigration, Joseph Smith told him that his "doctrine was of the devil."[487]

Confucianism and Taoism do not say whether there is any life after death or personal immortality:

Chi-lu asked how the spirits of the dead and the gods should be served. The Master said, 'You are not able even to serve man. How can you serve the spirits?'

'May I ask about death?'

'You do not understand even life. How can you understand death?'[488]

According to the Catechism of the Catholic Church:

The Church teaches that every spiritual soul is created immediately by God—it is not 'produced' by the parents—and also that it is immortal: it does not perish when it separates from the body at death, and it will be reunited with the body at the final Resurrection.[489]

The Christian who dies in Christ Jesus is 'away from the body and at home with the Lord.'[490]

For even dead we are not all separated from one another, because we all run the same course and we shall find one another again in the same place . . . we shall be together in Christ.[491]

In death, the separation of the soul from the body, the human

> *body decays and the soul goes to meet God, while awaiting its reunion with its glorified body. God, in his almighty power, will definitely grant incorruptible life to our bodies by reuniting them with our souls, through the power of Jesus' Resurrection.*[492]
>
> *All the dead will rise, those who have done good, to the resurrection of life, and those who have done evil, to the resurrection of judgment.*[493]
>
> *Christ is raised with his own body . . . . So, in him 'all of them will rise again with their own bodies which they now bear,' but Christ 'will change our lowly body to be like his glorious body,' into a 'spiritual body.'*[494]

Christianity teaches that Christ was the "firstfruits" of the resurrection.[495] When he appeared to his apostles following his resurrection he had a physical body:

> *And as they thus spake, Jesus himself stood in the midst of them, and saith unto them, Peace be unto you. But they were terrified and affrighted, and supposed that they had seen a spirit. And he said unto them, Why are ye troubled? And why do thoughts arise in your hearts? Behold my hands and my feet, that it is I myself: handle me and see; for a spirit hath not flesh and bones, as ye see me have. And when he had thus spoken, he shewed them his hands and his feet. And while they yet believed not for joy, and wondered, he said unto them, have ye here any meat? And they gave him a piece of a broiled fish, and of an honeycomb. And he took it, and did eat before them.*[496]

The Bible says that at the time of Jesus' resurrection the "graves were opened and many bodies of the saints which slept arose, and came out of the graves after his resurrection, and went into the holy city, and appeared unto many."[497] Professor Dummelow lists 12 appearances of Christ to various persons at various times after his resurrection as recorded in *The Bible*.[498] Paul writes that after his resurrection Jesus was seen by Peter, then the eleven apostles, and "after that he was seen of above five hundred brethren at once," and then he was seen by James and by Paul.[499] According to the New Testament, after his resurrection, Jesus ministered to his disciples for forty days and then ascended into heaven taking his body with him:

> *And when he had spoken these things, while they beheld, he was taken up; and a cloud received him out of their sight. And while they looked steadfastly toward heaven as he went up, behold two men stood by them in white apparel; which also said, Ye men of Galilee, why stand ye gazing up into heaven? This same Jesus, which is taken up from you into heaven, shall so come in like manner as ye have seen him go into heaven.*[500]

The Book of Mormon also records Christ's appearance to the people of the Americas.[501] Christianity teaches that all persons will be resurrected—both the righteous and the wicked,[502] that they will have memory, that they will be the same "person," and that they will have a glorified body. According to J. R. Dummelow:

> *From many points of view the Resurrection is the most important event in human history . . . (1) The Resurrection has brought new hope and happiness into the world by the light it sheds on human immortality . . . (2) The Resurrection vindicates God's justice and benevolence in the government of the world [because of rewards and punishments in the afterlife] . . . (3) The Resurrection indicates that the future life will not be of the soul only, but of the soul united to a suitable organ or 'body.' (4) The Resurrection sets the seal of divine approval upon the teaching of Jesus, and in particular, (5) Declares him to be the Divine Son of God.*[503]

Christianity also teaches that we will be rewarded or punished in accordance with our deeds. In regard to the suffering we must endure to be faithful to the commandments of Jesus Christ, Joseph Smith said, "All your losses will be made up to you in the resurrection, provided you continue faithful. By the vision of the Almighty I have seen it."[504] God told the prophet Moses, "This is my work and my glory—to bring to pass the immortality and eternal life of man."[505] We learn that the resurrection— immortality—comes as a free gift to every person that lives upon the earth:

For since by man came death, by man came also the resurrection of the dead. For as in Adam all die, even so in Christ shall all be made alive.[506]

But the quality of life that we have after the resurrection depends upon our repentance and obedience to Jesus' commandments. Paul teaches, "at the last day" "the dead in Christ will rise first."[507] The quality of life that God has is called "eternal life" because the living God is eternal. Those that obey the commandments of God will overcome both physical death—through the resurrection—and spiritual death—by returning to the presence of God.[508]

Islam also teaches a belief in the resurrection. "God will raise all the dead."[509] Sura 75 is entitled "Resurrection" and says, in part, "does man think We shall never put his bones together again? Indeed, We can remold his very fingers."[510] Each person will be judged by weighing his or her life in the balance:

Then those whose scales are heavy, they are successful. And those whose scales are light lose their souls, in hell abiding, the fire burns their faces and they are glum therein.[511]

In Islam the faithful shall dwell in bliss in a land of "shade," "gushing waters" and "abundant fruits," while the wicked will be "bound with chains," will "burn in hellfire" and will suffer "scorching winds and seething waters" in the "shade of pitch black smoke, neither cool nor refreshing," drinking "boiling water."[512]

The men are provided with "houris"—Black-eyed damsels said to be the reward of the faithful in the Muslim Paradise. Possessed of perpetual youth and beauty, they can renew their virginity at pleasure and are always equal in age with their husbands. According to The Koran, every believer will have seventy-two of these houris in Paradise and, depending on his wish, his intercourse may be fruitful or otherwise; if an offspring is desired, it will grow to full estate in an hour.[513]

8. EXISTENCE AND PURPOSE OF EVIL.

Hinduism teaches that evil is illusory, it is "maya." The world goes through cycles of creation or augmentation and decline or degradation. The degradation we experience as evil is in fact good. The Christian Scientists agree.[514] Will Durant commented:

> *[Hinduism] depicted life as inevitably evil, and broke the courage and darkened the spirit of its devotees; it turned all earthly phenomena into illusion, and thereby destroyed the distinction between freedom and slavery, good and evil, corruption and betterment.*[515]

Later Hinduism regards Shiva, one of the trinity of gods ("trimurti") as the Destroyer, but destruction is considered a natural part of the endless cycle of increase and decrease.

Buddhism, as the Hindu 'Protestantism," rejected that approach and taught that evil is real in the form of suffering, but comes from our own poor choices.

Confucianism and Taoism also teach that evil is real.

Christianity teaches that opposed to Christ is Satan, a spirit personage that was cast out of the presence of God along with one-third of the spirit children of God for rebellion and disobedience.[516] Satan and the spirits that followed him were denied bodies but have power to tempt humans and to cause suffering when humans succumb to such temptation. Evil is real and must be actively opposed in order to prevent its growth, but, ultimately, Christ will overcome the efforts of Satan and the earth will be freed from his influence. Evil is opposed to happiness.

The Catechism of the Catholic Church asks:

> *But why did God not create a world so perfect that no evil could exist in it? With infinite power God could always create something better. But with infinite wisdom and goodness God freely willed to create a world 'in a state of journeying' toward its ultimate perfection. In God's plan this process of becoming involves the appearance of certain beings and the disappearance of others, the existence of the more perfect alongside the less perfect, both constructive and destructive forces of nature. With physical good there exists also physical*

evil as long as creation has not reached perfection. Angels and men, as intelligent and free creatures, have to journey toward their ultimate destinies by their free choice and preferential love. They can therefore go astray. Indeed, they have sinned. Thus has moral evil, incommensurably more harmful than physical evil, entered the world. God is in no way, directly or indirectly, the cause of moral evil. He permits it, however, because he respects the freedom of his creatures and, mysteriously, knows how to derive good from it.[517]

The philosopher Gottfried Wilhelm von Leibniz wrote to show that the world that God created for the moral development of man was the best of all possible worlds. He said, "All is for the best in this best of all possible worlds."[518] Later, after the earthquake in Lisbon, Portugal, Voltaire wrote a book, *Candide*, which portrayed the characters as always doing good but always suffering evil, mocking the concept that this is the best of all possible worlds. Yet, Voltaire is not persuasive because (1) his book is a work of fiction—there is no evidence that those who do good always reap suffering or that those who do evil always obtain happiness—that idea is contrary to the real experience of mankind; (2) Christians concede that this world is not the best of "all possible" worlds—indeed, they are living to attain a better one— "heaven." Nevertheless, the doctrine of Christianity is that for persons to be prepared to live in the society of heaven they must experience evil and learn to eliminate evil and suffering as much as possible by their own choices. Furthermore, "the end does not justify the means," and "one may not do evil so that good may result from it."[519] Jesus told Joseph Smith, "woe unto him that lieth to deceive because he supposeth that another lieth to deceive."[520] In regard to individuals who commit evil:

Liberation in the spirit of the Gospel is incompatible with hatred of one's enemy as a person, but not with hatred of the evil that he does as an enemy.[521]

Joseph Smith taught:

All beings who have bodies have power over those who have not. The devil has no power over us only as we permit him.[522]

At another time Joseph

> *commenced his observations by remarking that the kindness of our Heavenly Father called for our heartfelt gratitude. He then observed that Satan was generally blamed for the evils which we did, but if he was the cause of all of our wickedness, men could not be condemned. The devil could not compel mankind to do evil; all was voluntary. Those who resisted the Spirit of God would be liable to be led into temptation, and then the association of heaven would be withdrawn from those who refused to be made partakers of such glory. God would not enter into any compulsory means, and the devil could not.*[523]

> *[F]or know assuredly, if we by our wickedness, bring evil on our own heads, the Lord will let us bear it till we get weary and hate iniquity.*[524]

The Catholic Catechism identifies many sources of "evil" in the world:

> *Ignorance of Christ and his Gospel, bad example given by others, enslavement to one's passions, assertion of a mistaken notion of autonomy of conscience, rejection of the Church's authority and her teaching, lack of conversion and of charity: these can be the source of errors of judgment in moral conduct.*[525]

Judaism and Islam also teach that evil is real, similar to Christianity. Moslems also believe in the existence of Satan.[526]

9. FREE WILL.

Hinduism teaches that the universe is "law abiding to the core, and yet that man is free to shape his own destiny in it."[527] A person is always free to choose, but the effect of man's choices are irrevocable—this cause and effect accumulates in a person as his or her "karma" and results in his increasing his status (caste) in the next cycle of reincarnation or in lowering his or her status, to an animal or less. The social restrictions of caste are a substantial limitation on free will during this life. The four main castes have "over three thousand" sub-castes with corresponding prohibitions against intermarriage and inter-dining.[528] Caste is hereditary and there is no change in caste throughout one's life. There is no "mercy" or forgiveness for one's actions—whatever one sows is what he or she will reap.

Buddhism also teaches that man has freedom of will to make choices. "Man remains a free agent, always at liberty to do something to affect his destiny."[529] In regard to people who believe in predestination, *The Teaching of Buddha* says:

> *First, some say that all human experience is based on destiny; second, some hold that everything is created by God and controlled by His will; third, some say that everything happens by chance without having any cause or condition.*
>
> *If all has been decided by destiny, both good deeds and evil deeds are predetermined, weal and woe are predestined; nothing would exist that has not been foreordained. Then all human plans and efforts for improvement and progress would be in vain and humanity would be without hope.*
>
> *The same is true of the other viewpoints, for if everything in the last resort is in the hands of an unknowable God, or of blind chance, what hope has humanity except in submission? It is no wonder that people holding these conceptions lose hope and neglect efforts to act wisely and to avoid evil.*[530]

In Confucianism, according to D.C. Lau:

> *Thus, there are certain things which are brought about, not by human agency, but by Destiny. These are things over which human endeavor has no effect. Whether or not a man is going to end with wealth, honour and long life is due to Destiny. No amount of effort on his part will make any difference to the outcome.*[531]

Judaism teaches that humans do have free will, and once a person has been taught the difference between good and evil, they are accountable before God for their choices. In Deuteronomy God tells the Israelites through Moses, "I have set before you life and death . . . therefore choose life."[532] Rabbi Akiba taught that, "All is foreseen yet freewill is given to man."[533] Rabbi Aknin commented, "The early

Sages used to say that at the time of his birth a person is not created to be by nature either of good works or bad works."[534] Rabbi Moses ben Maimon (Maimonides) said:

> *Do not think that because God knows what will happen things are predetermined and therefore a man is predestined to act as he does. It is not so. Man has the freedom to choose what he wants to do.*[535]

Rabbi Nahmias agreed.[536]

In regard to Islam Will Durant says:

> *Since Allah knows the future as well as the present and the past, all things are predestined; everything has been decreed and fixed from all eternity by the divine will, even to the final fate of every soul. Like Augustine's God, Allah not only knows from eternity who will be saved, but 'sendeth whom He will astray, and guideth Whom He will' (Sura 35:8; 126:31) . . . Allah says of unbelievers: 'We have thrown veils over their hearts lest they should understand The Koran, and into their ears a heaviness; and if thou bid them to the guidance, yet even they will not be guided'(Sura 18:58)... 'Had We pleased, says Allah, 'We had certainly given to every soul its guidance. But true shall be the word that has gone forth from me—I will surely fill hell with jinn [demons] and men together' (Sura 32:13).*[537]

But others do not completely agree with his view. Thomas Lippman says, "Many passages in *The Koran* can be taken to mean that the fate of every individual is sealed from the moment his soul is created [citing Suras 57:22, 54:48 and 9:51],"[538] but he also says in the eighth and ninth centuries the Mutazillite sect of Islam strongly rejected predestination. He says:

> *Islam has struggled to reconcile this belief that God has foreknowledge and that all events occur in conformity with a divine plan with the instructions of The Koran and the Prophet to do good works and live virtuously to find favor with Allah . . .*[539]

Christian belief on this subject is discussed in Part III, Section 7, "Election and Predestination."

10. UNIVERSAL APPLICATION.

Originally, Judaism taught that Judaism was the only true religion and that it began with the beginning of the earth and the creation of Adam and Eve by Jehovah. The House of Israel and the Jews were the "chosen" or elect of God. All those who wished to attain salvation must convert to Judaism up until the coming of the Messiah when new births of men will end. However, in modern Reform Judaism, all who are faithful in their religions will be saved.

Islam also teaches that it is the only true religion and that it began at the same time as Judaism, since Jehovah and Allah are the same God. A person must convert to Islam to receive the highest salvation, although the "People of the Book"—Christians and Jews—can obtain a limited salvation.

Buddhism requires believers to follow the Eightfold Path. Siddhartha Gautama did not teach that there were any "Buddhists" before his own time, but later, the Mahayana sect now teaches that Buddha has always existed since the beginning of the earth, that a Buddha has appeared on the earth from time to time, and that Buddhas will continue to appear—as a result, Buddhism is universally applicable in all time periods of the world.

Confucius and LaoTzu never claimed that their teachings would result in "salvation" in the next life—their teachings were designed to order society for this life. Nor did they contend that there were Confucianists or Taoists before their own time.

Many people believe or assume that Christianity began with Jesus. For example, Mortimer Adler refers to the teachings of Aristotle "four centuries before the advent of Christianity."[540] Islam teaches that Christianity began with Jesus. The concern about the "unfairness" of salvation only for those who have heard of and believed in Christ caused C.S. Lewis, the Christian apologist to write:

> *Isn't it frightfully unfair that this new life should be confined to people who have heard of Christ and been able to believe in Him? Well, the truth is God hasn't told us what His arrangements about the other people are. We do know that no man can be saved except through Christ; we don't know that only those who know Him can be saved through Him. But in*

the meantime, if you're worried about the people outside, the most unreasonable thing you can do is to remain outside yourself.[541]

However, the Roman Catholic Church teaches that the Jehovah of the Jews was God the Father of Christianity, that God the Father and Jesus are one "person," and that the religious teachings of Jesus were known in less complete form to Adam, Abraham, and the other righteous persons of the Old Testament. For example, the Catholic communion text refers to Melchizidek, as priest of the most high God, bringing bread and wine to Abraham in the Old Testament times.[542] Origen, an early Church "Father," said:

Jesus, who alone remained absolutely faithful to God, was chosen, because of merit, to be the leader of the Gospel plan. He was leader, not only while on earth, but also in Old Testament times 'for the Son . . . arranged all things from the beginning.'[543]

Justin Martyr, in his, *Dialogue with Trypho*, says:

But Jesus is indeed he who appeared and spoke to Moses, to Abraham and in a word, to all the other patriarchs, to serve the will of his Father; it is he who came to be born a man by the Virgin Mary, and is one still.[544]

Eusebius, the Christian bishop of Caesarea undertakes in an early chapter of *The History of the Church from Christ to Constantine*, written in about 324 A.D., to explain to his readers that, although the sect of "Christians" as known in the world at that time was relatively recent, in fact, the principles and doctrines of Christianity were the same throughout history:

All these, whose righteousness won them commendation, going back from Abraham himself to the first man, might be described as Christians in fact if not in name, without departing far from the truth.[545]

Eusebius also repeatedly states that the appearances of "God" recorded in the Old Testament were appearances of Christ in a human form, although he had not yet been born as a man.[546]

Blaise Pascal, a Catholic, believed, "No sect or religion has always existed on earth, but the Christian religion."[547] Further, he states:

> *The Messiah has always been believed in. The tradition from Adam was fresh in Noah and in Moses. Since then the prophets have foretold him, while at the same time foretelling other things, which being from time to time fulfilled in the sight of men, showed the truth of their mission, and consequently that of their promises touching the Messiah. Jesus Christ performed miracles, and the Apostles also, who converted all the heathen; and all the prophecies being thereby fulfilled, the Messiah is forever proved.*[548]
>
> *I find it convincing that, since the memory of man has lasted, it was constantly announced to men that they were universally corrupt, but that a Redeemer should come; that it is not one man who said it, but innumerable men, and a whole nation expressly made for the purpose and prophesying for four thousand years. This is a nation which is more ancient than every other nation. Their books, scattered abroad, are four thousand years old.*[549]

Luke states, "To him give all the prophets witness, that through his name whosoever believeth in him shall receive remission of sins,"[550] which seems to indicate that all the prophets before Christ also taught and testified of his mission. Paul said the "gospel" was preached in the days of Abraham.[551] The Roman Catholic scholar Femand Mourret, says:

> *Justin (106), Theophilus of Antioch (died 190), Irenaeus (martyred about 205), Tertullian (160-220 or 240), Clement of Alexandria (died before 216) and Origen (185-254), 'tried to convince the pagans that Christianity is not a new religion, but that it goes back to the birth of humanity.'*[552]

Eusebius and the Catholic Church teach that the doctrines of Christ were not known in their fullness before Christ, but Christ ultimately revealed all truth during his life. Christianity will exist until the end of time when Christ will return to the earth. In this sense the

Christian religion has been, and will be, universally applicable to all persons in all times. The translator for Eusebius comments:

> *We may think it is absurd to give the name of Christians to those who lived before Christ, but the same line of thought will be found in Hebrews 11 and I Corinthians 10; and Christ equated his own moral teaching with that of the time before Moses, at least as regards marriage. See Mark 10:1-12.*[553]

The "Reformed" Protestant Christians taught that the

> *[P]romises, prophecies, sacrifices, circumcision, the paschal lamb and other types and ordinances delivered to the people of the Jews, all foresignifying Christ to come, which were for the time sufficient and efficacious, through the operation of the Spirit, to instruct and build up the elect in faith in the promised Messiah, by whom they had full remission of sins and eternal salvation . . .*[554]
>
> *Although the work of redemption was not actually wrought by Christ till after the incarnation, yet the virtue, efficacy, and benefits thereof were communicated to the elect, in all ages successively, from the beginning of the world . . .*[555]

The Catholic Church taught that "limbo" was the "state of rest and natural happiness after death enjoyed by the just of pre-Christian times until they were admitted to heaven following the ascension of Christ."[556] Like Islam and its concept of limited salvation for the "People of the Book," Catholicism teaches complete salvation is only in joining the Catholic Church, but a limited salvation is given to good people in all religions everywhere, especially other Christians who have been baptized in other Christian sects—these become the "People of God."[557] They are "put in a certain, although imperfect, communion with the Catholic Church."[558] In regard to Jews, Muslims and other non-Christians, the Catholic Church "considers all goodness and truth found in these religions as a 'preparation for the Gospel and given by him who enlightens all men that they may have eternal life.'"[559]

Outside the Catholic Church there is no salvation for those "who, knowing that the Catholic Church was founded as necessary by God through Christ, would refuse either to enter it or to remain in it."[560] However,

> *Those who, through no fault of their own, do not know the Gospel of Christ or his Church, but who nevertheless seek God with a sincere heart, and, moved by grace, try in their actions to do his will as they know it through the dictates of their conscience—those too may achieve eternal salvation.*[561]

Jesus commanded that his gospel be taught to "all nations" and missionary work has always been a part of Christianity.[562]

The latter-day prophet Joseph Smith taught as follows:

> *Perhaps our friends will say that the Gospel and its ordinances were not known till the days of John, the son of Zacharias, in the days of Herod, the King of Judea. But we will here look at this point: For our own part we cannot believe that the ancients in all ages were so ignorant of the system of heaven as many suppose, since all that ever were saved, were saved through the power of this great plan of redemption, as much before the coming of Christ as since; if not, God has had different plans in operation (if we may so express it), to bring men back to dwell with Himself; and this we cannot believe since there has been no change in the constitution of man since he fell; and the ordinance or institution of offering blood in sacrifice, was only designed to be performed till Christ was offered up and shed His blood—as said before—that man might look forward in faith to that time. It will be noticed that, according to Paul, (see Gal. 3:8) the Gospel was preached to Abraham. We would like to be informed in what name the Gospel was preached, whether it was in the name of Christ or some other name. If in any other name was it the Gospel? And if it was the Gospel, and that preached in the name of Christ had it any ordinances? If not, was it the Gospel? And if it had ordinances what were they? Our friends say, perhaps, that there were never any ordinances except those of offering sacrifices before the coming of Christ, and that it could not be possible before the Gospel to have been administered while the law of sacrifices of blood was in force. But we will recollect that Abraham offered*

sacrifice, and notwithstanding this, had the Gospel preached to him. That the offering of sacrifice was only to point the mind forward to Christ, we infer from these remarkable words of Jesus to the Jews: 'Your Father Abraham rejoiced to see my day; and he saw it, and was glad.' (John 8:56). So, then, because the ancients offered sacrifice it did not hinder their hearing the Gospel; but served, as we said before, to open their eyes, and enable them to look forward to the time of the coming of the Savior, and rejoice in His redemption. We find also, that when the Israelites came out of Egypt they had the Gospel preached to them, according to Paul in his letter to the Hebrews, which says: 'For unto us was the Gospel preached, as well as unto them: but the word preached did not profit them, not being mixed with faith in them that heard it."'(see Heb. 4:2). It is said again, in Gal. 3:19, that the law of Moses (or the Levitical law) was "added" because of transgression. What, we ask, was this added to, if it was not added to the Gospel? It must be plain that it was added to the Gospel, since we learn that they had the Gospel preached to them. From these few facts, we conclude that whenever the Lord revealed Himself to men in ancient days, and commanded them to offer sacrifice to Him, that it was done that they might look forward in faith to the time of His coming, and rely upon the power of that atonement for a remission of their sins. And this they have done, thousands who have gone before us, whose garments are spotless, and who are, like Job, waiting with an assurance like his, that they will see Him in the latter day upon the earth, even in their flesh.[563]

Brigham Young states, "If we believe the plain, broad statements of *The Bible*, we must believe that Jesus Christ is the light that lighteth every man that cometh into the world; none are exempt."[564] The Church of Jesus Christ of Latter-day Saints also publishes to the world *The Book of Mormon* and *The Pearl of Great Price*. *The Book of Mormon* begins with an account of a family of Jews living in Jerusalem about 600 years before the birth of Jesus and describes their migration to the American continent and their subsequent civilization. These writings evidence a clear understanding of the future birth of Jesus Christ and the necessity of baptism and other Christian doctrines as taught by their prophets. *The Pearl of Great Price* includes writings describing the teaching of the Gospel to Adam and Eve and many of their posterity, including Enoch, concerning the future birth, life, death, atonement and resurrection of Jesus Christ. Indeed, if Christians accept that many prophecies in the Old Testament were of Christ and his life, it is certain that those who pronounced such prophecies and those who received them during many time periods before the birth of Christ understood that salvation was only to be gained and perfected by his work and mission. In regard to the salvation of those who have never heard the Gospel, Joseph Smith taught the following:

> *Q. If the 'Mormon' doctrine is true, what becomes of all those who died since the days of the Apostles?*
>
> *A. All those who have not had an opportunity of hearing the Gospel, and being administered unto by an inspired man in the flesh, must have it hereafter, before they can be finally judged.*[565]

This teaching will occur in the spirit world prior to the resurrection in accordance with the words of Jesus:

> *Verily, verily, I say unto you, The hours is coming, and now is, when the dead shall hear the voice of the Son of God; and they that hear shall live.*[566]

It is also in accordance with I Peter 3:18-19 and 4:6:

> *For Christ also hath once suffered for sins, the just for the unjust, that he might bring us to God, being put to death in the flesh, but quickened by the Spirit. By which also he went and preached unto the spirits in prison . . . For for this cause was the gospel preached also to them that are dead, that they might be judged according to men in the flesh, but live according to God in the spirit.*

The Roman Catholic Church teaches:

> *Jesus did not descend into hell to deliver the damned, nor to destroy the hell of damnation, but to free the just who had gone before him.*[567]

The gospel was preached even to the dead. The descent into hell brings the Gospel message of salvation to complete fulfillment. This is the last phase of Jesus' messianic mission, a phase which is condensed in time but vast in its real significance: the spread of Christ's redemptive work to all men of all times and all places, for all who are saved have been made sharers in the redemption.[568]

In summary, Christianity teaches that the Gospel of Christ has been and will be applicable throughout all the ages of the world and applies to all men, women and children.

11. NON-ATTACHMENT OR LOVE.

Radhakrishnan and Moore state, "The essential spirit of the philosophy of life of Hinduism, Buddhism and Jainism is that of non-attachment."[569] This state is called "sannyasin," defined in the *Bhagavad Gita* as "one who neither hates nor loves anything."[570] The Mahabharata Santiparva says:

Relatives, sons, spouses, the body itself, and all one's possessions stored with care, are unsubstantial and prove of no service in the next world.[571]

That man is said to be truly learned and truly possessed of wisdom who abandons every act, who never indulges in hope, who is completely dissociated from all worldly surroundings, and who has renounced everything that appertains to the world . . . who is never moved by joy or sorrow . . .[572]

As two pieces of wood floating on the ocean come together at one time and are again separated, even such is the union of living creatures in this world. Sons, grandsons, kinsmen relatives, are all of this kind. One should never feel affection for them, for separation with [from] them is certain.[573]

According to Buddhism, the cause of suffering in life is the attachment of a person to things or persons so that death and sickness of persons, which is inevitable, and the theft or loss of things, bring continual suffering. The Buddhist's solution is detachment or "non-attachment" to persons or things. By learning to perfectly control our emotions and restricting our desires we can achieve an indifference or equanimity to our good fortune or bad fortune that will bring us to release from the cycle of rebirths. According to *The Teaching of Buddha*:

> *A man who wishes to become My disciple must be willing to give up all direct relations with his family, the social life of the world and all dependence on wealth.*[574]

This, however, is the path in Mahayana Buddhism for those who choose to become monks. For "lay members" they should study, "[H]ow to serve their parents, how to live with their wives and children, how to control themselves, and how to serve Buddha."[575]

The historian Will Durant was not complimentary about the effects of this philosophy:

> *Despite its elements of nobility, Buddhism, like Stoicism was a slave philosophy, even if voiced by a prince; it meant that all desire or struggle, even for personal or national freedom, should be abandoned, and that the ideal was a desireless passivity.*[576]

Although Confucianism and Taoism teach that we should do our duty to the six relations—all family relationships—Taoism teaches:

> *There is no crime greater than having too many desires; There is no disaster greater than not being content; There is no misfortune greater than being covetous.*[577]

Jews do not believe in monks or nuns. *The Mishnah* says, "Do not withdraw from the community."[578] Judaism believes that even the study of Torah can become too extreme if one becomes too withdrawn from life. Rabbi Rabbi Joseph ben Judah ibn Aknin said:

> *Now this is something we know from psychology, that the association of men with each other and support of each other is an absolute good, for everybody helps his fellow. Withdrawal from human society is an absolute evil, unless of course, the people of one's time are utterly depraved and turn completely from the good way to the evil way and abandon the Lord.*[579]

Family relationships are very important in Judaism. Each Jew is blessed as a baby that he or she will be able to marry. The Sabbath dinner with the family and the blessing of the children each Sabbath make the family the center of Jewish life. But Judaism does not teach that family relations will continue after death.

Christianity teaches that love of God and love of fellow man is the heart of religion. In one scripture John says, "Beloved, let us love one another for love is of God."[580] Jesus teaches, "A new commandment I give unto you, That ye love one another; as I have loved you, that ye also love one another. By this all men shall know that ye are my disciples, if ye have love one to another" [581] John teaches, "We love him because he first loved us."[582] The Catholic Catechism says:

> *The entire Law of the Gospel is contained in the 'new commandment' of Jesus, to love one another as he has loved us.*[583]

Professor Dummelow says:

> *That 'God is love,' and cares with the intensity and impartiality of a father's affection for every individual soul that He has created, is the essence of the gospel (Matthew 10:31).*[584]

> *The chief stress, therefore, in Christian morality is laid upon love (Matthew 22:37). This love shows itself in various ways (1) In ready forgiveness . . . (2) In avoiding unkind criticism . . . (3) In a peaceful disposition . . . (4) In active benevolence . . . (5) In loving enemies and persecuton . . . (6) In not resisting or resenting injuries . . .*[585]

Joseph Smith taught:

> *Love is one of the chief characteristics of Deity and ought to be manifested by those who aspire to be the sons of God. A man filled with the love of God is not content with blessing his family alone, but ranges through the whole world, anxious to bless the whole human race.*[586]

Christianity teaches that one may very well experience persecution or estrangement from family for practicing Christianity and that one must be prepared to choose following the teachings of God over family relationships,[587] but it does not teach that men should renounce family relationships. One of the phenomena of Christianity has been monasticism. At first, individual hermits would seek seclusion in the desert. In 318 A.D. Pachomius established the first cenobitic (community) Christian monastery.[588] Around 370 A.D. Bishop Basil promulgated the first "rules" of a monastic order.

"Basil saw the monastic life as the climax of Christian achievement, with its aim of freeing the soul from the entanglements of the body through discipline."[589]

William James described a continuum along which some religious persons proceed where they progressively renounce business affairs, social life and then family to seek God in seclusion:

> *Amusements must go first, then conventional 'society,' then business, then family duties, until at last seclusion, with a subdivision of the day into hours for stated religious acts, is the only thing that can be borne. The lives of saints are a history of successive renunciations of complication, one form of contact with the outer life being dropped after another to save the purity of inner tone.*[590]

The Koran criticizes monasticism. In fact, the teachings of Jesus are that we should be engaged with our fellow man. To Peter, he said, "When thou are converted strengthen thy brethren,"[591] and, if thou lovest me, "Feed my sheep."[592] Christianity is a call to involvement in the lives of people—not withdrawal.

12. SCRIPTURES, REVELATION AND ENLIGHTENMENT.

The teachings of Hinduism are recorded in the *Vedas*, the later of which are called the *Upanishads*:

> *The word Veda means knowledge; a Veda is literally a Book of Knowledge. Vedas is applied by the Hindu to all the sacred lore of their early period; like our Bible it indicates a literature rather than a book. Nothing could be more confused than the arrangement and division of the collection. Of the many Vedas that once existed only four have survived: The*

Rg-Veda, or Knowledge of the Hymns of Praise; the Sama-Veda, or Knowledge of the Melodies; the Yajur-Veda, or Knowledge of the Sacrificial Formulas; and the Atharva-Veda, or knowledge of the Magic Formulas.[593]

The word [Upanishads] is composed of upa, near, and shad, to sit. From 'sitting near' the teacher the term came to mean the secret or esoteric doctrine confided by the master to his best and favorite pupils. There are one hundred and eight of these discourses composed by various saints and sages between 800 and 500 B.C.[594]

Durant further states:

All systems of Indian philosophy are ranged by the Hindus in two categories: Astika systems, which affirm, and Nastika systems, which deny [the authority of the Vedas].[595]

The Nastika systems are the Caravakas, the Buddhists and the Jains.

The *Vedas* form the basis for the six Astika sects or "darshana" of Hinduism. These record the activities of the gods and of men.

The interpretations of the Vedic texts depends on the philosophical predilections of the authors . . . The general conceptions of the Vedas were neither definite nor detailed, and so allowed themselves to be handled and fashioned in different ways by different schools of thought. Besides, the very vastness of the Vedas, from which the authors could select out of free conviction any portion for their authority, allowed room for original thought.[596]

Will Durant further comments on the six orthodox sects:

All six make certain assumptions which are the bases of Hindu thought: that the Vedas are inspired; that reasoning is less reliable as a guide to reality and truth than the direct perception and feeling of an individual properly prepared for spiritual receptiveness and subtlety by ascetic practices and years of obedient tutelage; that the purpose of knowledge and philosophy is not control of the world so much as release from it; and that the goal of thought is to find freedom from

> *the suffering of frustrated desire by achieving freedom from desire itself. These are the philosophies to which men come when they tire of ambition, struggle, wealth, 'progress,' and 'success.'*[597]

The six founders of the six Astika sects of Hinduism all interpreted the early *Veda* writings. To do so they wrote "sutras" that expressed their interpretations. The problem is that each verse of these sutras consists of "two or three words each" and "cannot be understood without a commentary."[598] No Hindus claim that the Vedas are the "revelations" of God or that they are literally true. These scriptures and the various commentaries thereon are designed only to recite events from which the truths of life may be deduced. As one does so well, he or she will be released from the cycle of reincarnation.

Siddhartha Gautama, the founder of Buddhism, wrote no books himself and the first of his words were not written until 150 years after his death, being preserved in oral tradition until that time.

> *The oldest extant documents purporting to be the teaching of Buddha are the Pitakas, or 'Baskets of the Law," prepared for the Buddhist Council of 241 B.C., accepted by it as genuine, transmitted orally for four centuries from the death of Buddha, and finally put into writing, in the Pali tongue, about 80 B.C.*[599]

No Buddhists regard Gautama's teachings or the subsequent commentaries as revelations from God. They are regarded as teaching a "Path" to enlightenment or understanding of the truth discovered by Buddha. The Buddhist Missionary Promotion Foundation, in their book, *The Teaching of Buddha*, states, "This book is valuable because it contains the essence of the Buddha's teachings as recorded in over 5,000 volumes."[600] Originally, in the teachings of Buddha, the precepts for the monks and the commentary were known as the *Triptaka* in Sanskrit. When Buddhism was introduced into China and translated the "number of books and volumes thus translated reached 1,440 scriptures in 5,586 volumes."[601] In other words, it is virtually impossible to reconstruct the original teachings of Siddhartha

Gautama or, even in an entire lifetime, to read what he reportedly taught.

The scriptures for the Sikhs is the *Guru Granth*. It contains "spiritual poetry" of the ten gurus of the Sikh religion.[602]

The teachings of Confucius were recorded in the *Five Ching*, apparently written or edited by his own hand, to which have been added four "Shu" or books to constitute the *Nine Classics*.[603] The first of the "Shu" is *The Analects*, written by his disciples and summarizing Confucius' opinions and pronouncements. None of the *Nine Classics* purport to be revelations from God—they claim only to be wisdom, not a guide to "salvation."

Lao Tzu supposedly recorded his beliefs in the *Tao Te Ching* as Taoism's only "scripture." It also does not claim to be a revelation from God or to teach how to achieve "salvation."

Shintoism does not have any scriptures or authoritative writings.

Judaism regards the *Torah* and the writings of the "prophets" as revealed directly by God. When Moses taught the Israelites the things he had learned after spending 40 days on Mount Sinai with God he said:

> *Now therefore hearken O Israel, unto the statutes and unto the judgments, which I teach you, for to do them, that ye may live, and go in and possess the land which the Lord God of your fathers giveth you. Ye shall not add unto the word which I command you, neither shall ye diminish ought from it, that ye may keep the commandments of the Lord God which I command you . . . . Keep therefore and do them; for this is your wisdom and your understanding in the sight of the nations, which shall hear all these statutes, and say, Surely this great nation is a wise and understanding people. For what nation is there so great who hath God so nigh unto them, as the Lord our God is in all the things that we call upon him for?*[604]

When Joshua succeeded Moses as the leader of the Israelites, God told him:

> *Only be thou strong and very courageous, that thou mayest observe to do according to all the law [Torah], which Moses*

> *my servant commanded thee: turn not from it to the right hand or to the left, that thou mayest prosper whithersoever thou goest. This book of the law shall not depart out of thy mouth; but thou shalt meditate therein day and night, that thou mayest observe to do all that is written therein; for then thou shalt make thy way prosperous, and thou shalt have good success.*[605]

Jewish devotion to their written scriptures was intense. Rabbi Nathan stated, "Men were created only on condition that they studyTorah."[606] Rabbi Machsor Vitry says of the *Torah*, "It was the instrument made use of by the Holy One at the very beginning—for God studied it and created the universe accordingly."[607] Rabbi Jonah ben Abraham was of the opinion:

> *Everything that was created was created only for the purpose of fulfilling the Torah. All the things under the heavens, all of them, are only the means of satisfying the needs of those who devote themselves to the Torah.*[608]

Historically, all Jews, and in modern times, Orthodox Jews, are extremely diligent in studying and preserving the scriptures. The scriptures consist of the first five books of the Old Testament (*Torah* or *Pentateuch*) and the remaining historical and prophetical books of the Old Testament. Taken together they are known as the *Tanakh*. Beginning about 500 B.C., the Soferin or "scribes" began developing interpretations of the *Torah* which were preserved orally.[609] Later, a written commentary on these scriptures, called *The Mishnah,* is considered authoritative on the "Oral Law" or tradition. This exegetical activity to interpret the scriptures is known as "Midrash."[610] A more detailed commentary is called the *Talmud*. The Palestinan version was completed about 400 A.D. and the Babylonian version was completed about 500 A.D. All young men of Orthodox families begin the study of *Torah* at the age of 5, and depending on their facility, continue through the age of 13. At that time the more gifted are allowed to enter the "university" to continue their study. Those who continue for many years become rabbis to teach others.[611] "Torah crowns" are created as decoration for the *Torah* scroll of the congregation "to signify that the *Torah* is for us our crowning possession."[612]

Because the *Torah* contains the word of God the text may never be changed. According to Rabbi Leo Trepp:

> *A group of Rabbis once counted every word, every paragraph, even every letter in it, to make sure there would be no errors or variations in the future; the text has never changed since.*[613]

Rabbi Jonah ben Abraham was of the opinion:

> *At the Final Judgment the first thing a person will have to account for is: why had he not set fixed times for studying Torah.*[614]

When the *Torah* scrolls become old or desecrated, they are even given a funeral service and buried.[615]

Islam has only one scripture, *The Koran* or *Qur'an*, written by just one prophet, Mohammed. Moslems believe that every word of *The Koran* is a direct revelation from God uttered by Mohammed at the command of the angel Gabriel. Many Moslems have memorized the entire Koran as a demonstration of their devoted faith to its teachings. Although *The Koran* "was recorded after a lapse of a hundred years," "not a syllable has been altered as God himself has guaranteed its preservation."[616] No more revelation is to be expected as Mohammed was the last prophet and in *The Koran* "all things are revealed."[617] Islam teaches that God revealed the truth to the Jews and the Christians, but they apostatized and corrupted the faith.[618] *The Koran* accepts the *Torah* given to Moses[619] and the other prophets identified in the rest of the Old Testament and purports to "confirm" those writings. According to Will Durant Islam believes:

> *God has given man 104 revelations, of which only four have been preserved—the Pentateuch to Moses, the Psalms to David, the Gospel to Jesus, The Koran to Mohammed; whoso rejects any one of these is, in Mohammed's view, an infidel. But the first three have suffered such corruption that they can no longer be trusted; and The Koran now replaces them.*[620]

While *The Koran* refers to the Holy Spirit in several places,[621] there is no doctrine of enlightenment by the Holy Spirit. In addition to *The Koran*, the sayings and deeds of Mohammed (Hadith or

Ahadith) were collected and transmitted by his followers. There are many collections of Hadith but six are most famous. Imam Muslim allegedly collected 3,000,000 Hadith but after evaluating their authenticity selected 4,000 for his compilation, *Sahih Muslim*.[622] The most famous and allegedly authentic Hadith collection is *Sahih Al-Bukhari*, which runs 9 volumes in English translation.[623]

Christians accept *The Bible*, including the Old and New Testament as their scriptures. Like the Jews, they accept the Old Testament as writings of authentic prophets called by God, and the New Testament as authentic writings by the apostles and disciples of Jesus Christ. Professor Dummelow states:

> *The central subject of The Bible is God. The Book opens with an account of His creation of the heavens and the earth and concludes with a description of the 'new heavens and the earth'—the ideal to which creation is moving and wherein God himself shall be the immediate source of illumination and the object of worship.* [624]
>
> *That is to say, the authority of the Scriptures through all the ages primarily rests upon the conviction which they themselves produced that they came from God.*[625]

In the Catholic Church the "Liturgy of the Word" includes "the writings of the prophets," that is, the Old Testament, and "the memoirs of the apostles" (their letters and the Gospels).[626]

The Liturgy of the Word is an integral part of sacramental celebrations. To nourish the faith of believers, the signs which accompany the Word of God should be emphasized: the book of the Word (a lectionary or a book of the Gospels), its veneration (procession, incense, candles), the place of its proclamation (lectern or ambo), its audible and intelligible reading, the minister's homily which extends its proclamation, and the responses of the assembly (acclamations, meditation, psalms, litanies and professions of faith).[627]

In the Reformation, there was a split between Protestants and Catholics on the importance of *The Bible*—many Protestants accepting *The Bible* literally, other Protestants discounting some of the things written in *The Bible*, and the Catholics who accept *The Bible*, but who also accept "tradition" as a valid source of teaching (see Part III, Section 1, "*The Bible*"). Christians believe that in addition to the scriptures, the "Light of Christ" enlightens every man and woman born in the world[628] and that God will grant the "gift" of the Holy Spirit to those who keep his commandments. The Light of Christ and the Holy Spirit will provide enlightenment and act as guides to truth in interpreting and understanding the scriptures.

13. CEREMONIES AND RITUAL.

All of the major religions of the world have various kinds of ceremonies and ritual, except perhaps some forms of Deism. These include such things as prayer, fasting, ordinances, worship services, pilgrimages, etc. Because of the wide variety it is probably not possible to decide what ceremonies and rituals are "true" without deciding first which religion one accepts, although what ceremonies and rituals a religion has may affect some people's opinion of the truthfulness of that religion.

One of the most ceremonial and ritualistic religions, at least in its Orthodox form, is Judaism. Although many of the laws of Moses are written in the *Torah* itself, in particular, the "law" of Deuteronomy, the Jewish rabbis developed elaborate interpretations and clarifications of the written scriptures. Rabbi Jonah justified this activity as follows:

> *It is a great and noble thing to make a hedge and fence about the commandments; in that way one who hears the words of the Lord will escape neglecting them. That is why he who carries out the words of the Sages, which are a hedge to the commandments of the Torah, gives evidence of greater love of piety than he who simply carries out the commandments itself. For carrying out the commandments is not a sufficient proof of piety.*[629]

The "traditions of the Elders" or the Oral Law for the prior 400 years, consisting of the "beliefs and religious practices as piety and custom had in the course of centuries, consciously or unconsciously, grafted on to or developed out of the Written Law [the *Torah*]," was compiled by Rabbi Judah the Patriarch at the end of the second century A.D.[630] Herbert Danby says:

> *Josephus, dealing with the controversy between Saducees and Pharisees in the time of John Hyrcanus (135-104 B.C) writes: 'The Pharisees have delivered to the people a great many observances by succession from their fathers which are not written in the law of Moses; and it is for that reason that the Saducees reject them, and say that we are to esteem those observances to be obligatory which are in the Written word, but are not to observe what are derived from the tradition of the forefathers.' It is a reasonable hypotheses that a result of this controversy—a controversy which continued for two centuries—was a deliberate compilation and justification of the unwritten tradition by the Pharisean party, perhaps unsystematic and on a small scale in the earlier stages, but stimulated and fostered from time to time both by opposition from the Saducees and by internal controversy (such as, e.g., the disputes between the Schools of Hillel and Shammai) within the ranks of the Phariesees, culminating in the collections of traditional laws (Halakoth) from which the present Mishnah drew its material.*[631]

"But the interpretation par excellence of *The Mishnah* is that given in the two Talmuds: the *Talmud Yerushalmi* or Palestinian Talmud, and the *Talmud Babli* or Babylonian Talumd."[632] For example, the Babylonian Talmud in English translation runs 68 volumes (tractates). In traditional Judaism the congregation assembles three times a day for prayer—morning, afternoon and evening.[633] Traditionally, each Jew was to recite 18 set prayers each day.[634] Despite Rabbi Simeon's teaching, "When thou prayest, make not thy prayer a fixed form, but make it an entreaty and supplication of love before the Almighty,"[635] prayers are written in a prayer book and are recited as a daily liturgy "because structured prayers express the thoughts and emotions of our soul more perfectly than individual prayers could possible do."[636] The Rabbis counted in the *Torah* that Jews were to obey 613 "Mitzvot"[commandments], and converts to Judaism must promise to obey all of them.[637] The Rabbis also appointed a "Berakah"—a blessing in set form for every occasion.

Rabbi Meir held that Jews should recite 100 Berakhot a day.[638] In regard to Sabbath observance, the scripture itself only enjoined the Israelites to keep the day holy, not to do any "work" on the Sabbath day, not to leave one's place on the Sabbath day, and not to kindle any fire in their settlements on the Sabbath day.[639] The Rabbis divided the "work" that could not be done into 7 major categories and 39 prohibitions. In addition to prohibitions against sports, dancing, swimming, boating and cooking—pens, pencils and the telephone could not be used; and travel from city to city, turning on electric lights, televisions, radios or heat; and opening an umbrella, were prohibited.[640] The strictness of these rules caused Jews to employ "Shabbes Goy"—non-Jews to perform such functions as turning on the lights, heating the stove and milking the cows.[641] The Jews also maintain a strict dietary law of "kasher,"[kosher] including a complete separate sets of dishes in their homes for meat dishes and milk dishes. At the time a Jew is near death, Orthodox Jews change the sick person's name just in case the death decree of God is limited to the person with the former name.[642] *The Koran* criticizes the Jews for "corrupting" the scriptures and claims that their corruption of the scriptures necessitated the revelation of *The Koran*. Jesus criticized the Jews for such things as their restrictions on the Sabbath day stating, "The Sabbath was made for man [as a day of rest], and not man for the Sabbath,"[643] and the evasion of duties to parents by declaring wealth to be "corban, " thereby "making the word of God of none effect through your tradition . . . and many such like things do ye."[644] Jesus taught that he had not come to destroy the law of Moses but to fulfill it.[645] Paul taught that Christ was the "end of the law."[646] Initially, there was some confusion as to whether Christian converts had to obey the law of Moses, such as circumcision, but the apostles determined that it was no longer necessary.[647] When the resurrected Jesus visited the Nephites as recorded in *The Book of Mormon*, he said, "[I]n me the law of Moses is fulfilled,"[648] and the people there "did not walk any more after the performances and ordinances of the law of Moses."[649] *The Book of Mormon* prophet, Jacob, a Jew by birth, wrote that the Jews went "beyond the mark" in their zeal to do God's will and embellish the commandments of God.[650]

The complexity of compliance with the Jewish Orthodox rules is sufficiently daunting that Rabbi Leo Trepp, the author of *The Complete Book of Jewish Observance*—whose stated purpose was to "help Jews become celebrants of Judaism"—commented, "The reader of this book…may feel that following Judaism, as outlined here, will become a full-time occupation, leaving no opportunity in thought and action ever to move into the secular field of life, its challenges, enjoyments, and satisfactions."[651] Many have come to believe that the practice of Orthodox Judaism is practical only when living in a community entirely of Jews where all of the members of the community can cooperate in assisting one another in their religious duties. Since the dispersion of Jews throughout the world (diaspora)—they are now living among many non-Jews—Conservative, Reform and Reconstructionist Judaism have arisen, all declaring it was necessary to make accommodations in the elaborate rules of Orthodox Judaism to different times and locations.

In Catholic Christianity there are seven "sacraments": baptism, confirmation, Eucharist (communion), penance, anointing of the sick (extreme unction), holy orders (entering the priesthood or clergy) and matrimony.[652] "The Church affirms that for believers the sacraments are necessary for salvation."[653]

> *Among the liturgical signs from the Old Covenant are circumcision, anointing and consecration of kings and priests, laying on of hands, sacrifices and above all the Passover. The Church sees in these signs a prefiguring of the sacraments of the New Covenant.*[654]

The Liturgy of the Mass has evolved and became very ceremonial. It "occupies a unique place as the 'Sacrament of sacraments:' all other sacraments are ordered to it as to their end."[655] However, the liturgical rites in the Catholic Church are not geographically uniform. Those in use include the Roman rite and the Ambrosian, Byzantine, Alexandrian or Coptic, Syriac, Armenian, Maronite and Chaldean rites.[656] In addition to the sacraments the Roman Catholic Church has "sacramentals." "These are "sacred signs that bear a resemblance to the sacraments," such as the blessings of persons, e.g., readers, acolytes, catechists, etc., the consecration of virgins, dedication of a church or an altar, the blessing of holy oils, vestments, bells, etc., and performing exorcisms.[657] In addition, the Roman Catholic Church determined in the Second Council of Nicaea in 787 A.D. that representations of Christ, Mary, angels and the saints (icons) are not idols.[658] The Eastern Orthodox Church, however, continues to reject all such representations. The Roman Catholic Church enjoins Sunday as the "foremost holy day of obligation," and also the "day of the Nativity of Our Lord, Jesus Christ, the Epiphany, the Ascension of Christ, the feast of the Body and Blood of Christ, the feast of Mary the Mother of God, her Immaculate Conception, her Assumption, the feast of Saint Joseph, the feast of the Apostles Saints Peter and Paul and the feast of All Saints" as holy days of obligation."[659]

In Islam there are five "pillars of faith." These are the profession of faith—"There is no God but God [Allah] and Mohammed is his messenger;" prayer facing in the direction of Mecca five times a day and congregational prayer at the mosque on Friday at mid-day in accordance with established formulas; the payment of the "zakat" or alms tax; fasting from food and drink during the daylight hours during the month of Ramadan; and the pilgrimage (hajj) to Mecca once during the life of the believer.[660]

In Hinduism, in the *Atharva Veda*, is listed "a medley of incantations . . . one must recite spells to obtain children, to avoid abortion, to prolong life, to ward off evil, to woo sleep, to destroy or harass enemies."[661]

At the other end of the spectrum of ceremonialism, in Amida Buddhism, Buddhahood is achieved by being reborn in the "Pure Land" through "repeating my name in sincere faith ten times."[662] Or, as expressed by another scholar in regard to Japanese Amida Buddhism:

> *He [Honen] taught that the mere recitation of the phrase 'adoration to the Lord of boundless light and infinite life' would give instantaneous and final assurance of rebirth in 'the pure land' if it were accompanied by faith.*[663]

In Nichiren Buddhism:

> *A Nichiren Buddhist believes that when he repeats the sacred formula 'Adoration to the sutra of the lotus of the true law'*

his soul becomes identified with the cosmic soul of the eternal Buddha. The sacred formula is, therefore, the means of salvation; it alone is sufficient.[664]

Professor Basil Chamberlain compares Buddhism and Christianity as follows:

Many writers, from St. Francis Xavier downwards, have drawn attention to the superficial resemblances between the Buddhistic and the Roman Catholic ceremonial—the flowers on the altar, the candles, the incense, the shaven heads of the priests, the rosaries, the images, the processions. In point of dogma, a whole world of thought separates Buddhism from every form of Christianity. Knowledge, enlightenment, is the condition of Buddhistic grace—not faith. Self perfectionment is the means of salvation, not the vicarious suffering of a Redeemer. Not eternal life is the end, and active participation in unceasing praise and thanksgiving, but absorption into Nirvana, practical annihilation. For Buddhism teaches that existence is itself an evil, springing from the double root of ignorance and the passions.[665]

In the Sikh religion, "For the early disciples who gathered around Nanak [the first guru], the goal of life was to devote themselves to dwelling upon the name of God, to sing and lodge within their hearts the hymns composed by their leader."[666] The Sikh religion rejected the Hindu Brahminic priesthood—there are no priests—anyone can conduct the worship service.[667]

14. TOLERANCE AND FANATICISM.

Religions can also be distinguished by their attitudes about other religions. Some people are respectful of other persons and their religious beliefs, and even though almost all of the major religions have some form of the Golden Rule, some religions are zealous, even fanatical. The historian Will Durant was of the view, "[N]o man can be tolerant except where he is indifferent."[668]

Hinduism is perhaps the most tolerant. Although there are six schools of Hinduism, and some have diametrically opposing beliefs, the overall attitude of Hinduism is that "all is one" and that "all roads lead to heaven."

The Hindu is prone to believe even that all the six systems, as well as their varieties of subsystems are in harmony with one another, in fact, that they are complementary to one another in the total vision, which is one.[669]

In the nineteenth century the Hindu leader Ramakrishna taught:

All religions are good...each is a way to God, or a stage on the way, adapted to the mind and heart of the seeker. To be converted from one religion to another is foolishness; one need only continue on his own way and reach to the essence of his own faith. 'All rivers flow to the ocean. Flow, and let others flow, too!'[670]

Will Durant ascribes to this Hindu toleration the virtual extinction of Buddhism in modern India:

Brahmanism [Hinduism] had always been tolerant; in all the history of the rise and fall of Buddhism and a hundred other sects we find much disputation, but no instance of persecution. On the contrary Brahmanism eased the return of the prodigal by proclaiming Buddha a god (as an avatar of Vishnu), ending animal sacrifice, and accepting into orthodox practice the Buddhist doctrine of the sanctity of all animal life. Quietly and peacefully, after half a thousand years of gradual decay,Buddhism disappeared from India.[671]

Still, Hinduism is strict about the separation of the castes and regards the caste each person is born into as evidence of his or her righteousness in previous incarnations.

Buddhism teaches its own "Way" and the "Eightfold Path." It teaches that a person who does not follow the Eightfold Path is to some extent deluded, so Buddhists could be described as intolerant but not fanatical. In Japan, a compromise was effected between the native Shinto religion and the imported Buddhism:

There developed a division of duties: Shinto deities presided over the affairs of this world, while the life hereafter became the concern of Buddhism. Births, marriages, seasonal festivals, and victories in battles were in the sphere of Shinto interest. Preaching doctrinal matters, ecclesiastical organization and funerals were the responsibility of Buddhism. Ancestral worship, however, which under strong Confucian influence had become a universal practice, was the affair of both.[672]

Confucianism and Taoism are concerned with an orderly society and rules to help reduce friction and maintain harmony. As such they are quite tolerant—Confucius "refused to be inflexible"[673]— but tend to enforce their rules by social pressure. In some countries such as Japan such pressure has brought about social conformity but also high rates of suicide. When Confucius was asked, "Should one love one's enemy, those who do us harm?" he replied, "By no means. Answer hatred with justice and love with benevolence. Otherwise you would waste your benevolence."[674] But, he also taught that "tolerance" is one of the five aspects of benevolence.[675] Nevertheless, according to the *Shih Chi*, the ancient record of China, when Confucius was made Prime Minister, "Thereupon, he killed Shao Cheng Mao, a Counsellor of Lu, who caused disorder in the government."[676]

Judaism is quite strict about its beliefs, at least in the Orthodox sect, and although Jews are required to be hospitable to strangers,[677] they require that visitors and strangers abide by the Jewish precepts when mingling with Jews.[678] A modern rabbi, Morris Kertzer, in response to the question, "Do Jews believe that Judaism is the only true religion?" said:

Jews do not presume to judge the honest worshiper of any faith.Our prayer book tells us: 'The righteous of all nations are worthy of immortality.' We Jews know that there are many mountain tops—and all of them reach for the stars.[679]

Christianity, in its Biblical teachings, is tolerant. The teachings of Jesus that you should "Love your enemies, bless them that curse you, do good to them that hate you, and pray for them that despitefully use you, and persecute you"[680] has resulted in innumerable actions of self-sacrifice in Christian history. Jesus, himself, was the model of the man of peace, suffering evil rather than doing evil, he amply demonstrated that he had sufficient power to avoid the designs of his enemies, but he accepted suffering and death to bring about the atonement for all who would accept him and keep his commandments. Despite the teachings and example of Jesus, there are numerous instances of Christian fanaticism in later ages, including the Crusades, the religious wars of Europe and the Inquisition. The Fourth Lateran Council in 1215 declared that no man could be saved outside the [Catholic] Church.[681] Both Catholics and Protestants supported the death penalty for being an Anabaptist. John Calvin, once he obtained political power in Geneva, Switzerland, was severe on heresy. He had Michael Servetus, who disagreed with Calvin's views about the Trinity, burned. Fifty-eight persons were put to death in Calvin's Geneva for heresy. Calvin said, "When his [God's] glory is to be asserted, humanity must be almost obliterated from our memories."[682] Luther was fanatical in later years in regard to the Jews, denouncing them as wicked and abominable, demanding that their schools and synagogues be razed with fire, advocating the burning of their houses, forbidding preaching by their rabbis on pain of death, calling for destruction of their prayer books and Talmud and confiscation of their money, "and if this be not enough, let them be driven like mad dogs out of the land."[683] Jews and Moslems were expelled from Spain and Portugal in 1492 by the Christians, and Jews were persecuted and killed in Italy, England, France, Germany, Austria and Belgium in "pogroms." According to Will Durant, John Knox, the founder of Presbyterianism in Scotland "rejoiced in that 'perfect hatred which the Holy Ghost engendereth in the heart's of God's elect against the contemners of His holy statutes.' In conflicts with the reprobate all methods were justified—lies, treachery, flexible contradictions of policy."[684] When Edward II, King of England was induced to arrest members of the Catholic Order of Templars, Pope Clement V wrote to Edward, "We hear that you forbid torture as contrary to the laws of your land. But no state law can override canon law. Therefore, I command you at once to submit these men to torture."[685] Voltaire refers to a book written by the Catholic Bishop Bartolome de Las Casas of Chiapas, Mexico "from which it appears that in America ten million infidels had been slaughtered or burned or drowned in order to convert them."[686] It is almost as if Jesus' maxim, "Whatsoever ye would that men should do to you, do ye even so to them" was totally forgotten. The most famous chronicle of persecution was John Fox's *Book of Martyrs*. Published in 1563, it detailed the early Christian persecutions by pagans and the later persecutions of the Protestants. Joseph Smith once wrote:

> *We have learned by sad experience that it is the nature and disposition of almost all men, as soon as they get a little authority, as they suppose, they will immediately begin to exercise unrighteous dominion.*[687]

The Catholic Church currently teaches that, "All men are bound to seek the truth," but then says:

> *It does not contradict a 'sincere respect' for different religions which frequently 'reflect a ray of that truth which enlightens all men,' nor the requirement of charity, which urges Christians 'to treat with love, prudence and patience those who are in error or ignorance with regards to the faith.'*[688]

In regard to tolerance and respect in connection with differing religious beliefs, Joseph Smith said:

> *If it has been demonstrated that I have been willing to die for a 'Mormon,' I am bold to declare before Heaven that I am just as ready to die in defending the rights of a Presbyterian, a Baptist, or a good man of any other denomination; for the same principle which would trample upon the rights of the Latter-day Saints would trample upon the rights of the Roman Catholics or of any other denomination who may be unpopular and too weak to defend themselves.*[689]

Tolerance is one of the Articles of Faith of The Church of Jesus Christ of Latter-day Saints:

> *We claim the privilege of worshiping Almighty God according to the dictates of our own conscience, and allow all men the same privilege, let them worship how, where or what they may.*[690]

The true test of any religion is how the minority is treated when that religion is in the majority and has the power to persecute.

In 1841, when The Church of Jesus Christ of Latter-day Saints was headquartered in Nauvoo, Illinois and the vast majority of the citizens were members of that Church, the City Council passed "An Ordinance in Relation to Religious Societies:"

> *Be it ordained by the City Council of the City of Nauvoo that the Catholics, Presbyterians, Methodists, Baptists, Latter-day Saints, Quakers, Episcopals, Universalists, Unitarians, Mohammedans and all other religious sects and denominations whatever, shall have free toleration, and equal privileges in this city; and should any person be guilty of ridiculing, and abusing or otherwise depreciating another in consequence of his religion, or of disturbing or interrupting any religious meeting within the limits of this city, he shall, on conviction thereof before the Mayor [Joseph Smith] or Municipal Court, be considered a disturber of the public peace, and fined in any sum not exceeding five hundred dollars, or imprisoned not exceeding six months, or both, at the discretion of said Mayor or Court.*[691]

Islam teaches that, "The only true faith in Allah's sight is Islam,"[692] and "He that chooses a religion other than Islam, it will not be accepted from him in the world to come; he will be one of the lost."[693] In one place *The Koran* teaches, "There shall be no compulsion in religion,"[694] and, in another, "Fight for the sake of Allah those that fight against you, but do not attack them first. Allah does not love the aggressor."[695] But there are also numerous passages that teach that unbelievers should be put to death, including the following:

> *Mohammed is Allah's apostle. Those that follow him are ruthless to the unbelievers but merciful to one another.*[696]

> *Make war on them [the unbelievers] until idolatry is no more and Allah's religion reigns supreme.*[697]

> *When the sacred months are over slay the idolaters wherever you find them. Arrest them, besiege them, and lie in ambush everywhere for them.*[698]

Those who have embraced the faith and fled their homes and fought for Allah's cause with their wealth and their persons are held in higher regard by Allah.[699]

Prophet, make war on the unbelievers and the hypocrites and deal rigorously with them. Hell shall be their home: an evil fate.[700]

Seek out your enemies relentlessly.[701]

According to the historian Will Durant, during the time Mohammed was in Medina "he planned sixty-five campaigns and raids, and personally led twenty seven."[702]

After Mohammed's death, a struggle ensued over succession. Three of the next successors (caliphs) were assassinated, two of them by other Muslims.[703] Islam spread through much of the Middle East by conquest and forced conversions. Even in modern times, some sects of Islam have openly violent doctrines and behavior. Thomas Lippman says flatly:

Throughout The Koran, the principal motivation to accepting God and believing in His revelations appears to be fear—fear of the last judgment and fear of eternal damnation. Though God is described as generous and beneficent, He is always the God who punishes unbelievers and destroys corrupt societies. Islam places less stress upon love of the Deity as a motivation for piety than does Christianity.[704]

15. SEPARATION OF CHURCH AND STATE

Strongly related to the foregoing topic, different religions have different attitudes about the proper relationship of church and state. The Moslems have always maintained that there should be no separation of religion and civil government. As Thomas Lippman states it, "There is technically no separation between church and state in Islam."[705] In the 1800's, with freer immigration and commerce and mixed religious groups within one country, democratic constitutions have been adopted guaranteeing religious freedom and civil rights in many Moslem countries, but many Moslem groups have continuously advocated the establishment of Moslem religious teachings—the "Shariah"—as the sole law governing the state, with the effect that residents must practice Islam or emigrate.

In Confucianism we read:

> *Heaven cares profoundly about the welfare of the common people and the Emperor is set up expressly to promote that welfare. He rules in virtue of the Decree of Heaven and remains Emperor only so long as he fulfills that purpose. As soon as he forgets his function and begins to rule for his own sake, Heaven will withdraw the Decree and bestow it on someone more worthy.*[706]

Confucianists and Taoists have shown religious tolerance and have not sought to combine Church and State for the purpose of oppressing unbelievers.

Hindus can be said to be indifferent to the State—they believe that happiness and release from reincarnation can be achieved without regard to the political government and are quite comfortable with complete separation of Church and State.

In Judaism, even when the Jews were captured by their oppressors, Jeremiah instructed:

> *Seek the peace of the city where I have caused you to be carried away captive, and pray unto the Lord for it; for in the peace thereof ye shall have peace.*[707]

The prophet Ezra taught, "And pray for the life of the king, and of his sons."[708]

Since A.D. 70, Jews have not been in a position to have a State where they could have a choice to separate government from religion until the establishment of Israel in 1948. Prior to that time, they strongly favored separation of Church and State as the only way to prevent the majority Christian and Islamic adherents from oppressing them. In Israel, though Jews constitute the political majority and despite efforts by Orthodox Jews to integrate the government and religion, religious freedom and separation of Church and State have been maintained.

When Christ's disciples asked if they should pay taxes to the Roman rulers, Jesus taught that men should, "[R]ender unto Caesar the things that are Caesar's and to God the things that are God's,"[709] and, on another occasion, he sent his apostle to obtain a coin from the fish's mouth to pay the taxes he owed.[710] Paul also taught Timothy:

> *I exhort, therefore, that, first of all, supplications, prayers intercessions, and giving of thanks be made to all men; for kings, and for all that are in authority; that we may lead a quiet and peaceable life in all godliness and honesty.*[711]

Peter taught:

> *Honor all men. Love the brotherhood. Fear God. Honor the king.*[712]

Paul declared to the Roman members of the Church:

> *Let every soul be subject unto the higher powers; for there is no power but of God: the powers that be are ordained of God. Whosoever resisteth the power resisteth the ordinance of God and they that resist shall receive to themselves damnation.*[713]

Unfortunately, we have seen many political leaders who relied on the foregoing scriptures to abuse their authority, and religious leaders who have coerced political leaders to establish or maintain their religion or to discriminate against other religions.

Christianity was a persecuted minority until about A.D. 325 when Constantine, the emperor of Rome, accepted Christianity and made it the state religion. Thereafter, there was serious cross interference in church and state affairs. In 380 A.D. the Emperor Gratian "proclaimed the Nicene Creed as compulsory 'on all the peoples subject to the governments of our clemency' and denounced as 'mad and insane' the followers of other faiths."[714] According to Professor Todd:

> *The dramatic change at the end of the fourth century, when the church came to dominate the Emperor, was due to Ambrose, the great bishop of Milan.*[715]

In the late fifth century the bishop of Rome, Gelasius I, developed the view that the Emperor was directly subject to the head of the church.[716] According to Professor Rosenberg the general pattern of early medieval conversions to Christianity was "essentially a matter of royal policy; the ruler's conversion decided the religion of his subjects."[717] For example, Charlemagne, the first "Holy Roman Emperor," conquered on the basis that those who refused baptism were to be punished by death.[718] Around 988, Vladimir, the pagan prince of Kiev, accepted Eastern Orthodox Christianity and "then ordered the mass baptism of the Russians according to the Orthodox form. Orthodoxy thus became the state religion of Russia, which it was to remain until 1917."[719] In the eighth century a document appeared known as the "Donation of Constantine" asserting that Constantine had donated to the pope the secular rule of Rome, Italy and the West, but in the fifteenth century it was proven a forgery.[720] In 756 A.D. Pepin the Short gave all central Italy to the pope, whereby he had his own state, and in 800 A.D. the pope returned the favor by conferring the title of "Emperor of the Holy Roman Empire" on Charlemagne—thereafter for 500 years no man could be an accepted emperor in the West without anointment by a pope.[721] Pope Innocent III (1198-1216) declared, "The Lord left to Peter the government not only of all the Church, but of the whole world,"[722] perhaps forgetting that Christ had said, "My kingdom is not of this world." [723]

In the eleventh century political leaders appointed bishops and priests—"lay investiture"—and in the twelfth and thirteenth centuries the Church asserted its authority by Pope Gregory VII excommunicating the Emperor Henry IV and deposing the Emperor Frederick II.[724]

> *[Pope] Innocent III also led the papacy to victory over the kings of France and England. In 1205 King John argued with the pope over the appointment of the Archbishop of Canterbury, and Innocent arranged the election of Stephen Langton to the post. John refused to accept him, so England was placed under an interdict in 1208, with the result that the church refused to marry, baptize or bury people. John retaliated by seizing church lands and forcing most of the bishops out of England. In 1209 Innocent excommunicated the English king and in 1212 declared the throne of England vacant, inviting the French to invade the land. This proved effective, and John agreed to accept Langton and return church property. He resigned the crown of England to receive*

it back as a feudal retainer of the pope.[725]

In 1338, the Diet of Rhense finally declared that papal confirmation was not necessary to appoint the Emperor.[726]

Unfortunately, Christianity did not always treat minority religions with tolerance and it persecuted Jews and Muslims, as well as Christian "heretics." In many countries both Catholics and Protestants sought to drive the others out and establish political majority and control. The Catholic Church, forbidden by its canons from "shedding blood," nevertheless encouraged or required political governments to carry out corporal punishment for Church judgments of blasphemy and heresy. In that manner, the Inquisition, in which tens of thousands were killed became a blot on Christianity:

> *[Pope Innocent III's] successor Honorius III, allowed the Albigensian Crusade to intensify, assisted by the French King Louis VIII, who in 1226 issued an ordinance under which bishops would judge, and French law punish, heretics. Emperor Frederick II had issued a similar decree in 1220, and in 1224 he ordered the burning of heretics. When in 1231 another great pope, Gregory IX, in Excommunicamus, issued further decrees against heretics, he repeated this law of 1224. Execution by the secular authorities had finally and officially become papal policy. Under Gregory the Inquisition as a church institution was practically completed, and the new orders of friars, especially the Dominicans, had become the favored papal agents of the Inquisition. The finishing touches were supplied by Pope innocent IV who, in the bull, Ad Extirpanda (1252), incorporated all earlier papal statements about the organization of the Inquisition, as well as condoning the use of torture.*[727]

According to Will Durant:

> *The most rigorous code of suppression was enacted by Frederick II in 1220-39. Heretics condemned by the Church were to be delivered to the 'secular arm'—the local authorities—and burned to death. If they recanted they were to be let off with imprisonment for life. All their property was to be confiscated, their heirs were to be disinherited, their children*

were to remain ineligible to any position of emolument or dignity unless they atoned for their parents' sin by denouncing other heretics. The houses of heretics were to be destroyed and never rebuilt . . . Pope Innocent III, in 1215, required all civil authorities, on pain of being themselves indicted for heresy, to swear publicly 'to exterminate, from the lands subject to their obedience, all heretics who have been marked out by the Church for animadversion debita—'due punishment.'[728]

Usually a part of the confiscated goods went to the secular ruler of the province, part to the Church; in Italy one third was given to the informer; in France the crown took all. These considerations stimulated individuals and the state to join in the hunt, and led to trials of the dead.[729]

The Catholic Franciscan writer Felician Foy says:

In 1231 A.D. Pope Gregory IX authorized establishment of the Papal Inquisition for dealing with heretics. It was a creature of its time, when crimes against faith and heretical doctrines of extremists like the Cathari and Albigenses threatened the good of the Christian community, the welfare of the state and the very fabric of society. The institution, which was responsible for excesses in punishment, was most active in the second half of the century in southern France, Italy and Germany.[730]

The Baptist Alfred Henry Newman says:

Obstinate heretics were condemned to the stake; those that recanted were to be imprisoned for life; those that relapsed were to be executed; the property of heretics was to be confiscated; houses of heretics and their friends were to be destroyed and never rebuilt; the lands of civil rulers who should neglect to purge them of heresy were to be open for occupancy by any Catholic who would extirpate heresy therefrom . . . The civil authorities were required to act in entire subserviency to the inquisitors and to have lists of all heretics made out, to be read three times a year in public. The local inquisitors were to receive a third of the proceeds of confiscations and fines, the cities a third, and the bishops the other third . . .[731]

Lars P. Qualben in *A History of the Christian Church* says:

After the close of the war against the Albigenses in 1229, Gregory IX made heresy a capital offense, and insisted that the state must assist the Church in suppressing heresy. All the kings of Europe agreed to make heresy punishable by death, except England where it was not made a capital offense until 1401.[732]

In 1207 Pope Innocent III offered the feudal lords of central and northern France the same plenary indulgence (remission of the temporal punishment for sins) as had been granted to the Crusaders to Jerusalem if they would take part for 40 days in the effort to crush the Albigensian heretics in Southern France. This was the first "crusade" against fellow Christians. Instead of 40 days, the crusade lasted for 22 years until 1229, during which 100,000 heretics were killed.[733]

Pope Innocent IV (1252) authorized torture in the church courts when the inquisitors were convinced of the accused man's guilt, and later popes condoned its use.[734] The Inquisition was revived in the 1500's in Italy, Spain and France:

The Inquisition commonly used terror and torture to obtain confessions [of heresy]. If the death penalty was required, the convicted heretic was handed over to the civil authorities for execution, since canon law forbade churchmen to shed blood.[735]

The Catholic historian Boulenger says torture "was commanded by Pope Innocent IV, in 1522, as a means of obtaining the confession of the guilty."[736] Both Luther and the Calvinists taught that it was acceptable for the civil authorities to "suppress" "blasphemers" and "stubborn heretics."[737] In Zurich, Switzerland, where the Reformer Ulrich Zwingli held political authority, the Anabaptists, who taught a different doctrine, were subjected to the death penalty.[738] Luther came to the opinion that those worshipping in different ways could not live together in peace; therefore, according to his biographer:

The outcome was the territorial church, in which the confession was that of the majority in a given locality, and the minority were free to migrate to favorable terrain.[739]

Luther stated, "I cannot admit that false teachers are to be put to death. It is enough to banish."[740] However, at a later point he agreed the political leaders could impose the penalty of death for sedition and "blasphemy." [741] In one of his later tracts, when he learned that Jews were attempting to convert Christians, he proposed that all Jews be deported to Palestine, that their synagogues should be burned and their books, including *The Bible,* should be taken away from them.[742] But Martin Luther also taught that the king was not to be obeyed if a war is manifestly unjust.[743] After substantial fighting between the Lutherans and the Catholics, the Peace of Augsburg in 1555 "provided for the co-existence of Lutheran and Roman Catholic expressions of Christianity in Germany on the basis of 'whose the rule, his the religion.' That is, the prince could decide the faith of his subjects."[744] The Durants say:

The Diet of Augsburg (1555) had brought the religious strife to a geographical truce on the principle Cuius regio eius religio, 'Whose region, his religion'—i.e.,in each state the religion of the ruler was to be made the religion of his subjects; dissidents were to leave. The agreement represented a mite of progress, since it substituted emigration for execution; but it was restricted to Lutheranism and Catholicism, and the painful uprooting of many families added to the chaos and bitterness in Germany. When a ruler of one creed was succeeded by another of another, the population was expected to change its faith accordingly. Religion became the tool and victim of politics and war.[745]

The Protestants all came to support separation of church and state. Luther demanded that clergy guilty of crimes be subject to the civil, not just the church, courts, that citizens should be free from ecclesiastical extortion, and that the state should be free from clerical interference.[746] The Thirty-Nine Articles of Religion of the English Anglican Church stated:

The Power of the Civil Magistrate extendeth to all men, as well Clergy as Laity, in all things temporal; but hath no authority in things purely spiritual. And we hold it to be the duty of all men who are professors of the Gospel, to pay respectful obedience to the Civil Authority, regularly and legitimately constituted.[747]

But the history of Europe in the sixteenth to nineteenth centuries is one round of persecution by the dominant religious authority of minorities in France, Spain, Netherlands, England, Sweden, Germany, Italy, Portugal, Russia, Belgium, and the notorious persecution of Catholics in Ireland.

In 1864 Pope Pius IX published an encyclical, "Quanta Cura," to which was annexed a Syllabus or "catalogue of the principal errors of contemporary society." Among other things, the Syllabus condemned the separation of church and state, freedom of worship, the neutrality of the state in religious matters and the "the right for all to manifest openly and publicly all the thoughts and opinions."[748] Later, Popes Leo XIII and Pius X reaffirmed the doctrine of the Syllabus.[749] The temporal power of the pope continued until 1870, when the Republic of Italy was established and the Pope's secular dominion was confined to the Vatican city.[750]

Today, the Catholic Church's official doctrine is:

If because of the circumstances of a particular people special civil recognition is given to one religious community in the constitutional organization of a state, the right of all citizens and religious communities to religious freedom must be recognized and respected as well.[751]

[But] the right to religious liberty is neither a moral license to adhere to error, nor a supposed right to error, but rather a natural right of the human person to civil liberty, i.e., immunity within just limits, from external constraint in religious matters by political authorities.[752]

The scripture, as recorded in Romans, "the powers that be are ordained of God," was used by kings to justify their rule, even the most wicked and vicious tyranny. While the Catholic Church still accepts this scripture as the basis that the "moral order derives from

God," it has recognized that there are limits to this doctrine:

> *Authority is exercised legitimately only when it seeks the common good of the group concerned and if it employs morally licit means to attain it. If rulers were to enact unjust laws or take measures contrary to the moral order, such arrangements would not be binding in conscience. In such a case, 'authority breaks down completely and results in shameful abuse.'*[753]

Now, in regard to religious persecution, the Catholic Church teaches:

> *It is also blasphemous to make use of God's name to cover up criminal practices, to reduce peoples to servitude, to torture persons or put them to death. The misuse of God's name to commit a crime can provoke others to repudiate religion.*[754]

> *In times past, cruel practices were commonly used by legitimate governments to maintain law and order, often without protest from the Pastors of the Church, who themselves adopted in their own tribunals the prescriptions of Roman law concerning torture. Regrettable as these facts are, the Church always taught the duty of clemency and mercy. She forbade clerics to shed blood. In recent times it became evident that these cruel practices were neither necessary for public order nor in conformity with the legitimate rights of the human person. On the contrary these practices led to ones even more degrading. It is necessary to work for their abolition. We must pray for the victims and their tormentors.*[755]

In the modern Catholic Church's canons it "acknowledges and defends religious liberty for all persons: they are to be free from all coercion to lead their religious lives, privately and publicly, according to their consciences."[756]

As far as religious liberty was concerned, it wasn't until the establishment of the United States that religious freedom was established by the Constitution, and separation of Church and State was guaranteed. The United States Constitution rejected all religious tests for officeholders.[757] The First Amendment laid down that there should be neutrality in religion—the government could neither "establish" a state religion nor could it prohibit "the free exercise" of religion. Fourteen years after the adoption of the First Amendment, Joseph Smith, the "Mormon" prophet was born in a land where the restoration and spread of the Restored Gospel of Jesus Christ could be effected. Related to the proper church-state relationship, Joseph Smith was informed by Jesus Christ that the scripture in Romans should read, [F]or there is no power "**in the church but of God**." [emphasis added], and that not all political governments were righteous. Nevertheless, The Church of Jesus Christ of Latter-day Saints, consistent with I Peter 2:13-17, teaches:

> *We believe in being subject to kings, presidents, rulers, and magistrates in obeying, honoring, and sustaining the law.*[758]

One of the Church's declarations is:

> *We believe that all religious societies have a right to deal with their members for disorderly conduct, according to rules and regulations of such societies; provided that such dealings be for fellowship and good standing; but we do not believe that any religious society has authority to try men on the right of property or life, to take from them this world's goods, or to put them in jeopardy of either life or limb, or to inflict any physical punishment upon them. They can only excommunicate them from their society, and withdraw from their fellowship.*[759]

The Book of Mormon teaches that freedom of religion protects freedom of belief, but if religious practices or conduct infringe the civil liberties of others, such actions may be punished by the government.[760]

* * *

In summary of this Part, Christianity is a monotheistic religion enjoining duties on its believers to both God and man. Its God is a personal, loving God. Its chief teacher claimed he was the Son of God and the purpose of his mission was to teach the truth and to atone for the sins of all men and women who would accept him and keep his commandments in order that they could return to the presence of

God. Those who knew him best testified that he was the Son of God. The purposes of life are to obtain a body by birth in this world and to learn to keep the commandments through using our free will to overcome evil in many types of temptation and adversity. Through such efforts our strength to do good increases, and we will attain a fullness of joy after the resurrection and judgment. The Christian religion applies to all men born in all ages of the world. Its scriptures give guidance to our personal lives and, in particular, enables us to understand how God treats his children who obey—and those who do not obey—his commandments. Through these scriptures we understand his nature and attributes, including his power, justice and mercy, which results in obeying his commandments from appreciation and love, not duty or constraint. Christianity's ceremonies and rituals have inspiring symbolism and, although there are differences of opinion among Christians, they are a middle road between the deist who accepts no ceremony or ritual and the formalism of Orthodox Judaism. We have ended this Part by discussing the failings of Christianity—the intolerance, fanaticism and abuses that took place. In the next Part we will discuss why these occurred.

PART III

IS THE CHURCH OF JESUS CHRIST OF LATTER-DAY SAINTS ["MORMON"] THE TRUE FORM OF CHRISTIANITY?

INTRODUCTION

For some or all of the reasons discussed in Part II, or for other reasons, a person may be fully satisfied that Christianity is the true religion. Despite that, there are approximately 275 sects of Christianity just in the United States with varying and conflicting doctrines.[761] These include, Roman Catholicism (with its varying rites such as Latin, Byzantine, Maronite, Melkite, Armenian and Chaldean),[762] Eastern or Greek Orthodox (which severed all relations with the Roman Catholics), Baptist, Lutheran, Methodist, Presbyterian, Anglican, Mennonite, Pentecostal, Society of Friends (Quakers), Adventist, Church of God, Jehovah's Witnesses, Christian Scientist, The Church of Jesus Christ of Latter-day Saints [Mormon], Church of Christ, Assembly of God and others. One can become overwhelmed, despairing of ever being able to sort through all the alternatives to find the truth. However, there are some historical facts and doctrines that can be considered which will greatly simplify the search. In this section we will discuss such doctrines and why a "restoration" was necessary.

WHY A "RESTORATION" WAS NECESSARY

"The Catholic Church is the Church founded by Christ," asserts the Catholic Franciscan writer Felician Foy.[763] The current *Catechism of the Catholic Church* further states:

> *God graciously arranged that the things he had once revealed for the salvation of all peoples should remain in their entirety,throughout the ages, and be transmitted to all generations.*[764]

BUT—ALL OF THE PROTESTANT SECTS OF CHRISTIANITY ARE IN AGREEMENT ON ONE POINT: THE ROMAN CATHOLIC CHURCH DEPARTED FROM THE ORIGINAL TEACHINGS OF JESUS CHRIST IN ITS DOCTRINE AND PRACTICES.

The New Testament prophesied that this would occur. Paul told Timothy:

> *For the time will come when they will not endure sound doctrine; but after their own lusts they shall heap to themselves teachers having itching ears; And they shall turn away their ears from the truth, and shall be turned unto fables.*[765]

Paul told the Christians in Thessalonia—who anticipated that the Second Coming of Jesus Christ would be soon:

> *Now we beseech you, brethren, by the coming of our Lord Jesus Christ, and by our gathering together unto him, that ye be not soon shaken in mind, or be troubled, neither by Spirit, nor by word, nor by letter as from us, as that the day of Christ is at hand. Let no man deceive you by any means: for that day shall not come, except there come a falling away first, and that man of sin be revealed, the son of perdition; who opposeth and exalteth himself above all that is called God, or that is worshipped; so that he as God sitteth in the temple of God, shewing himself that he is God.*[766]

These, and other scriptures,[767] foretold an apostasy from the original teachings of Jesus Christ. Eusebius, the "Father of Ecclesiastical History," writing in 324 A.D.,said:

> *In describing the situation at that time Hegesippus [who belonged to the first generation after the apostles] goes on to say that until then the Church had remained a virgin, pure and uncorrupted, since those who were trying to corrupt the wholesome standard of the saving message, if such there were, lurked somewhere under cover of darkness. But when the sacred band of the apostles had in various ways reached the end of their life, and the generation of those privileged to listen with their own ears to the divine wisdom had passed on, then godless error began to take shape, through the*

deceit of false teachers, who now that none of the apostles was left threw off the mask and attempted to counter the preaching of the truth by preaching the knowledge falsely so called.[768]

Eusebius names 47 heretics and 10 different sects of Christianity in a period of two centuries who taught conflicting doctrines and contributed to confusion and the corruption of Christianity.[769] The first bishop of Jerusalem was James, the "Lord's brother," but when he was martyred a dispute arose as to his successor. As a result,

From these came Simon and his Simonians, Cleobius and his Cleobienes, Dositheus and his Dositheans, Gorhaeus and his Gorathenes and the Masbotheans. From these were derived the Menandrianists, Marcionists, Carpocratians, Valentians, Basilidians, and Saturnilians, every man introducing his own opinion in his own particular way. From these in turn came false Christs, false prophets, false apostles, who split the unity of the Church by poisonous suggestions against God and His Christ.[770]

Will Durant says:

Celsus himself had sarcastically observed that Christians were 'split up into ever so many factions, each individual desiring to have his own party.' About 187 [A.D.] Irenaeus listed twenty varieties of Christianity; about 384 [A.D.] Epiphanius counted eighty.[771]

By the fifth century, Augustine could list "no fewer than eighty-eight different heresies.[772]

In his writing, "The Babylonian Captivity of the Church," Luther said:

As the Jews had suffered a long captivity in Babylonia, so the Church as established by Christ, and as described in the New Testament, had undergone over a thousand years of captivity under the papacy in Rome. During that period the religion of Christ had been corrupted in faith, morals and ritual.[773]

At other times he said:

I have sought nothing beyond reforming the Church in conformity with the Holy Scriptures.[774]

I simply say Christianity has ceased to exist among those who should have preserved it—the bishops and scholars . . . .[775]

Professor McNair has written:

Martin Luther reckoned that things began to go badly wrong with the Christian church in the eighth century. Today most Catholics and Protestants alike say that several generations before Luther's protest against indulgences it was evident that there was something radically wrong with the Roman Catholic Church.[776]

The Reformers were not the only ones that railed against the wickedness in the Christian church.In 1513 Niccolo Machiavelli said:

Had the religion of Christianity been preserved according to the ordinances of its Founder, the states and commonwealths of Christendom would have been far more united and happy than they are. Nor can there be a greater proof of its decadence than the fact the nearer people are to the Roman Church, the head of this religion, the less religious are they. And whoever examines the principles on which that religion is founded, and sees how widely different from those principles its present practice and application are, will judge that her ruin or chastisement is near at hand.[777]

In Luther's own day, Pope Adrian VI (1521) said:

We know well that for many years things deserving of abhorrence have gathered around the Holy See. Sacred things have been misused, ordinances transgressed, so that in everything there has been a change for the worse. Thus it is not surprising that the malady has crept down from the head to the members, from the popes to their hierarchy. We all, prelates and clergy, have gone astray from the right way, and for long there is no one that has done good, no, not one . . . [Romans 3:12]. Therefore . . . we shall use all diligence to reform before all else the Roman Curia, whence perhaps these evils have had their origin. The whole world is longing for such reforms.[778]

Bishop Safileo, preaching to the Rota (a branch of the Roman Catholic Curia) in 1528 said, "Because all flesh has become corrupt; we are citizens not of the holy city of Rome, but of Babylon, the city of corruption." The renowned jurist, Giovani Battista Caccia presented Pope Paul III a treatise in 1533 which began, "I see that our Holy Mother the Church . . . has been so changed that she seems to have no tokens of her evangelical character; and no trace can be found in her of humility, temperance, continence and Apostolic strength." [779]

In 1534 Rothman declared:

The world has fallen from the truth, in that it has been misled by the papacy and by the so-called Evangelical [Lutheran] teachers, but the time is at hand when Christ shall restore the world lost in sin, and this restitution or restoration of the world shall take place by means of the lowly and unlearned.[780]

In its "Homily Against Peril of Idolatry," written in the middle of the sixteenth century and approved in the *Book of Common Prayer*, the Church of England stated:

So that laity and clergy, learned and unlearned, of all ages, sects and degrees of men, women and children of the whole Christendom—an horrible and most dreadful thing to think—have been at once drowned in abominable idolatry; of all other vices most detested by God and most damnable to man; and that by the space of eight hundred years and more.[781]

In 1713 Peter Poiret wrote:

Christianity, having degenerated into a beast and a Harlot, receives sentence of condemnation, which God is pleased not to execute without calling men to repentance by one more, and that the last dispensation of his Grace . . .

In the world's sixty, which is its old age, it shall be the favor of Jesus Christ to receive one more Dispensation of His

Grace, which will be the last the wicked world is ever to expect. It will consist, as the former did, in appearing, revelation and reestablishment of some ordinances.[782]

Johann Goethe, the author of *Faust*, writing in 1786 said, "I have arrived at a vivid conviction that all trace of original Christianity are extinct here [in Rome]."[783]

Roger Williams, the first minister of the oldest Baptist Church in the United States said there was

[N]o regularly constituted church on earth, nor any person qualified to administer any church ordinances; nor can there be until new apostles are sent by the Great Head of the Church for whose coming I am seeking.[784]

Thomas Jefferson said:

The religion builders have so distorted and deformed the doctrines of Jesus, so muffled them in mysticisms, fancies and falsehoods, have caricatured them into forms so inconceivable as to shock reasonable thinkers to revolt against the whole, and drive them rashly to pronounce its founder an impostor.[785]

Happy in the prospect of a restoration of primitive Christianity, I must leave to younger persons to encounter and lop off the false branches which have been engrafted into it by the mythologists of the middle and modern ages.[786]

All of the Protestant leaders, William Ockham, John Wyclif, John Hus, Jerome of Prague, Martin Luther, Philip Melanchthon, Andreas Carlstadt, Ulrich Zwingli, John Calvin, William Tyndale, John Knox, and others, identified various doctrines and practices that they believed were not in accordance with the original teachings of Christ or the early Christian church. These included such things as the veneration of Mary, saints and relics, canonical hours (fixed prayers framed for certain hours in the day and chanted or oft-repeated), the fast of Lent, worship services only in Latin, stations of the cross, rosaries, stigmata, the crucifix, the signing of the cross, incense, separate courts for trying offenses by the clergy, "dispensations" (release) from Church laws, restrictions on owning and discussing *The Bible*, last rites, processions and religious dances, baptism by aspersion (sprinkling), etc. Professor James Atkinson gave a concise summary of the Reformation:

> *But the Reformers rejected the authority of the pope, the merit of good works, indulgences, the mediation of the Virgin Mary and the saints, and all sacraments which had not been instituted by Christ. They rejected the doctrine of transubstantiation (the teaching that the bread and wine of communion became the body and blood of Christ when the priest consecrated them), the view of the mass as a sacrifice, purgatory and prayers for the dead, private confession of sin to a priest, celibacy of the clergy, and the use of Latin in the services. They also rejected all the paraphernalia that expressed these ideas—such as holy water, shrines, chantries, wonder-working images, rosaries, paternoster stones, images and candles.*[787]

They all attempted to "reform" the then-current form of Christianity to their idea of the original teachings of Christ. This was done by referring back to, and interpreting, *The Bible*. Despite their sincere attempts, however, they could not agree on what the correct doctrines should be and to this day remain in disunity. The Church of Jesus Christ of Latter-day Saints is in agreement with the Protestants that the Roman Catholic Church departed from the original teachings of Jesus Christ, but maintains that only a "restoration" by Jesus Christ himself could accomplish the Reformer's intention. According to Joseph Smith, it was his concern for "which of all the sects was right" for "the teachers of religion of the different sects understood the same passages of scripture so differently as to destroy all confidence in settling the question by an appeal to *The Bible*" that led to his prayer to God for guidance.[788] In answer to this prayer, according to his testimony, God the Father and Jesus Christ appeared to him. Thereafter, Jesus Christ and various angels instructed Joseph and others in the "restoration." He said:

> *The time has at last arrived when the God of Abraham, of Isaac, and of Jacob has set his hand again the second time to recover the remnants of his people . . . and with them to bring*

in the fullness of the Gentiles, and establish that covenant with them, which was promised when their sins should be taken away. See Isaiah 11, Romans 11:25-27, and also Jeremiah 31:31-33.[789]

Peter had prophesied a Restoration in Acts 3:19-21:

Repent ye therefore, and be converted that your sins may be blotted out when the times of refreshing shall come from the presence of the Lord, and he shall send Jesus Christ, which before was preached unto you: Whom the heavens must receive until the times of restitution of all things which God hath spoken by the mouth of all the holy prophets since the world began.[790]

Isaiah had prophesied of a time of spiritual desolation saying, "The earth also is defiled under the inhabitants thereof; because they have transgressed the laws, changed the ordinance, broken the everlasting covenant."[791] When Jesus Christ began instructing Joseph Smith how to restore The Church of Jesus Christ he told him:

[A]nd the day cometh that they who will not hear the voice of the Lord, neither the voice of his servants, neither give heed to the words of the prophets and apostles shall be cut off from among the people; For they have strayed from mine ordinances and broken mine everlasting covenant.[792]

Joseph also referred to the prophecy of Daniel, that in the "latter days" the God of heaven would set up a kingdom which would roll forth and fill the whole earth as a stone cut out without hands.[793] Isaiah had recorded:

Wherefore the Lord said, Forasmuch as this people draw near me with their mouth, and with their lips do honor me, but have removed their heart far from me, and their fear toward me is taught by the precept of men: Therefore, behold, I will proceed to do a marvelous work among this people, even a marvelous work and a wonder: for the wisdom of their wise men shall perish and the understanding of their prudent men shall be hid.[794]

When the Father and the Son appeared to Joseph Smith, Jesus

told him the professors of religion of his day "draw near to me with their lips, but their hearts are far from me, they teach for doctrines the commandments of men, having a form of godliness, but they deny the power thereof."[795] Subsequently, an angel told Joseph the prophecy of Isaiah that the Lord would "set his hand again the second time to recover the remnant of his people" to "assemble the outcasts of Israel, and gather together the dispersed of Judah from the four corners of the earth" was about to be fulfilled.[796] Later, after heavenly messengers ordained Joseph Smith and Oliver Cowdery to the priesthood, in a revelation to Joseph, Jesus Christ said:

> *The keys of the kingdom of God are committed unto man on the earth, and from thence shall the gospel roll forth unto the ends of the earth, as the stone which is cut out of the mountain without hands shall roll forth until it has filled the whole earth.*[797]

In the sections that follow we will review some of the major doctrines that were the basis for the Reformation and what Joseph Smith learned during the Restoration.

1.THE BIBLE.

The direct cause of the Reformation was the invention of the printing press, the printing of *The Bible* by Gutenberg in 1456, and the widespread publication and reading of *The Bible*. Prior to that time, the number of copies of *The Bible* was so small, they were maintained in monasteries and so few other, mostly inaccessible locations, and so few people were able to read, that the knowledge that most Christians had of *The Bible* came solely from the Sunday masses and preaching of the priests. The "creeds" were developed as short-form summaries of key doctrines that the illiterate could memorize and understand. Around 400 A.D. Augustine acknowledged the existence of many different interpretations of *The Bible* in his own day and recognized that one interpretation must be abandoned for a better one if there is better evidence for the new interpretation.[798] Jerome, the Catholic bishop and translator of the "Vulgate" Latin version of the scriptures from the original Hebrew and Greek used by the Roman Catholic Church "says plainly" there were errors in the existing manuscripts for Matthew 13:35 and 27:9.[799] While certain priests and those with the ability to read and study the scriptures may have entertained doubts about the conformity of the teachings and practices of the Roman Catholic Church with *The Bible*, it was not until the common person could read and verify for themselves the objections raised by the Reformers that widespread support grew and alternate Christian churches were established. Will Durant says, "[T]he spread of the New Testament among the people prepared them for Luther's challenging contrast between the Gospels and the Church,"[800] and, "Printing was the Reformation; Gutenberg made Luther possible."[801] At that time, it was the official position of both the Roman Catholic Church and the Eastern Orthodox Church that the scriptures should only be read and taught by the clergy, lest the common man become confused. Indeed, the efforts of such men as William Tyndale to publish *The Bible* met with burning at the stake. In 1200 Pope Innocent III ordered a French version of *The Bible* to be burned.[802] In 1229 the Council of Narbonne forbade the possession of any part of *The Bible* by laymen.[803] In 1280 a bull of Pope Nicholas III said, "We prohibit all laymen to discuss matters of the Catholic faith; if anyone does so he shall be excommunicated."[804] In 1534 King Henry induced Parliament to rule that only nobles and property owners might legally possess *The Bible* and only priests might preach on it or discuss it publicly. [805] Today, the Roman Catholic Church encourages all of its members to read *The Bible*:

> *The Church 'forcefully and specifically exhorts all the Christian faithful . . . to learn the surpassing knowledge of Jesus Christ, by frequent reading of the divine Scriptures.'*[806]

But the Eastern Orthodox Church still reserves *Bible* reading to the clergy.

Martin Luther was a Catholic priest and an Augustinian monk for 19 years. During that time he was a diligent student of *The Bible* (eventually preparing a German translation). Although it was the sale of indulgences and the accumulation of relics that provoked Luther to post his 95 "theses" on the Wittenburg, Germany church door in 1517 A.D., his "protest" came from his conviction that all these practices were inconsistent with *The Bible*. He also concluded from his study of *The Bible* that certain books—the 15 books of the "Apocrypha"—were not inspired. The Jews had rejected them, and Jerome, the Catholic bishop, was of the opinion that "they may be read for edification, as they contain valuable lessons for the conduct of life, but they are not to be used as a basis of doctrine."[807] On the other hand, another Catholic bishop, Augustine, had accepted the Apocrypha as inspired. (The Greek Orthodox Church adds 2 Esdras and 3 Maccabees to the Apocrypha, placing 4 Maccabees in an appendix. The Russian Orthodox Church adds 3 Esdras and omits 4 Maccabees. The Ethiopian *Bible* canon, which claims links back to the fourth century, contains eighty-one books—as opposed to the traditional Protestant *Bible*, which contains only sixty-six,[808] and the Catholic *Bible* which contains seventy-three.[809]) During the early centuries the books that were considered authentic was very much in dispute—such books in the present Bible as Hebrews, James, 2 Peter, 2 & 3 John and Jude were considered of doubtful authenticity, and certain books not in our present *Bible* were considered orthodox at various times, including The Shephered of Hermas, Letter of Barnabas, Teaching of the Twelve Apostles, and the Didache.[810] The canon of the Catholic *Bible* was not established until A.D. 382[811] (and the Apocrypha was not officially added until 1546[812]).

When Luther was excommunicated by the Catholic Church, they sought to have Charles, Emperor of the Holy Roman Empire impose a corporal punishment on him. In response to the prosecution by Eck, the Roman Catholic accuser, Luther stated his famous reply:

> *I ask you, Martin—answer candidly and without horns—do you or do you not repudiate your books and the errors which they contain? Luther replied, 'Since then Your Majesty and your Lordships desire a simple reply, I will answer without horns and without teeth. Unless I am convicted by Scripture and plain reason—I do not accept the authority of popes and councils for they have contradicted each other—my conscience is captive to the Word of God. I cannot and I will not recant anything, for to go against conscience is neither right nor safe. God help me. Amen.'*[813]

Luther had repeatedly expressed his desire to maintain the unity of the Church and reform the Church from within. It was only when he became convinced that the Roman Catholic Church would not reform itself in conformity with the teachings of *The Bible* that he determined that the only course was to break from the Catholic Church and establish a new church. The other Reformers were in agreement with this view, but each of them disagreed with Luther and with each other regarding the proper interpretation of certain scriptural passages. At one point, three "prophets" from Zwickau visited Luther and taught that *The Bible* was not necessary—they relied directly on guidance by the Holy Spirit. Luther, however, distrusted them, partly because they taught the speedy establishment of the kingdom of the godly through the slaughter of the ungodly, but more importantly, because *The Bible* must be maintained as a standard by which to test the teachings of any man.[814] Another reformer, Thomas Muntzer, was skeptical of relying on the words of *The Bible* and suggested that those who relied solely on the letter of the law were like the scribes against whom Christ inveighed. Muntzer held that *The Bible* needed an interpreter, that the "the letter killeth, but the spirit giveth life,"[815] and that this interpreter would be a prophet inspired by the Holy Spirit. Robert Barclay, the formulator of the Quaker theology, argued that to know God was life eternal, that no man knoweth the Father but the Son and he to whom the Son reveals him, and that the revelation of the Son is in and by the [Holy] Spirit.[816] Consequently,

> *[The scriptures] are only a declaration of the fountain, and not the fountain itself, therefore they are not to be esteemed as the principal ground of all truth and knowledge, nor yet the primary rule of faith and manners . . . [T]hey are and may be esteemed a secondary rule, subordinate to the Spirit . . . [S]o they testify that the Spirit is the guide by which the saints are led into all truth: therefore, according to the scriptures, the Spirit is the first and principal leader.*[817]

Luther was concerned that revelation in the present could destroy the uniqueness of Christian revelation in the past.[818] In more modern times this concept is found in Pentecostalism:

> *Pentecostalism belongs to that stream within Christianity*

> *which places a personal experience of the Holy Spirit high among the marks of a Christian. In contrast the Catholic has normally tended to 'channel' the Spirit through bishop and the sacrament, and the Protestant through The Bible.*
>
> *The most important figure within that stream in previous centuries was John Wesley. Indeed, Wesley—whose own heart was 'strangely warmed,' who emphasized the inner 'witness of the Spirit,' and taught that sanctification was a second work of grace distinct from and following justification—might well be called the great-grandfather of Pentecostalism.*[819]

(As we have discussed above, if truth is a unity, there should never be a conflict between true scripture—properly interpreted—and the revelations of the Holy Spirit. We will discuss the Holy Spirit further in Section 4, hereafter). The Protestant churches adopted a "Presbyterian" form of government by the elders of the churches. They taught that delegates of the churches could convene in councils or synods and that such councils could determine "controversies of faith." However, they made clear that the ultimate authority was *The Bible*:

> *All synods or councils since the apostles' times, whether general or particular, may err, and many have erred; therefore, they are not to be made the rule of faith or practice, but to be used as a help in both.*[820]

The Council of Trent, convened by the Catholic Church after the Protestant revolt, essentially reaffirmed their own interpretation of the scriptures and stated, "No one may in matters concerning faith and morals, attribute to the Scriptures any other meaning than that which the Church has given and gives to it."[821] The Church admitted the justness of some of the Reformer's criticisms but characterized the problems as abuses of correct doctrine by certain men, such as Tetzel, the seller of indulgences. They also strongly urged the authority of "tradition" as the basis for interpretation of ambiguous passages of scripture.[822] The current *Catechism of the Catholic Church* says, "The Church . . . does not derive her certainty about all revealed truths from the holy Scriptures alone. Both Scripture and Tradition must be accepted with equal sentiments of devotion and reverence."[823] The Protestants to this day rely exclusively on *The Bible* for doctrine and are referred to by some as "fundamentalists" as a result. Calvinists taught that *The Bible* was "immediately inspired by God, and by his singular care and providence kept pure in all ages."[824] In fact, one of the accusations the Protestants have faced is that they worship *The Bible*—they engage in "Bibliolatry." In the nineteenth century, there arose many critics of *The Bible*. Asserting what they called the "Higher Criticism," they pointed out doctrinal and historical inconsistencies and translation problems. This was regarded as the "scientific" study of *The Bible*, superior to blind acceptance, and caused many to question the confidence they could place in the churches' and their own interpretation of any passage of *The Bible*. Julius Wellhausen questioned the Old Testament as an inspired book. Later H.S. Reimarus, D.F. Strauss, Ernest Renan, J.R. Seeley, Johan Semler, F.C.Baur, Karl Bahrdt, Rudolf Bultmann and Georg Wilhelm Hegel, all questioned the historicity and divinity of Christ and the New Testament.[825] This led the Deists to affirm their belief in God but to discard the authority of *The Bible*.

In the beginning, Joseph Smith had only *The Bible* and it was his family's practice to read regularly from it. It was while reading James 1:5 that he gained the idea that he could ask God directly what church was true:

> *If any of you lack wisdom let him ask of God, who giveth to all men liberally and upbraideth not, and it shall be given him.*

When Jesus Christ appeared to him he was informed that the "creeds" were an "abomination" and that all of the existing churches had errors in doctrine. The first major restoration consisted of Joseph Smith being guided by an angel to the place of burial of ancient gold plates on which were inscribed the history of the Indians on the American continent. These writings were made by prophets of God among their people—similar to those prophets that were active among the Jews and who had written the Old Testament. These gold plates were based in part on a set of "brass plates" which recorded the writings of the prophets we have in the Old Testament that were carried to the American continent in approximately 600 B.C. When Joseph translated this "Book of Mormon" he had the opportunity of comparing the doctrines as taught in *The Bible* with those recorded by the American prophets, which were in part based on the writings of the Hebrew prophets. Although Joseph had been told by Jesus himself that his teachings had been corrupted—in exact agreement with the conclusion of the Reformers—until Joseph received *The Book of Mormon* he had no idea which of the various doctrines were still being correctly interpreted and by which sect. Indeed, he reports that he assumed that at least one of the churches on the earth was true, and it came as a shock to him that they all contained some errors in doctrine. Later, students have shown that there were many sacred writings that existed anciently that are referred to in *The Bible,* but they have not been included in *The Bible* as we have it in modern times, such as the Book of the Covenant,[826] the Book of the Wars of the Lord,[827] the Book of Jasher,[828] the Book of the Acts of Solomon,[829] the Book of Samuel the Seer,[830] the Book of Nathan the Prophet,[831] the Book of Gad the Seer,[832] the Book of Shemaiah the Prophet,[833] the Book of Iddo the Seer,[834] the Book of Jehu,[835] the Book of the Acts of Uzziah written by the prophet Isaiah,[836] the Prophecies of Enoch,[837] the prophecy that Jesus would be a Nazarene,[838] and certain epistles of Paul.[839] He also learned that *The Bible* itself prophesied of the coming forth of *The Book of Mormon* (see Section 13, "Continuing Revelation," infra). He received many other revelations directly from Jesus Christ and instruction by angels, which are now known as *The Doctrine and Covenants* and *The Pearl of Great Price*. Through *The Book of Mormon* and these revelations, Joseph was able to identify and ascertain the correct interpretation of *The Bible* with a confidence that went far beyond his mere opinion or guesswork. As a result of this work, Joseph realized that the Higher Critics were right in some respects, not because *The Bible* was not from God, but because it contained translation and copying errors, some of which were intentional. One of the things that Joseph was commanded to do by Jesus Christ was to correct certain passages of *The Bible* to the intent of the original authors by the gift of the Holy Ghost. Joseph never set out to revise *The Bible* and, initially had no conception that there were any errors in *The Bible*. Since that time many students of *The Bible* have concurred that there are errors in the text of *The Bible*. Professor Dummelow, in *A Commentary on the Holy Bible*, says:

> *The scribes who copied were undoubtedly very careful, butsometimes the same consonant was written twice. Sometimes, of two consonants of the same form one was omitted; or a word might occur twice in the same verse, and the scribe going on to the second as he copied the first would omit the intervening words.*[840]
>
> *A copyist would sometimes put in not what was in the text, but what he thought ought to be in it. He would trust a fickle memory, or he would even make the text accord with views of the school to which he belonged. Besides this, an enormous number of copies are preserved. In addition to the versions and quotations from the early Christian Fathers, nearly four thousand Greek MSS [manuscripts] of the New Testament are known to exist. As a result the variety of readings is considerable.*[841]

Professor Larry Hurtado in his article, "How the New Testament Has Come Down to Us" in *Eerdman's Handbook to the History of Christianity*, states that "5,355" Greek manuscripts of the New Testament exist. "Most of these date from the eighth century or later, and few have been studied in detail." Commenting on the variations in the manuscripts he says:

> *The overwhelming mass of variations in the many manuscripts studied consist of accidental spelling differences or omissions, but some variations are clearly deliberate. Most of these appear to be attempts to 'improve' the style, to remove the ambiguity or sometimes to harmonize parallel accounts in different books. A few of the variations appear to be caused by a copyist's concern about doctrines . . . Because of its rather non-literary style Mark's Gospel appears to have suffered most often from these kinds of deliberate alterations during copying.*[842]

Origen, one of the "Fathers" of the early Christian church, says:

> *Today the fact is evident, that there are many differences in the manuscripts, either through the negligence of certain copyists, or the perverse audacity of some in correcting the text.*[843]

Eusebius, the "Father of Ecclesiastical History," writing in 324 A.D. in regard to 10 sects of Christianity in existence at that time says:

> *They have not hesitated to corrupt the word of God; they have treated the standard of the primitive faith with contempt . . . So it was that they laid hands unblushingly on the Holy Scriptures, claiming to have corrected them.*[844]

Peter Abelard, in his famous work, *Sic et Non* [Yes and No] (c. 1120) set forth 157 questions of the Christian religion as interpreted by the Catholic Church at that time and pointed out many contradictions between the interpretations of various Church spokesmen over hundreds of years. He asserted that the "sacred text had sometimes been corrupted by interpolation or careless copying."[845]

Professor Thomas Hanlon said:

> *The difficulties that beset the modern bible translator are legion and need not be enumerated here, but not least is the constant need to remind oneself that the translator is not an expositor and therefore has no right to allow his own theological opinions to intrude into the translation. It must be acknowledged now that, in the past, translators both Catholic and Protestant, did not always avoid this danger, and this, coupled with the fact that the manuscripts from which the translations were made were comparatively recent and corrupt, rendered their translations suspect.*[846]

The great English poet John Milton felt that *The Bible* should be the "sole basis of [religious] creed" but admitted that the Biblical text had suffered "corruptions, falsifications and mutations." [847]

The additions and changes that were made to manuscripts (interpolations) did not occur just to Christian writings. Many scholars, especially Jewish, have long asserted that the short paragraph about Jesus Christ in the Jewish historian Flavius Josephus' *The Antiquities of the Jews* was an interpolation by a later Christian that survived in the only known manuscripts.[848]

Consistent with all of this Joseph Smith expressed one of the Articles of Faith of the restored Church of Jesus Christ as follows:

> *We believe The Bible to be the word of God as far as it is translated correctly. We also believe The Book of Mormon to be the word of God.*[849]

He further said:

> *I believe the Bible as it read when it came from the pen of the original writers. Ignorant translators, careless transcribers, or designing and corrupt priests have committed many errors.*[850]

In response to his inquiry about the Apocrypha, Joseph was also told by Jesus Christ:

> *There are many things contained therein that are true, and it is mostly translated correctly; there are many things that are contained therein that are not true, which are interpolations by the hands of men.*[851]

One irony of the publication of *The Book of Mormon*, *The Doctrine and Covenants* and *The Pearl of Great Price* is that they have re-affirmed the existence of God, the truthfulness of the Christian religion and the authority of *The Bible*. Initially, many criticized the publication of *The Book of Mormon* on the basis that it would undermine belief in *The Bible*, that *The Book of Mormon* was intended as an alternate to *The Bible*, and that *The Bible* was complete and sufficient and any conflicts between them would cast doubt on *The Bible*. In fact, widespread lack of faith in *The Bible* began with the Higher Critics and the "scientific method." Today, those who do not want to believe in *The Bible* will gain no comfort from these new scriptures. Each of them affirms that *The Bible* is the word of God and Jesus Christ is the Son of God. *The Book of Mormon* speaks of the scriptures of the Jews and prophesies of the compilation of *The Bible*,[852] consisting of the revelations given by Jesus Christ to Joseph Smith, declares that the principles of the gospel are contained in the "Bible and the Book of Mormon."[853] Mormon, the compiler of *The*

Book of Mormon, states on the front page of his work that one of his purposes is to the "convincing of the Jew and Gentile that Jesus is the Christ . . ."[854] What these books do, however, is give new insight to the correct interpretation of *The Bible* that eliminates many of the criticisms of the "Higher Critics." One example from the Old Testament is, "Thou shall not suffer a witch to live."[855] This single passage of scripture was used as the primary basis for incredible persecution in Europe, and later, the United States:

> *Pope Innocent VIII issued the celebrated bull Summis Desiderantes in 1484, directing inquisitors and others to put to death all practitioners of witchcraft and other diabolical arts, and it has been computed that as many as nine million persons have suffered death for witchcraft since that date.*[856]

> *German scholars estimate a total of 100,000 executions for witchcraft in Germany in the seventeenth century.*[857]

> *The popes took literally a passage in Exodus (22:18): 'Thou shalt not suffer a witch to live . . . . In 1554 an officer of the Inquisition boasted that in the preceding 150 years the Holy Office had burned at least 30,000 witches.'"*[858] *'Between 1560 and 1600 some eight thousand women were burned as witches in a Scotland having hardly a million souls.'*[859]

Joseph Smith was informed that the passage as originally written read, "Thou shall not suffer a murderer to live." Other examples, include the doctrine of the "divine right" of kings discussed in Part II, Section 15, "Separation of Church and State," Paul's teachings against marriage,[860] the teaching of Jesus to pluck out your own eye and cut off your right hand if they offend you,[861] the criticism that Jesus and his disciples expected his Second Coming to be within their same generation,[862] Paul's instructions to the Corinthians not to let women speak in the church,[863] the two similar but different accounts of the Creation in Genesis,[864] etc. Of course, no one is going to accept any of the changes made by Joseph Smith to *The Bible* unless they are satisfied that he was a prophet of God and that his changes were authorized by and came from God. However, one of the very best ways to come to that determination is to study the changes he made.

When one sees the consistency they bring to doctrines that are conflicting even in *The Bible* (for example, salvation by grace or works), and the answers they provide to the Higher Critics, one is led to exclaim that such changes could not have come from the mere opinions of an unlearned man. (Joseph Smith had little formal schooling and was never a student at a religious seminary). Indeed, the insight they provide are startlingly beyond the conflicting opinions and interpretations of the Reformers.

Before concluding this Section we should mention that here are those who believe that *The Bible* was the end of all revelation from God, or at least "public" revelation. We will examine that belief later in Section 13.

2. AUTHORITY IN THE MINISTRY.

The Roman Catholic and Eastern Orthodox Churches claim authority directly from the apostles from the time of Jesus Christ in an unbroken succession. The Roman Catholics claim that Peter, as the chief apostle, established the Christian church in Rome and was its first bishop. Further, that he ordained his successor and that such succession has continued to the present. According to Catholic belief, the ordination of a minister must come by a "minister capable of communicating it;"[865] in other words, authority must be obtained from a person who already has it.

When the Reformation began, the issue of authority in the ministry was central. Luther, as a Catholic priest and monk, had always accepted the pope as the head of Christianity, and Luther's authority to perform his religious responsibilities was derived indirectly from the pope and directly through his ordination by the bishop when he became a priest. The Roman Catholic Church taught that the Church's "magisterium" or teaching authority, entitled it to settle all doctrinal disputes and determine what was heresy. In the New Testament Matthew records:

> *When Jesus came into the coasts of Caesarea Philippi, he asked his disciples, saying, Whom do men say that I the Son of man am? And they said, some say that thou art John the Baptist, some Elias; and others, Jeremias or one of the*

prophets. He saith unto them, But whom say ye that I am? And Simon Peter answered and said, Thou art the Christ, the Son of the living God. And Jesus answered and said unto him, Blessed art thou Simon Barjona, for flesh and blood hath not revealed it unto thee, but my Father which is in heaven. And I say also unto thee, That thou art Peter, and upon this rock I will build my church; and the gates of hell shall not prevail against it. And I will give unto thee the keys of the kingdom of heaven: and whatsoever thou shalt bind on earth shall be bound in heaven: and whatsoever thou shalt loose on earth shall be loosed in heaven.[866]

In Luther's day the Catholic Church taught that Peter and his successors the popes were the "rock" on which the Church was built. Pope Leo had also declared that it did not matter how unworthy any particular pope might be, as long as he was the successor of Peter and was acting according to canon law.[867] Augustine, the extremely influential Catholic bishop of Hippo, taught that Christ is the chief minister of the sacraments, so that they remain valid even if administered by unworthy men.[868]

John Eck challenged Luther to a debate on the authority of the Church:

Eck asserted that the primacy of Peter went back to the very earliest days of the Church. By way of proof he introduced letters ascribed to a bishop of Rome in the first century affirming 'The Holy Roman and Apostolic Church obtained the primacy not from the apostles but from our Lord and Savior himself, and it enjoys preeminence of power above all of the churches of the whole flock of Christian people'; and again, 'The sacerdotal order commenced in the period of the New Testament directly after our Lord Christ, when to Peter was committed the pontificate previously exercised in the Church by Christ himself.' Both of these statements had been incorporated into canon law. 'I impugn these decretals,' cried Luther. 'No one will ever convince me that the holy pope and martyr said that.' Luther was right. They are today universally recognized by Catholic authorities as belonging to the spurious Isidorian decretals. Luther had done an excellent piece of historical criticism, and without the help of Lorenzo Valla, whose work he had not yet seen. Luther pointed out that actually in the early centuries bishops beyond Rome were not confirmed by nor subject to Rome and the Greeks never accepted the Roman primacy. Surely the saints of the Greek Church were not on that account to be regarded as damned.[869]

According to Will Durant:

These early documents [Isidorian Decretals] were designed to show that by the oldest traditions and practice of the Church no bishop might be deposed, no Church council might be convened, and no major issue might be decided without the consent of the pope.[870]

Luther and the other Reformers disputed the authority of the pope in two ways: First, they challenged the "primacy" of the Roman bishop over the other bishops; second, they challenged the succession from the early popes to their own day. In regard to these issues they began by questioning the accuracy of the supposed historical records of succession back to Peter and were quite successful in showing that there were no reliable records. For example, the "official" book of succession for the popes, the *Liber Pontificalis*, not compiled until 715 A.D., states that Peter was the first bishop of Rome, but only after being the bishop of Antioch for seven years.[871] Another Catholic chronology, the *Liberian Catalogue* of 324 A.D., says that Peter became the bishop of Rome within a year after the death of Jesus, which conflicts with the account in Acts of Paul's visit to Rome at a time when Peter was not the bishop.[872] Indeed, at the Council of Nicaea in 325 A.D., it was the Patriarch of Alexandria, Egypt, where one of the two leading Christian schools was located (the other being in Antioch), who held the title of "Pope"—Pater Patrum—father of fathers.[873] (The historian Will Durant says, "The term 'papa,' 'father,' which became in English 'pope,' was applied in the first three centuries to any Christian bishop").[874] Eusebius, writing in 324 A.D. states that Peter was the first bishop of Antioch, that the title "Pope" was applied to the Bishop of Alexandria, and that all bishops were considered equal.[875] The Eastern Orthodox Church also claimed that

Peter established a Christian church in Antioch and that the other apostles established other churches, each of them appointing bishops for the churches. They claimed that there were five churches established by the apostles and they were all considered equal in the time of the apostles. It was not for some 200 years—in the time of Pope Leo—before Rome first made the claim of preeminence over the other Christian churches. Indeed, it was only because Rome was the headquarters for the civil government—the Roman Empire—and Constantine, the emperor, converted to Christianity in 310 A.D.—that Rome was able to assert political supremacy over the other Christian churches. The Eastern bishops rejected Pope Leo's claims to supremacy based on being the successor of Peter at the Council of Chalcedon in 451 A.D. The twenty-eighth canon of the Council of Chalcedon "affirmed the equal authority of the bishop of Constantinople with that of Rome."[876] The Eastern Orthodox Church never accepted Rome's primacy and severed its relationship with the Roman Church in 855 A.D. The Eastern Orthodox Church maintained that the church should be governed by the five "patriarchs" of Antioch, Alexandria, Jerusalem, Rome and Constantinople (after the Eastern Orthodox Church excommunicated the Bishop of Rome in 1054 A.D. Moscow replaced Rome)[877] The Catholic Church, in its recent Catechism, agrees that the Eastern Churches have maintained the authority of the priesthood through apostolic succession, but still claims the "primacy:"

> *These Churches, although separated from us, yet possess true sacraments, above all—by apostolic succession—the priesthood and the Eucharist . . .*[878]

Luther demonstrated that, originally, the popes were elected by the people and the bishops near Rome, and the election of the pope by the cardinals was not established until the eleventh century.[879] The authority of the pope had been contested within the Catholic church many times—in 1324 by Marsilius of Padua and in 1414 by the Ecumenical Council of Constance.[880]

According to the Protestant historian Philip Schaff:

> *[T]he Roman bishop . . . was on an equality with other*

bishops until Constantine made him pope. It was then he began to usurp authority.[881]

The modern Catholic writer James Coriden says:

In the Code [of Canon Law], the preferred title for the Pope is 'Roman Pontiff.' Pontiff (from pons, bridge, and facere, to make, meant one who bridged the chasm between gods and humankind) is the ancient term used for the priest in the Roman Empire; the Pontifex Maximus was the high priest in pagan Rome. The title was applied to bishops in the early church and gradually its use was reserved to the Bishop of Rome.[882]

In regard to the establishment of the Church on Peter as the "rock," some of the Reformed churches believed that Christ was referring to himself (on "this"—perhaps pointing to himself) as the "rock" when Peter confessed that Jesus was the son of God.[883] Others, quoting the early Church writer Hippolytus believed the "rock" was the Holy Ghost:

By this Spirit Peter spake the blessed word 'Thou art the Christ, the Son of the living God.' By this Spirit the rock of the church was established. This is the Spirit, the Comforter, that is sent because of thee, that he may show thee to be the child of God.[884]

Hilary of Poitiers said:

This faith [Peter's confession] is the foundation of the church . . . This faith is a gift of revelation from the Father . . . [He] knew the Son of God by revelation from the Father . . . He confessed the Son of God and for that was blessed. This is the revelation of the Father, this is the foundation of the church . . .[885]

The modern Protestant Professor Dummelow says:

The Roman Catholic Launoy reckons that seventeen Fathers [writers in the early Christian church] regard Peter as the rock; forty-four regard Peter's confession as the rock; sixteen regard Christ himself as the rock; while eight are of the opinion that the Church is built on all the apostles.[886]

Professor Dummelow states the traditional Protestant position as follows:

> *The next question is, 'Was the promise made to Peter exclusively, or did Christ address Peter as the representative of the Twelve, intending to give to all the same powers that He gave to Peter? The answer can hardly be doubtful. The whole text speaks of the future. Christ says not 'I build,' but 'I will build'; not 'I give,' but 'I will give,' referring to the future for the explanation. The rest of the N.T. shows in what sense the words of Christ are to be understood. On the evening of Easter Day He fulfilled His promise to Peter, by giving all the Apostles present even greater powers than those which are here promised—'As my Father hath sent me, even so send I you. And...he breathed on them and saith unto them, Receive ye the Holy Ghost: Whosoever sins ye remit, they are remitted unto them; and whosoever sins you retain, they are retained'(John 20:22-23). No power of any kind was then given to Peter which was not given equally to all the Apostles, and in harmony with this all the Apostles are jointly regarded in the NT as the foundation on which the Church is built (John 19:28, Ephesians 2:20, Revelations 21:14) . . . What was the nature of the primacy that Peter possessed? It was a primacy of personal character and ability. He excelled the other apostles not in office but in zeal, courage, promptness of action, and firmness of faith.*[887]

The Reformers also challenged the succession of priesthood authority by referring to well-known historical events. Will Durant summarizes a period of a little over 100 years as follows:

> *By the tradition of the Church no pope could be elected without the consent of the Roman clergy, nobles and populace. The rulers of Spoleto, Naples and Tuscany, and the aristocracy of Rome divided into factions as of old; and whichever faction prevailed in the city intrigued to choose and sway the pope. Between them they dragged the papacy, in the tenth century, to the lowest level in history.*
>
> *In 878 Duke Lambert of Spoleto entered Rome with his army, seized Pope John VIII, and tried to starve him into favoring*

Carloman for the Imperial throne. In 897 Pope Stephen VI had the corpse of Pope Formosus (891-6) exhumed, dressed in purple robes, and tried before an ecclesiastical council on the charge of violating certain church laws; the corpse was condemned, stripped, mutilated, and plunged into the Tiber. In the same year a political revolution in Rome overthrew Stephen, who was strangled in jail. For several years thereafter the papal chair was filled by bribery, murder, or the favor of women of high rank and low morality. For half a century the family of Theophylact, a chief official of the papal palace, made and unmade popes at will. His daughter Marozia secured the election of her lover as Pope Sergius III (904-11); his wife Theodora procured the election of Pope John X (914-28). John has been accused of being Theodora's paramour, but on inadequate evidence; certainly he was an excellent secular leader, for it was he who organized the coalition that in 916 repulsed the Saracens from Rome. Marozia, after having enjoyed a succession of lovers, married Guido, Duke of Tuscany; they conspired to unseat John; they had his brother killed before his face; the Pope was thrown into prison, and died there a few months later from causes unknown. In 931 Marozia raised to the papacy John XI (931-5), commonly reputed to be her bastard son by Sergius III. In 923 her son Alberic imprisoned John in the Castle of Saint Angelo, but allowed him to exercise from jail the spiritual functions of the papacy. For twenty-two years Alberic ruled Rome as the dictatorial head of a 'Roman Republic.' At his death he bequeathed his power to his son Octavian and made the clergy and people promise to choose Octavian pope when Agapetus II should die. It was done as he ordered; in 955 Marozia's grandson became John XII, and distinguished his pontificate by orgies of debauchery in the Lateran palace.

Otto I of Germany, crowned Emperor by John XII in 962,learned the degradation of the papacy first hand. In 963, with the support of the Transalpine clergy, Otto returned to Rome,and summoned John to trial before an ecclesiastical council.Cardinals charged that John had taken bribes for consecrating bishops, had made a boy of ten a bishop, had committed adultery with his father's concubine and incest with his father's widow and her niece, and had made the papal palace a very brothel. John refused to attend the council or answer the charges; instead he went out hunting. The council deposed him and unanimously chose Otto's candidate, a layman, as Pope Leo VIII (963-5). After Otto had returned to Germany John seized and mutilated the leaders of the Imperial party in Rome, and had himself restored by an obedient council to the papacy (964). When John died (964) the Romans elected Benedict V, ignoring Leo. Otto came down from Germany, deposed Benedict, and restored Leo, who thereupon officially recognized the right of Otto and his Imperial successors to veto the election of any future pope. On Leo's death Otto secured the election of John XIII (965-72). Benedict VI (973-74) was imprisoned and strangled by a Roman noble, Bonifazio Francone, who made himself pope for a month, then fled to Constantinople with as much papal treasury as he could carry. Nine years later he returned, killed Pope John XIV (983-4), again appropriated the papal office, and died peaceably in bed (985). The Roman Republic again raised its head, assumed authority, and chose Crescentius as consul. Otto III descended upon Rome with an irresistible army, and a commission from the German prelates to end the chaos by making his chaplain Pope Gregory V (996-9).The young Emperor put down the Republic, pardoned Crescentius, and went back to Germany. Crescentius at once re-established the Republic, and deposed Gregory (997). Gregory excommunicated him, but Crescentius laughed, and arranged the election of John XVI as pope. Otto returned, deposed John, gouged out his eyes, cut off his tongue and nose, and paraded him through the streets of Rome on an ass, with his face to the tail. Crescentius and twelve Republican leaders were beheaded, and their bodies were hung from the battlement of Sant' Angelo (998). Gregory resumed the papacy, and died, probably of poison, in 999 . . .[888]

At first, Luther's position was that the Church's leaders were corrupt, including Leo X, the pope, and Tetzel, the seller of indulgences, and others. Eventually, however, Luther became convinced that the entire system of the Roman Catholic Church had become corrupt and that the corruption did not depend on who was serving in the office of pope:

> *Whereas [the Fraticelli, Wycliffites and Hussites] identified particular popes, because of their evil lives, with Antichrist, Luther held that every pope was Antichrist even though personally exemplary, because Antichrist is collective: an institution, the papacy, a system which corrupts the truth in Christ.*[889]

The "Reformed" churches believed:

> *There is no other head of the Church but the Lord Jesus Christ: nor can the Pope of Rome, in any sense be the head thereof; but is that Antichrist that man of sin and son of perdition, that exalteth himself in the Church against Christ, and all that is called God.*[890]

The Reformers also pointed to the numerous contests throughout the centuries over the position of the pope, usually settled by violence or political interference. Many times, "antipopes" were elected or assumed the office and made ecclesiastical appointments and issued doctrinal decrees. The Catholic Felican Foy in *A Concise Guide to the Catholic Church* identifies two such "antipopes" in each of the third, fourth, fifth, sixth, seventh, eighth and ninth centuries, three in the tenth, five in the eleventh century, ten in the twelfth century, two in the fourteenth century and four in the fifteenth century. One significant period was the "Great Schism:"

> *After armed battles for control of Rome between the forces of the rival popes, Clement VII retired to Avignon [France] in 1381. This marked the beginning of the Great Schism, a split of the very top of the government of the Church. It had political as well as religious repercussions. Some countries, such as Italy, the Empire, the eastern and Scandinavian areas, Hungary and England, supported Urban VI of Rome. France*

and its territories, Spain and Scotland supported Clement VII in Avignon. In the earlier medieval period two and even three popes had occasionally co-existed. But this Schism was far more serious. Unlike earlier schisms, the problem originated within the papal court itself, among the cardinals . . . . Finally, since neither pope would agree to give way, some of their cardinals called a council to meet in Pisa in 1409...The popes refused to attend. The cardinals deposed both of them and elected in their place Alexander V (1409-10). Neither the Avignon nor the Roman pope recognized this new man, so the result of the council was the creation of three popes where there had been two. More significantly, the Council of Pisa raised an important principle by its actions: a council may be superior in power to a pope. This in effect called papal supremacy into question.[891]

The Durants wrote:

Philip IV secured the election of a Frenchman to the papacy, and persuaded him to move the Holy See to Avignon on the Rhone. For sixty-eight years, the popes were so clearly the pawns and prisoners of France that other nations gave them a rapidly diminishing reverence and revenue.[892]

The Reformers further argued that the sale of ecclesiastical offices (simony), even the position of pope, and "lay investiture," where kings, princes and secular rulers selected the clergy, was well known in history and the succession of original authority had been corrupted and interrupted. The modern Catholic scholar, Donald Attwater agreed that, "At certain times and in certain places this abuse has been rife in the church.[893] For example, such men as Pope Sixtus IV (1471-1484) showed "the most flagrant nepotism—of the 34 cardinals he elevated, 6 were his own nephews."[894] James Coriden, in *An Introduction to Canon Law*, tells how the feudal system and the concept of vassalage impacted the Church:

For instance, the local lord gave priests the revenue from certain lands in exchange for the performance of their parochial duties. The pastorate became a benefice, an office tied to a source of income. And the lord, owner and protector of the land, dispensed the pastoral offices to whomever he wished, often without regard for the priest's qualifications or the spiritual welfare of the people. The same was true of bishoprics and monasteries . . . .

Many other elements of this tradition found their way into the church's discipline; e.g., the extensive use of oaths in judicial proceedings, stipends and stole fees on the occasion of sacramental ministries, personal penances replaced by offerings of money or performed by a substitute, etc.

Although such arguments provided the Reformers with sufficient evidence to reject the authority of the pope, the question still remained where they would obtain their authority to organize or govern a church in the name of God. The Reformers found their most important answer to the question of authority in the ministry in the doctrine of the "priesthood of all believers." In Luther's two publications, "To the Christian Nobility of the German Nation" and "The Liberty of the Christian Man," he emphasized this concept. According to this doctrine, derived in part from certain passages in the writings of Paul in the New Testament, all believers in Christ had the priesthood and could exercise it in organizing churches and ordaining ministers as long as it was done in accordance with the teachings of *The Bible*. For example, one formulation of this belief was in the *Second Helvetic Confession*:

The apostles of Christ do term all those who believe in Christ 'priests;' not in regard to their ministry, but because that all the faithful, being made kings and priests, may through Christ, offer up spiritual sacrifices unto God (Exodus 19:6, I Peter 2:5,9; Rev. 1:6). The ministry, then, and the priesthood are far different from the other.[895]

(The Quakers eventually rejected completely the concept of a professional ministry).[896]

The Lutherans held:

[N]obody should publicly teach or preach or administer the sacraments in the church without a regular call.[897]

The Reformed Churches agreed, stating that the ministers of the church should "be called and chosen by a lawful and ecclesiastical election," "ordained by the elders with public prayer, and laying on of hands," condemning "all those who run of their own accord, being neither chosen, sent, nor ordained."[898]

When Luther initiated the Reformation, the Catholic Church began to examine itself. In 1536 Pope Paul III invited various cardinals and leaders of the Oratory of the Divine Love to discuss reform. Sadoleto opened the conference by "boldly stating that the popes themselves by their sins, crimes, and financial greed, had been the prime source of ecclesiastical deterioration."[899] In March, 1537 the group presented the Pope with its report, "Counsel of the Appointed Cardinals on Reforming the Church." The report said:

Some popes had assumed the right to sell ecclesiastical offices and this simony had spread venality and corruption so widely through the Church that now the great organization was on the verge of destruction through men's lack of trust in its integrity. The report urged strict supervision of all Curial activities, a check on dispensations, an end to money payments for them, a higher standard in all appointments and in eligibility to the cardinalate and the priesthood, and a prohibition of plural or absentee holding of benefices.[900]

The Church also convened the Council of Trent which met in 17 sessions from 1545 to 1562 to consider the doctrinal issues raised by the Reformers. Its attempt at reform was summarized by Will Durant as follows:

In Italy—less visibly beyond it—the Church had reformed her clergy and her morals, while leaving her doctrines proudly intact.[901]

However, for Luther and the other Reformers, reform of doctrine was essential for true reform and the moral reform of the clergy came as too little, too late for them.

The Catholics objected to Luther's doctrine of the "priesthood of all believers," questioning who had the authority to issue this "call" to a minister, citing the scripture which says, "And no man taketh this honor to himself but he that is called of God as was Aaron [by Moses, the prophet].[902] Other examples in the Old Testament included Moses' laying a "charge" and some of his "honor" on Joshua by the laying on of hands,[903] the appointment and consecration of priests to minister in the Tabernacle,[904] the appointment of the seventy men of the elders of Israel,[905] and the numerous cases of retribution upon some who presumed to officiate without authority.[906] There was Christ's example in calling and ordaining the twelve apostles[907]—in regard to which it is recorded that he emphasized, "Ye have not chosen me, but I have chosen you, and ordained you,"[908] and his calling of the "seventy."[909] Following Christ's example, during New Testament times, there were the seven men chosen and ordained by the laying on of hands,[910] the laying on of hands to Saul and Barnabas,[911] and the "ordaining" of "elders" in every church."[912] Paul reminded Timothy not to neglect the gift that is in him "which was given by prophecy, with the laying on of the hands of the presbytery [elders]."[913] The Catholics argued that the whole pattern of the scriptures was that the authority came from God—from the top down—and recognized Church leaders passing the authority on to newly consecrated priests and bishops, not from an election by the congregation.

After the Protestant Reformation, the struggle over the leadership of the Catholic Church was renewed. During the 1700's and 1800's the "Gallicans" of France, the "Febronians" of Germany and the "Josephins" in Austria asserted that all the bishops of the Church were successors to the apostles, and that a council of the bishops of the Church had supreme authority. For example, J.N. von Hontheim, the bishop of Trier argued that the keys of the kingdom of God had been committed to the entire church, not only to Peter and his successors. The church councils, not the pope, were the primary source of authority. The pope was in fact only first amongst equals.[914]

However, the "Ultramontanists" prevailed, and in the First Vatican Council of 1870, the pope was declared to be the supreme authority in the Church, and that he was "infallible" in matters of faith and morals.[915] Today, no bishop can consecrate another bishop without a mandate from the pope.[916] The pope can also grant dispensations or "indults" "giving permission to do something not allowed by the canon law of the Church."[917] For example, historically the popes have granted divorces to kings that would not otherwise have been allowed by Church law. One irony is that the modern Catholic Church has recognized Luther's doctrine of the "priesthood of all believers:"

> *The Christian tradition considers Melchizedek, 'priest of God Most High,' as a prefiguration of the priesthood of Christ, the unique 'high priest after the order of Melchizedek . . .'*[918]
>
> *Christ, high priest and unique mediator, has made of the Church, 'a kingdom, priests for his God and Father.' The whole community of believers is, as such, priestly . . . Through the sacraments of Baptism and Confirmation the faithful are 'consecrated to be . . . a holy priesthood.'*[919]

The current Catholic Catechism states, "The ordained ministry or ministerial priesthood is at the service of the baptismal priesthood,"[920] refers to "the royal priesthood of the baptized,"[921] and says, "Baptism gives a share in the common priesthood of all believers."[922] The Catholic Church accepts joint administration of the Mass or communion with the Eastern Orthodox Church but it does not accept joint administration with Protestant churches because they deny the authority of the Protestant clergy to administer ordinances or sacraments.[923] While the Catholic Church does not regard it as necessary for a person performing baptism to hold the priesthood—"in case of necessity, any person may baptize, even someone not baptized, can baptize if he has the right intention,"[924]—the Church also teaches, "No one can give himself the mandate and the mission to proclaim the Gospel."[925] The Catholic Church teaches, "[T]he fullness of the sacrament of Holy Orders . . . is called the high priesthood . . ."[926]

When Joseph Smith saw the Father and the Son he was commanded to organize a new church. Joseph was told that those holding the authority of the priesthood necessary to act for and in the name of God would give those "keys" of the priesthood to him. Subsequently, John the Baptist, as a resurrected personage appeared and ordained Joseph Smith and Oliver Cowdery to the Priesthood of Aaron, or the lesser priesthood.[927] Later, Peter, James and John, also resurrected from New Testament times, appeared and ordained them to the Priesthood of Melchizidek, or the "high priesthood."[928] Joseph was told that God's kingdom is a "house of order"[929] and

> *[I]t shall not be given to any one to go forth to preach my gospel, or to build up my church, except he be ordained by someone in authority, and it is known to the church that he has authority and has been regularly ordained by the heads of the church.*[930]

From this they understood no person should be performing ordinances (sacraments) in the new church without the knowledge and consent of their church leaders, and records should be kept to keep track of who had received such authority so that the members might know who was authorized to act on behalf of God. Later, other messengers from heaven, including Moses, Elijah, Elias, Michael, Gabriel, Raphael and others visited Joseph Smith, Oliver Cowdery and Sidney Rigdon to give them the "keys" of certain priesthood work, such as the gathering of Israel (missionary work), and temple worship.[931] It is important to note that, except for Joseph Smith's initial interview with God the Father and Jesus Christ, he was never alone for the subsequent visits of these heavenly messengers and those present affirmed to the end of their lives the reality of these experiences and the spiritual efficacy of the priesthood authority to act in the name of God which they received. Through this authority they could baptize persons for the forgiveness of sins, confirm them as members of The Church of Jesus Christ and promise them the gift of the Holy Ghost with confidence that God and Jesus Christ would recognize and honor these ordinances performed in their name. Brigham Young, the second president of the Church, taught:

> *The Priesthood of the Son of God, which we have in our midst, is a perfect order and system of government, and this alone can deliver the human family from the evils which now afflict its members, and insure them happiness and felicity hereafter.*[932]

When other Christians sought to join the new church, some objected to receiving baptism on the ground that they had already been baptized in their previous church (some churches taught that baptism could only be performed once in a person's life). Joseph decided to inquire of the Lord and was told:

Behold, I say unto you that all my covenants have I caused to be done away with in this thing [the restoration of the Church]; and this is a new and everlasting covenant, even that which was from the beginning. Wherefore, although a man be baptized an hundred times it availeth him nothing, for you cannot enter inat the strait gate by the law of Moses, neither by your dead works. For it is because of your dead works that I have caused this last covenant and this church to be built up unto me, even as in the days of old. Wherefore, enter ye in at the gate, as I have commanded, and seek not to counsel your God.[933]

At another time, Joseph was told:

Behold, I am Alpha and Omega, even Jesus Christ. Wherefore, let all men beware how they take my name in their lips; for behold, verily I say, that many there be who are under this condemnation, who use the name of the Lord, and use it in vain, having no authority.[934]

Not to mention that this revelation put an enlightening interpretation on the commandment, "Thou shalt not take the name of the Lord thy God in vain"[935] that Joseph and others had probably not considered before, through these and other instructions, Jesus made clear that those who purport to act in the name of God must be authorized to do so. Joseph learned that "feeling a call" from God to preach or become a minister of the gospel, even if elected or ordained by a congregation of believers in Christ, was not sufficient to become an interpreter and teacher of the gospel or to perform ordinances or make promises in God's name without express authority from him. Although, it may have seemed tedious for Joseph, Oliver Cowdery, Sidney Rigdon and others to have to wait for these divine messengers to ordain them and authorize them to perform various priesthood work, Joseph and the other church leaders were repeatedly told not to proceed more quickly or to take actions until the Lord was ready to authorize them to proceed in the Lord's own timetable. Since that time all those who have been authorized to perform any work of the Church have been authorized by priesthood authority, by the laying on of hands, by those who are superior to them in the church in accordance with the pattern of the New Testament.[936] Joseph wrote: We believe that a man must be called of God, by prophecy and by the laying on of hands by those who are in authority, to preach the Gospel and administer in the ordinances thereof.[937]

One may justly question if the Roman Catholic or Eastern Orthodox Churches had the proper priesthood authority to act on behalf of God, which they received from the apostles, how did they lose such authority? Many historians, Catholic and Protestant alike, have catalogued the many changes that were made in the doctrine and rituals of the Christian church. However, if these changes were made by divine authorization no reformation or restoration would have been necessary, and the Roman Catholic Church would be entitled to claim exclusive allegiance from Christians, no matter how apparently contradictory or inconsistent such changes may appear to be to humans. The short answer is that all such changes would need to be made by revelation from God the Father or Jesus Christ by means of the Holy Ghost. The apostles were given the Holy Ghost by Jesus Christ[938] and told, "It is not ye that speak but the Holy Ghost"[939] and "For the Holy Ghost shall teach you in the same hour what ye ought to say."[940] Luke states:

> *The former treatise have I made, [the gospel of Luke], O Theophilus of all that Jesus began both to do and teach, until the day in which he was taken up, after that he through the Holy Ghost had given commandments unto the apostles whom he had chosen.*[941]

Peter taught:

> *For the prophecy came not in old time by the will of man: but holy men of God spake as they were moved by the Holy Ghost*[942]

The Holy Ghost is a revelator[943] and was the means promised and actually used by the early apostles to know the will of God and govern the Church. The will of God as expressed through holy prophets and apostles was the "power of God unto salvation."[944] But *The Bible* is equally clear that the Holy Ghost would not remain with a person if they committed serious sins, and revelation would not be given by God unless a person was living in obedience to his commandments. Although these conditions existed in the time of the apostles, they did not continue. This was a result of three principal developments: (1) during the period of "Caesaro-papism" political leaders, such as emperors and kings exercised control over the appointments of church leaders (lay investiture). They called and presided over church councils. According to Professor Barker, "The first eight ecumenical councils were called by the emperors and held in the East. Not until the ninth general council, the first to be held in the West, was a general council called by the pope and held in the papal palace of the Lateran (1123 A.D.)." [945] At these councils political leaders made doctrinal decisions, for example, Constantine at the Council of Nicaea on the doctrine of the Trinity, and Honorius on the doctrine of original sin. Father McSorley said:

> *They [the emperors] decided theological questions by Imperial decree, treated bishops as court officials, and in general, followed the theory that the church was to be ruled from the throne—a policy later called "Byzantium" or "Caesaropapism."*[946]

Will Durant says:

> *As bishops in England, Germany, France and Italy administered profane as well as ecclesiastical affairs, and were feudally endowed with lands or villages or even cities to supply their necessary revenues, ambitious men paid secular powers great sums for such appointments, and greedy potentates overrode all decencies to earn these bribes . . . The French kings, following a tradition established by Charlemagne, regularly appointed the bishops of Sens, Rheims, Lyons, Tours and Bourges; elsewhere in France the bishops were appointed by dukes or counts. Many bishoprics became in the eleventh century the hereditary patrimony of noble families . . . in Germany one baron possessed and transmitted eight bishoprics.*[947]

The result was that persons who were not Christians by faith or practice held positions in the Church; as such they could not receive either the Holy Ghost or the priesthood—for even if it was conferred upon them, it would not abide with them.

Secondly, Church leaders appointed other Church leaders based, not on their qualifications, but on the sale of the Church office to the highest bidder (simony). This occurred as a way to raise revenue for the Church and the bidder was willing to make such "contributions" because the tithes, rents and revenues of the bishop's diocese were kept by him as personal income. Will Durant says:

> *An 'annate'—theoretically the whole, actually half the first year's revenue of a newly elected bishop—was required by the popes as a fee for confirming his appointment; and large sums were expected from recipients of the archiepiscopal pallium.*[948]
>
> *Such appointees were men of the world; many lived in luxury, engaged in war, allowed bribery in episcopal courts, named relatives to ecclesiastical posts, and worshiped Mammon with undivided loyalty . . . The purchase of sees became so usual that practical men accepted it as normal; but reformers cried out that Simon Magus had captured the Church.*[949]

He says in 1728 in France:

> *Of 740 monasteries, 625 were in commendam, i.e., they were governed by assistant abbots on behalf of absentee abbots who received the title and half or two-thirds of the revenue without being required to live an ecclesiastical life.*[950]

Again, this resulted in a situation where unworthy men were administering the affairs of the Church and the Holy Ghost could not inspire them.

Third, the church leaders, including the very highest, became immoral, corrupt, and did not live in accordance with the teachings of Christ. "The morals of the clergy are corrupt," said the Bishop of Torcello (1458), "they have become an offense to the laity."[951] "Of the four orders of friars founded in the thirteenth century—Franciscans, Dominicans, Carmelites, Augustinians—all but the last [Luther's order] had become scandalously lax in piety and discipline."[952] "Thousands of priests had concubines; in Germany nearly all. In Rome it was assumed that priests kept concubines; and some reports estimated the prostitutes there at 6,000 in a population not exceeding 100,000."[953] The corruption of the popes themselves in the tenth century was described by the historian Will Durant as quoted above. With the corruption of the highest leaders of the Church, the Holy Ghost could not guide the Church and doctrinal and ceremonial changes instituted in the Church were not authorized by God, no matter how sincere and faithful the parish priest or the lay believer might be. Joseph Smith taught:

> *[T]he rights of the priesthood are inseparably connected with the powers of heaven, and that the powers of heaven cannot be controlled or handled only upon the principle of righteousness. That they may be conferred upon us, it is true; but when we undertake to cover our sins, or to gratify our pride, our vain ambition, or to exercise control or dominion or compulsion upon the souls of the children of men, in any degree of unrighteousnss; behold, the heavens withdraw themselves; the Spirit of the Lord is grieved; and when it is withdrawn, Amen to the priesthood or the authority of that man.*[954]

"Amen" means "the end," as the end of a prayer.

In regard to the "rock" Joseph Smith taught:

> *Jesus in his teaching says, 'Upon this rock I will build my church; and the gates of hell shall not prevail against it.' What rock? Revelation.*[955]

In one of the revelations given to Joseph Smith by Jesus Christ, Jesus said:

> *Yea, repent and be baptized, every one of you, for a remission of your sins; yea, be baptized even by water, and then cometh the baptism of fire and of the Holy Ghost. Behold, verily, verily, I say unto you, this is my gospel; and remember that they shall have faith in me or they can in nowise be saved; And upon this rock I will build my church; yea, upon this rock*

ye are built, and if he continue, the gates of hell shall not prevail against you.[956]

The Church of Jesus Christ of Latter-day Saints accepts that Peter was selected by Jesus as the chief apostle and spokesman for the Twelve Apostles and did hold the keys to bind on earth and seal in heaven (sealing power or authority) along with the other apostles during the time period immediately following the ascension of the Lord Jesus Christ into heaven. But, the authority given to Peter and the other apostles did not continue in succession to the present day.

It is not the intention of the author to further recount the wickedness of certain leaders of the Christian church in the "Dark Ages"[957]—the previous quotations are sufficient to show there was adequate reason for the Lord to withdraw his authority from the Church leaders and to conclude, as Luther did, that "the tree was dead at its roots."

In summary, The Church of Jesus Christ of Latter-day Saints agrees with the Roman Catholic Church that no man can call himself to establish a church in the name of God or Jesus Christ; therefore, despite the sincerity of the Reformers and their conclusion that the Roman Catholic Church no longer had the authority of God, they could not establish a church in which the doctrines they taught or the ordinances they performed were recognized by God. Joseph Smith and the other early Church leaders received their authority, not from reading *The Bible*, or election by the members, but by being called directly by Jesus Christ and direct ordination by the laying on of hands by heavenly messengers holding the keys to the priesthood authority of God.

3. PENANCE AND FORGIVENESS OF SIN.

Martin Luther was an Augustinian monk.

Augustine, who lived around the year 400 A.D., was very concerned about sin and the sinful nature of man. He was the first to formulate the Roman Catholic Church's doctrine of "original sin," i.e., through Adam and Eve's disobedience to God's commandment not to partake of the Tree of Good and Evil, they had fallen and were thrust out of the garden prepared for them by God. This sin was entailed upon their own children and all their future posterity so that men were naturally sinful. Only through baptism could a man or a woman overcome this sin. Not all Catholics found this doctrine reasonable. For example, Blaise Pascal wrote:

> *For it is beyond doubt that there is nothing which more shocks our reason than to say the sin of the first man has rendered guilty those who, being so removed from this source, seem incapable of participation in it. This transmission does not only seem to us impossible, it seems also very unjust. For what is more contrary to the rules of our miserable justice than to damn eternally an infant incapable of will, for a sin wherein he seems to have so little a share that it was committed six thousand years before he was in existence.*[958]

(The doctrine of original sin and its relation to baptism will be discussed in the next section.) Moreover, despite baptism, people continued to commit sins. What is to be done in such cases? The practice of the Roman Catholic Church was to administer "penance." This consisted of the penitent expressing remorse and committing to refrain from such sins, the imposition of some penalty, such as fasts, and the "absolution" or forgiveness granted by the priesthood authority of the priest. However, the original concept began to change. The Roman Catholic theologian, Franz Zaver von Funk said:

> *The practice of redeeming penance . . . now led to an alteration of far-reaching consequences in the penitential discipline. Among the penalties into which due penance might be commuted was that of alms-giving, and it had also, even earlier, been a custom among penitents to seek the aid of others in performing the penance imposed; thence it was an easy step to the practice of buying off a penance at the price of money. Subsequent to the Eighth Century the Penitentials [books] contain tariffs showing the sums which, should he be unable to fast, the penitent must devote to pious work.*[959]

Forgiveness of sins was promised for undertaking pilgrimages. For example, at the Council of Clermont in 1095, Pope Urban II called for the first Crusade to capture Jerusalem from the Moslems and the Jews. He promised complete forgiveness of sins for all who would join in the Crusade and promised "like Mohammed" that "Those who die will enter the mansions of Heaven."[960] In his speech he said, "Undertake this journey eagerly for the remission of your sins, and be assured of the reward of imperishable glory in the Kingdom of Heaven."[961]

The two things that most provoked Luther were the sale of indulgences by the Roman Catholic Church and the accumulation of relics in Christian churches. The sale of indulgences was based on the concept that certain people in Christ's Church, including Christ himself, Mary, the apostles and certain of the martyrs had lived lives more than sufficiently good to merit salvation. This excess goodness was part of the "treasury" of the Church and could be "supererogated" by the pope and distributed to less righteous persons. In particular, it was the Roman Catholic doctrine that persons who were not sufficiently righteous to merit entrance into God's presence at their death would enter "purgatory" where they would be purged from their "venial" or lesser sins for a sufficient time, in some cases, very long periods. Charles Clarke says with regard to indulgences:

> *Learned men set to work to discover a theological basis for what seems an innovation, and to an English Franciscan, Alexander of Hales, belongs the credit of having developed the theory of the treasury of merit. The theory was that the church possessed a treasury of merits accumulated by the sufferings of Christ and the supererogatory merits of our lady and the saints, upon which the pope was entitled to draw and to assign the merits to the credit of the indulgenced, thus making the power to grant indulgences the peculiar prerogative of the pope.*[962]

According to Professor Bainton:

> *The practice grew out of the crusades. Pope Sixtus IV had promised immediate release of all souls in purgatory and Pope Leo X had promised crusaders plenary remission of sins in 1513. At first, indulgences were conferred on those who sacrificed or risked their lives in fighting against the infidel, and then were extended to those who, unable to go to the Holy Land, made contributions to the enterprise. The*

device proved so lucrative that it was speedily extended to cover the construction of chapels, monasteries and hospitals. The gothic cathedrals were financed in this way. Frederick the Wise [Elector of Saxony in Germany] was using an indulgence to reconstruct a bridge across the Elbe.[963]

Luther was very concerned about the fact that Pope Leo X, in order to raise funds to build the present Vatican headquarters of the Catholic Church, negotiated with the German political leader, Albert of Brandenburg, to appoint him to three bishoprics (which represented a substantial annual income and was in derogation of the Church's prohibition on pluralism), in return for a contribution of 10,000 ducats and 50 percent of the profits from indulgences to be sold in Albert's territory for a period of eight years:

Subscribers would enjoy a plenary and perfect remission of all sins. They would be restored to the state of innocence which they enjoyed in baptism and would be relieved of all the pains of purgatory, including those incurred by an offense against the Divine Majesty. Those securing indulgences on behalf of the dead already in purgatory need not themselves be contrite and confess their sins.[964]

For one thing, Luther was concerned that these indulgences were promoted as a method for living Catholics to release dead ancestors from the pains of purgatory by the payment of money. At the Wittenburg Castle Church twenty-five priests were employed to celebrate Mass for the souls of the departed members of the House of Saxony.[965] Will and Ariel Durant wrote:

Almost as mercenary as the sale of indulgences was the acceptance or solicitation, by the clergy, of money payments, grants, legacies, for the saying of Masses supposed to reduce a dead soul's term of punishment in purgatory. Large sums were devoted to this purpose by pious people, either to relieve a departed relative or friend, or to shorten or annul their own purgatorial probation after death. The poor complained that through their inability to pay for Masses and indulgences it was the earthly rich, not the meek, who inherit the kingdom of heaven; and Columbus ruefully praised money because, he said, 'he who possesses it has the power of transporting souls into paradise.'[966]

'Chantries' were now a frequent form of contribution: persons expecting death paid for the building of a chapel and for the chanting of Masses to expedite their souls into paradise.[967]

But most important to Luther was his concern that sale of indulgences would foster sin. Some believed that they could purchase an indulgence now to apply to a sin they were planning or might commit in the future. Luther believed indulgences were inconsistent with the need for contrition and change of life required for true repentance.

The saints have no extra credits. Every saint is bound to love God to the utmost. There is no such thing as supererogation...If the pope does have the power to release anyone from purgatory, why in the name of love does he not abolish purgatory by letting everyone out. If for the sake of miserable money he released uncounted souls, why should he not for the sake of most holy love empty the place?[968]

According to Durant, "Priests complained that most people put off thought of hell to their deathbed, confident that however sinful their lives, 'three words' (ego te absolvo—I absolve you) will save me."[969]

Luther discovered that the Latin Vulgate version of Matthew 4:17 contained a mistranslation—sinners were not to "do penance" but were to "be penitent."(King James version—"repent").[970]

The "Reformed" Christians taught:

They who in their obedience attain to the greatest height which is possible in this life, are so far from being able to supererogate and to do more than God requires, as that they fall short of much in duty they are bound to do . . . but when we have done all we can we have done but our duty, and are unprofitable servants.[971]

The Eastern Orthodox Church never accepted the doctrines of supererogation or indulgences.[972]

The Roman Catholic Church responded by checking the worst

abuses, but in the Council of Trent, reaffirmed the basic efficacy of indulgences and the veneration of relics. It "laid down . . . that the power of granting indulgences had been left by Christ to his church and that their use was specially salutary to Christian people."[973] In the current Catholic Catechism, the Catholic Church says, "Because sin is always an offense against God, only he can forgive it,"[974] and "only God forgives sins"[975] "[b]ut he entrusted the exercise of the power of absolution to the apostolic ministry which he charged with the 'ministry of reconciliation.'"[976]

Indeed, bishops and priests, by virtue of the sacrament of Holy Orders, have the power to forgive all sins 'in the name of the Father, and of the Son, and of the Holy Spirit.'[977] It is called the sacrament of forgiveness, since by the priest's sacramental absolution God grants the penitent 'pardon and peace.'[978] There is no offense, however serious, that the Church cannot forgive.[979] The Church must be able to forgive all penitents of their offenses, even if they should sin until the last moment of their lives.[980]

Further,

> *Absolution takes away sin, but it does not remedy all the disorders sin has caused. Raised up from sin, the sinner must still recover his full spiritual health by doing something more to make amends for sin: he must 'make satisfaction for' or 'expiate' his sins. This satisfaction is also called 'penance.' The penance the confessor imposes must take into account the penitent's personal situation and must seek his spiritual good."*[981]

In regard to indulgences:

> *'An indulgence is a remission before God of the temporal punishment due to sins whose guilt has already been forgiven, which the faithful Christian who is duly disposed gains under certain prescribed conditions through the action of the Church which, as the minister of redemption, dispenses and applies with authority the treasury of the satisfactions of Christ and the saints.' 'An indulgence is partial or plenary according as it removes either part or all of the temporal punishment due to sin.' Indulgences may be applied to the*

living or the dead . . . . [E]very sin, even venial, entails an unhealthy attachment to creatures, which must be purified either here on earth, or after death in the state called Purgatory. This purification frees one from what is called the 'temporal punishment' of sin.[982]

[T]he 'treasury of the Church' is the infinite value, which can never be exhausted, which Christ's merits have before God . . .' This treasury includes as well the prayers and good works of the Blessed Virgin Mary . . . In the treasury, too, are the prayers and good works of all the saints . . .[983]

The current Catechism also teaches, "[I]t is a wholesome thought to pray for the dead that they may be loosed from their sins" and, "Our prayer for them is capable not only of helping them, but also of making their intercession for us effective."[984] The Catechism says:

This teaching [purgatory] is also based on the practice of prayer for the dead, already mentioned in Sacred Scripture: [Apocrypha] 'Therefore [Judas Maccabeus] made atonement for the dead, that they might be delivered from their sin.'[985]

From the beginning the Church has honored the memory of the dead and offered prayers in suffrage for them, above all the Eucharistic sacrifice, so that thus purified, they may attain to the beatific vision of God. The Church also commends almsgiving, indulgences, and works of penance undertaken on behalf of the dead.[986]

The Catechism says:

Through indulgences the faithful can obtain the remission of temporal punishment resulting from sin for themselves and also for the souls in Purgatory.[987]

The Catholic scholar James Coriden says in regard to the faithful:

They obtain from God forgiveness for their sins through the absolution of the minister, and they are reconciled with the church (Canon Law 959) . . .

The Council of Trent of 1551 described the priest's absolution as a judicial act. The council linked the notion to the

> *gospel references to binding or loosing, forgiving sins or retaining them (Matthew 16:18; John 20:23).*[988]

Apparently not as a condition of forgiveness, but as a "substitute for a penal sanction" for sin, the priest can impose a "penance," consisting of "some work of religion or charity . . ., e.g. a retreat, a fast, alms, abstinence, a specific task or service, etc."[989] It must correspond as far as possible to the gravity and nature of the sins committed. It can consist of prayer, an offering, works of mercy, service of neighbor, voluntary self-denial, sacrifices, and above all the patient acceptance of the cross we must bear.[990]

After confession and agreement to perform the penance imposed by the priest, the penitent offers a prayer and then the priest pronounces the words, "I absolve you from your sins in the name of the Father and of the Son and of the Holy Spirit."[991] As one of the "precepts" of the Church, Catholic faithful must participate in confession and Penance at least once a year.[992] When a person is dying the priest says:

> *By the authority which the Apostolic See has given me, I grant you a full pardon and the remission of all your sins in the name of the Father, and of the Son and of the Holy Spirit.*[993]

The Catholic Church continues to grant indulgences at various times. For example, in 1950 Pope Pius XII proclaimed an indulgence for visiting Rome:

> *[D]uring the year of expiation, to all Christians, of both sexes, who duly confessed and having had communion, will visit the same day or in several days the basilicas of St. John Lateran of Saint Peter of the Vatican, of Saint Paul on the Ostian Way, of Saint Mary Maggiore on the Esquiline and will recite three Paters, Aves, Glorias, plus another Pater, Ave, Gloria " a nos intentions," to which they will add a Credo in each basilica, we grant mercifully in the name of the Lord, a plenary indulgence from all punishments which their sins have merited . . . We grant besides to the faithful this indulgence, valid for themselves as well as for the dead, as many times as they will be able to fulfill the prescribed ritual conditions.*[994]

Indulgences are also available for reciting the Rosary prayers, meditating on the "Stations of the Cross," and wearing the "Miraculous Medallion."[995]

The revelations given to Joseph Smith relate to several of the foregoing issues. To begin with, when translating *The Book of Mormon*, he read writings of the ancient American prophets relating to the sin of Adam. These taught that through Adam's disobedience that mankind did "fall" and became "carnal, sensual and devilish" and an "enemy" to God.[996] They taught that in this state men commit sin "by nature," and if men persevere in that state and do not call upon God and "yield to the enticings of the Holy Spirit" and become "born of God" through faith in Jesus Christ, repentance, baptism and receiving the Holy Ghost, they cannot be saved, that is, return to the presence of God.[997]

But, Joseph learned that Jesus Christ had atoned for "original guilt."[998] In other words, Adam and Eve's sin would not be the basis for judgment of any of their posterity—it was only a person's own sins that could prevent him or her from returning to the presence of God. Eventually, he formulated this knowledge into a simple Article of Faith:

> *We believe that men will be punished for their own sins and not for Adam's transgression.*[999]

Joseph also learned a substantial amount regarding life after death. Most of this will be discussed in Section 14 hereafter, but, in regard to purgatory, he learned that such a place does exist, but it is different than the Christian churches were teaching. He learned that for the wicked who will not accept Jesus Christ and his atonement, either in their earthly life or in the spirit world after their death, their resurrection will be postponed at the Second Coming of Jesus Christ. While Christ reigns on the earth for a 1,000 year (Millennial) period with the righteous, these persons will remain in the world of spirits, suffering for their own sins.[1000] This suffering, however, is not physical because they will not be resurrected and regain their body until the end of that period—it will be emotional and mental. He taught, "What is the damnation of hell? To go with the society who have not obeyed His commands."[1001] In one of the poignant pleas of Jesus

Christ about this matter he said in a revelation to Joseph:

> *For behold I, God, have suffered these things for all, that they might not suffer if they would repent; But if they would not repent they must suffer even as I; which suffering caused myself, even God, the greatest of all, to tremble because of pain, and to bleed at every pore, and to suffer both body and spirit—and would that I might not drink the bitter cup and shrink; nevertheless, glory be to the Father, and I partook and finished my preparations unto the children of men.*[1002]

At the end of this time of suffering for the wicked, they will enter into a measure of "glory," but not that which will be received by the righteous. Joseph was further taught, "[B]y this ye may know if a man repenteth of his sins—behold, he will confess them and forsake them."[1003] As a result, serious sins are to be confessed to the bishop in private for the purpose of receiving counsel and advice, but the bishop has no authority to forgive sins. If the bishop believes that discipline is appropriate that person may be excommunicated from the Church, disfellowshipped or placed on probation for a time suitable to complete the repentance process. True repentance consists in recognizing that a particular action or thought was contrary to God's commandments, feeling remorse for the sin, making restitution insofar as possible to those harmed by the sin, and resolving not to commit the sin again. Joseph taught:

> *Repentance is a thing that cannot be trifled with every day. Daily transgression and daily repentance is not that which is pleasing in the sight of God.*[1004]

He also learned in *The Book of Mormon* that postponing, or "deathbed" repentance, was of no avail:

> *For behold, if ye have procrastinated the day of our repentance even until death, behold, ye have become subjected to the spirit of the devil, and he doth seal you his; therefore, the spirit of the Lord hath withdrawn from you, and hath no place in you, and the devil hath all power over you; and this is the final state of the wicked.*

4. BAPTISM, CONFIRMATION AND THE HOLY GHOST

Colin Buchanan has written:

> *During the second five hundred years of the Christian era in the West the doctrines of baptism and of communion developed considerably—both in a slightly 'magical' direction. Baptism was greatly affected by Augustine's controversy with Pelagius and his followers. The doctrine of original sin, which Augustine set out, made it vital for the church to believe in the absolute necessity of baptism for salvation. People took this to imply that unbaptized infants went to hell, or at least to 'limbo' on the borders of hell. The high rate of infant mortality at this period led to baptism being carried out within minutes of birth, often by midwives. (A carry-over survives to this day when newborn infants are in danger of death) . . . The older tradition of Easter baptisms decreased. It also became impossible for the bishop to lay on hands (or anoint) at baptism. Indeed, in the larger dioceses of France and Britain, this practice was often neglected entirely, so that many people were never 'confirmed' at all. Acquinas even argued that confirmation was not necessary for ordination.*[1005]

The Roman Catholic Church has consistently taught that baptism is essential to salvation based on John 3:3-5, Matthew 28:19 and Mark 16:16.[1006] "By Baptism all sins are forgiven, original sin and all personal sins, as well as all punishment for sin."[1007] Catholics also teach that baptism as an ordinance of salvation began at the time of Christ's death.[1008] In regard to the method of baptism, the Roman Catholic Church expressly states that, in its "original and complete" form, it was administered by complete immersion and that now the prevalent form is pouring or sprinkling.

Among the Reformers the Anabaptists were most critical of the practice of infant baptism.[1009] To them, infants could not exercise faith in Christ, understand who he was, his mission, his commandments, or make promises of obedience. They argued that the Catholic practice of using "godfathers" to profess faith and promise obedience on behalf of the infant was not supported by any scriptures or examples in *The Bible*. They further demonstrated that the method of pouring or sprinkling only developed because it was risky to immerse infants and because some elderly persons were too infirm to be immersed. They pointed to historical records establishing that some early Christians, such as the Emperor Constantine, although professing to accept Christianity, postponed baptism to the end of their life in order to be certain that the forgiveness of sins would cover the longest possible time period.[1010] The practice of instructing baptismal candidates for as long as three years and conducting baptisms only at Easter was gradually replaced by infant baptism between the third and sixth centuries. Durant says:

> *By the ninth century the early Christian method of baptism by total immersion had been gradually replaced by aspersion—sprinkling—as less dangerous to health in northern climes.*[1011]

It was only after Augustine developed his doctrine of "original sin" entailed upon newborns that the Roman Catholic Church began to practice infant baptism to avoid the risk that a child would die without baptism, and, thereby, be consigned to hell. At that time period, the Church taught, "Infants not baptized, who die before the age of reason go to hell."[1012] During his lifetime, Augustine was able to prevail upon a Council of the Church to adopt the position:

> *[W]hosoever says that between the kingdom of heaven and hell there is a third intermediate sojourn where children who have died without baptism live happily . . . let him be anathema (Canon 3).*[1013]

According to Will Durant:

> *Augustine reluctantly concluded that infants dying before being baptized went to hell . . . The Church softened the doctrine by teaching that unbaptized infants went not to hell but to limbo—Infernus puerorum—where their only suffering was the pain of the loss of paradise."*[1014]

Dante Alighieri, in *The Divine Comedy* (1318), consigned those who were not baptized to limbo, the second level of hell, just below the "neutrals," along with those who "were before Christianity" who did not "duly worship God."[1015]

However, it was not until the Councils of Olmutz (1318 A.D., Canon 19) and Salamanca (1335 A.D., Canon 6) that it was decreed, in general, children should be baptized soon after birth.[1016] Certain early Christian "Fathers' (Gregory of Nyssa (d. A.D. 389), Gregory Nazianzen (d. A.D. 389) and John Chrysostom taught that newly-born children are exempt from sin.[1017] The Anabaptists insisted upon baptism by immersion of adults as they found in the New Testament. Luther, steeped in the teachings of Augustine, believed in "original sin" and condemned to the "eternal wrath of God" all those who were not born again through baptism, including infants.[1018] "Luther taught that infants were regenerated in baptism (through infant faith!)."[1019] The "Reformed" churches accepted baptism as a sacrament, but deemed confirmation (and extreme unction [last rites]) as "mere devices of men, which the Church may well spare, without any damage or inconvenience at all."[1020] The Reformed churches also taught the necessity of infant baptism to overcome "original sin" and baptism either by immersion or sprinkling.[1021] Apparently, partly due to their concern about the justice of God for damning a person who had never been baptized, they downplayed the necessity of baptism:

> *Although it be a great sin to condemn or neglect this ordinance, yet grace and salvation are not so inseparably annexed unto it, as that no person can be regenerated or saved without it, or that all that are baptized are undoubtedly regenerated.* [1022]

> *Elected infants, dying in infancy, are regenerated and saved by Christ through the Spirit, who worketh when, and where, and how he pleaseth.*[1023]

As indicated above, the transition from baptisms performed either in old age or annually at Easter time to the immediate baptism of infants came about as a direct result of Augustine's doctrine that children inherited the sin of Adam and Eve in the Garden of Eden through their parents. When his critics argued that this made God unjust because it made men responsible for sins they had not committed, Augustine responded:

Original sin is indeed said to be the sin of another because each one of us derives it from his parents; but not without reason is it said to be our own, because, as the apostle says in that one man (Adam) all sinned [Romans 5:12].[1024]

When Pelagius, a monk, and Celestius, a Roman lawyer, opposed Augustine's doctrine of original sin, Pope Zosimus sided with Pelagius. However, Augustine persuaded the Roman Emperor Honorius of the correctness of his views. On April 30, 418 A.D. the Emperor ordered the expulsion of Pelagius and Celestius. As a result, Pope Zosimus reversed his position. A new council held:

Whosoever says that it is not necessary to baptize new-born infants...because they have not in them the original sin transferred from Adam . . . so that indeed the formula for baptism 'for the remission of sins' would have no meaning properly speaking or have an improper meaning, let that one be anathema; for according to the Epistle to the Romans (5:12), the fall of Adam is imputable to all his descendants (Canon 2).[1025]

Augustine relied on the scripture Romans 5:12, as it existed in the then-current Latin translation by Jerome (the "Vulgate"), "Wherefore, as by one man sin entered into the world, and death by sin; and so death passed upon all men, in whom all have sinned." However, when Erasmus made his new translation of the original Greek manuscripts, he saw that the correct translation of the last phrase was "for that all have sinned." In other words, Augustine understood from the translation he was working from that all men had sinned by Adam, but the more accurate translation indicated that spiritual death—separation from the presence of God—passes upon men due to their own sins. "For all have sinned and come short of the glory of God."[1026] According to Professor Barker, "The most eminent Catholic and Protestant authorities today are agreed on this translation, "for that all have sinned."[1027]

In 1947 Boulenger stated the then-current Catholic position on infant baptism:

[C]hildren themselves cannot go to heaven if they have not

been baptized; hence the obligation for parents to have their children baptized as soon as possible, in order not to expose them to the danger of dying before having received baptism.[1028]

Today, the Catholic Church recognizes that their baptismal practice has changed over time:

This initiation has varied greatly through the centuries according to circumstances. In the first centuries of the Church, Christian initiation saw considerable development. A long period of catechumenate included a series of preparatory rites, which were liturgical landmarks along the path of catechumenal preparation culminated in the celebration of the sacraments of Christian initiation.

Where infant Baptism has become the form in which this sacrament is usually celebrated, it has become a single act of encapsulating the preparatory stages of Christian initiation in a very abridged way. By its very nature infant Baptism requires a post-baptismal catechumentate . . . The second Vatican council restored for the Latin Church 'the catechumenate for adults, comprising several distinct steps.[1029]

The Catholic Church says:

The Church and the parents would deny a child the priceless grace of becoming a child of God were they not to confer Baptism shortly after birth.[1030]

The current Catholic Catechism says:

As regards children who have died without baptism, the Church can only entrust them to the mercy of God, as she does in her funeral rites for them. Indeed, the great mercy of God who desires that all men should be saved, and Jesus' tenderness toward children which caused him to say: 'Let the children come to me, do not hinder them,' allow us to hope that there is a way of salvation who have died without Baptism. All the more urgent is the Church's call not to prevent little children coming to Christ through the gift of holy Baptism.[1031]

In addition, in the current *Catechism of the Catholic Church*, it appears that the Church's traditional position that "outside of the Church there is no salvation" does not apply to those who

> *Through no fault of their own, do not know the Gospel of Christ or his Church, but who nevertheless seek God with a sincere heart, and moved by grace, try in their actions to do his will as they know through the dictates of their conscience—those too may achieve eternal salvation."*[1032]

> *It may be supposed that such persons would have desired Baptism explicitly if they had known of its necessity."*[1033]

> *Those who suffer death "for the sake of the faith" (baptism by blood) and catechumens who die before baptism are also free from the necessity of baptism.*[1034]

In regard to "original sin," today, the Roman Catholic Church teaches:

> *Following St. Paul [Romans 5:12, 18], the Church has always taught that the overwhelming misery which oppresses men and their inclination toward evil and death cannot be understood apart from their connection with Adam's sin and the fact he has transmitted to us a sin with which we are all born afflicted—a sin which is the 'death of the soul.' Because of this certainty of faith, the Church baptizes for the remission of sins even tiny infants who have not committed personal sins.*[1035]

This inclination to sin is called "concupiscence."[1036] However, the Catholic Church does not believe that Adam's sin totally corrupts man (Calvin believed that man was "totally depraved"), since that would predestine all men to hell. The Catholic Church believes that Adam's sin has "wounded" man's nature and that baptism "erases original sin."[1037] As a result, "infants are to be baptized within the first weeks after their birth," and an infant in danger of death may lawfully be baptized "even if its parents are unwilling and the parents are not Catholic."[1038] Each baptized person is to have a sponsor (godfather).[1039] As part of the pre-baptismal prayer the priest says, "We pray for these children: set them free from original sin.'[1040]

As for the rite of baptizing, the Catechism says:

This sacrament is called 'Baptism', after the central rite by which it is carried out: to baptize (Greek baptizein) means to 'plunge' or 'immerse'; the 'plunge' into the water symbolizes the catechumen's burial into Christ's death, from which he rises up by resurrection with him, as 'a new creature.'[1041]

But, either immersion—full body or just the head—"which is more suitable as a symbol of participation in the death and resurrection of Christ, or pouring may lawfully be used."[1042]

Baptism is performed in the most expressive way by triple immersion in the baptismal water. However, from ancient times it has also been able to be conferred by pouring the water three times over the candidate's head.[1043]

Adults (at least 14 years of age) are baptized once a year during Easter.[1044] If an infant dies before baptism the Catholic Church permits a Church funeral if the parents intended to have the child baptized.

The role of confirmation was also interpreted differently at different times. Originally, according to the Catholic Catechism, "[f]rom that time on, the apostles, in fulfillment of Christ's will, imparted to the newly baptized by the laying on of hands the gift of the Spirit that completes the grace of baptism."[1045] Later, "an anointing with perfumed oil (chrism) was added to the laying on of hands."[1046] However, with the rise in infant baptisms, "confirmation" was postponed to the age of reason (seven years),[1047] but the anointing with sacred chrism at the time of baptism continued and "signifies the gift of the Holy Spirit to the newly baptized."[1048] The Catechism describes these changes succinctly:

In the first centuries Confirmation generally comprised one single celebration with Baptism, forming with it a 'double sacrament,' according to the expression of St. Cyprian. Among other reasons, the multiplication of infant baptisms all through the year, the increase of rural parishes, and the growth of dioceses often prevented the bishop from being present at all baptismal celebrations. In the West the desire

> *to reserve the completion of Baptism caused the temporal separation of the two sacraments. The East has kept them united, so that Confirmation is conferred by the priest who baptizes. But he can do so only with the 'myron' [oil]consecrated by a bishop.*[1049]

For adults, confirmation follows immediately after baptism by the priest laying hands on the candidate's head, dipping his right thumb in the chrism [anointing oil], and making the sign of the cross on the forehead of the one being confirmed, saying, "Be sealed with the Gift of the Holy Spirit,"[1050] which signifies the royal priesthood of the baptized and the enrollment into the company of the people of God.[1051]

Baptism was for the remission of sins, but when confirmation was separated in time from baptism, there was a possibility that sins would intervene; as a result, now a candidate for confirmation "should receive the sacrament of Penance in order to be cleansed for the gift of the Holy Spirit."[1052] Candidates for confirmation should have a "sponsor"— who can be one of the baptismal godparents.[1053]

Part of the "apostolic succession," which the Catholic Church claims, is Christ giving the Holy Spirit to the apostles and their entrustment of this power to their successors.[1054] From the disputes between the Catholics—who claimed that the Church, the Church's traditions and the popes (or at least the Church councils)—had the supreme authority to decide doctrine and to prescribe orthodoxy, and the Protestants—who held that *The Bible* was the supreme authority—arose those who followed the "third way." This was the view that the Holy Ghost was the supreme guide for the personal life of each Christian. This was the view of the "three prophets" from Zwickau who visited Luther, the Quakers and the Pentecostals, as discussed in Section 1, "The Bible," above.

Over time and currently, the practices of Protestant churches have varied in regard to the necessity, proper age and proper method of baptism and confirmation.[1055] For example, Christian Scientists and Quakers do not practice baptism, Presbyterians practice baptism, but do not believe baptism is necessary for salvation, and Baptists, Disciples of Christ and Jehovah's Witnesses do not baptize infants.[1056] The Unitarians do not believe in the Holy Ghost.[1057]

When Joseph Smith was taught by Jesus Christ in the restoration of the gospel, baptism was reaffirmed as essential for the higher degrees of salvation. Joseph learned that even Adam had been taught about the plan of salvation, including faith in Jesus Christ (who would be born later), and that Adam and Eve and many others in later time periods were also baptized, "looking forward" to the coming of Christ. [1058] Baptism was not to be postponed until old age, but should be performed as soon as the person had faith in Jesus Christ and repented of his or her sins. However, there was no need to baptize infants. As explained in the previous Section, *The Book of Mormon* taught that Christ had atoned for Adam's sin and that only personal sin was of concern for salvation. Since infants had not committed any personal sins, indeed they did not even understand what conduct would violate the commandments of Jesus Christ, baptism of infants would be of no efficacy and would deny the atonement of Christ.[1059]

In regard to the concern that children might die without baptism and thus be consigned to hell, Joseph Smith learned that those who have not had a chance to learn and understand the teachings of the gospel during their earthly life would receive that opportunity in the spirit world prior to the resurrection. Although baptism is required for the highest degree of salvation to live in the presence of God as Jesus had taught,[1060] baptisms for persons who accepted the gospel in the spirit world could be performed in temples and during the Millenium. Jesus Christ instructed that children were to be taught and prepared by their parents to receive baptism at the age of eight years old, the age of "accountability." While some could question whether an eight year old child is sufficiently mature to understand and commit to living the gospel of Jesus Christ (they are certainly more mature than an infant), the additional consideration is the gift of the Holy Ghost. By receiving baptism and confirmation, the influence of the Holy Ghost could begin operating more effectively in assisting in the prevention of sin and strengthening the believer. He learned the ordinance of baptism should be administered only by immersion as a symbol of the burial and resurrection of Jesus Christ as taught by Paul to the Romans.[1061] Since infants were not to be baptized there was no health hazard. The Holy Ghost was to be confirmed upon the newly baptized person by those holding the proper priesthood authority. Joseph Smith said:

> *Baptism is a holy ordinance preparatory to the reception of the Holy Ghost; it is the channel by which the Holy Ghost will be administered. The Gift of the Holy Ghost by the laying on of hands cannot be received through the medium of any other principle than the principle of righteousness; for if the proposals are not complied with, it is of no use, but withdraws.*[1062]

5. COMMUNION.

If the Roman Catholics accused the Protestants of worshiping *The Bible*, the Protestants retorted that the Catholics worshiped the Eucharist. Even today, the Catholic theologian James Coriden states:

> *The most holy Eucharist is the most august of all the sacraments; all the others are ordered to it. In the Eucharist Christ the Lord himself is contained, offered and received...The faithful are to hold the Eucharist in highest honor, actively participating in its celebration, receiving it frequently and devoutly, and worshiping it.*[1063]

"The Eucharist is the source and summit of the Christian life."[1064] Adults being baptized into the Catholic Church receive their first communion—"which is the climax of their initiation and the center of the whole Christian life."[1065]

The other sacraments, like every ministry of the Church and every work of the apostolate, are linked with the holy Eucharist and have it as their end. For the Eucharist contains the Church's entire spiritual wealth, that is Christ himself . . . The Eucharist therefore stands as the source and apex of all evangelization.[1066]

The Roman Catholic Church had blessed the bread and wine and administered it to believers in accordance with the teachings of Jesus Christ from earliest times. This ritual of the "Holy Eucharist" was a part of the Sunday worship service (Mass).

Michael Smith writes:

> *From the third century, Old Testament ideas of priesthood*

were used by some to interpret the Eucharist as the 'Christian sacrifice.' At first the sacrifice was thought to consist of praises, but gradually it came to be held that an offering was made to God to gain forgiveness of sins. By the Middle Ages this had been developed to make the Eucharist a re-offering of Christ's sacrifice on the cross. There also arose magical ideas concerning the bread and wine. By the fourth century it was held that either when words of the Last Supper were repeated (in the Western Church), or when the Holy Spirit was invoked on the bread and wine (at the prayer called the epiclesis in the Eastern church) a change took place. It was felt right to venerate the bread and wine as representing Jesus visibly.[1067]

According to the Catholic historian, Boulenger, in the seventh century the private Mass and the practice of placing the "host" on the tongue of the communicant by the priest was instituted. In the twelfth century children were no longer permitted to take communion until the age of reason [seven years], communion was limited to the bread, and the practice of elevating the "host" for adoration was instituted.[1068] The Eastern Orthodox Church continued to permit all newly-baptized and confirmed—"even little children"—to partake of the communion.[1069] They also administered both the bread and the wine to communicants.[1070]

While the Reformers had differences with the Catholic Church over various aspects of communion, including whether both bread and wine should be given to the communicants,[1071] the major disagreement was over the doctrine of "real presence" or transubstantiation, and whether each Mass was a new sacrifice of Jesus Christ for sins. The Catholics interpreted the teachings of Jesus as requiring believers to "eat" the body and blood of Christ as given in Jesus' "bread of life" sermon:

I am the living bread which came down from heaven: if any man eat of this bread, he shall live forever and the bread I will give is my flesh, which I will give for the life of the world . . . Except ye eat the flesh of the Son of man, and drink his blood, ye have no life in you . . . For my flesh is meat indeed, and my blood is drink indeed. He that eateth my flesh, and

> *drinketh my blood, dwelleth in me, and I in him. As the living Father hath sent me, and I live by the Father: so he that eateth me, even he shall live by me. This is that bread which came down from heaven: not as your fathers did eat manna and are dead: he that eateth of this bread shall live for ever.*[1072]

The Roman Catholic Church had come to the doctrine that when the priest blessed the bread and wine they were transformed (transubstantiated) into the actual body and blood of Jesus Christ, although they retained their appearance and the taste of bread and wine, and that the bread and wine were offered as sacrifices for sins. Because of increasing concern that the actual flesh of Christ was in the crumbs left behind in partaking of the bread, a one-piece wafer was developed. In the twelfth century the custom arose that only the priest was allowed to partake of the wine lest it be spilled, and a straw called a fistula was used to drink the wine to prevent spillage.[1073]

> *[W]hen some conservatives . . . demanded communion in both forms to make sure they received the blood as well as the body of the Lord, theologians explained that the blood of Christ was 'concomitant' with His body in the bread, and His body was 'concomitant' with His blood in the wine. A thousand marvels were told of the power of the consecrated Host to cast out devils, cure disease, stop fires, and detect perjury by choking liars. Every Christian was required to communicate at least once a year; and the First Communion of the young Christian was made an occasion of solemn pageantry and happy celebration.*[1074]

Although some in the Roman Catholic Church argued that there had always been some Church doctors who had taught the concept of the "real presence."

> *The influential Abbot of Corbie, Paschasius Radbertus, [in the ninth century] wrote a treatise On the Body and Blood of the Lord. This was the first clear statement of a doctrine of the 'real presence' of Christ's body and blood in the Eucharist, suggesting what was later called transubstantiation.*[1075]

According to Professor Colin Buchanan:

> *A controversy concerning the use of unleavened bread (azymes) in the eight century standardized the use of wafers at communion in the Western church. Ratramnus in the ninth century describes the elements of the Eucharist as 'symbols', but his book was condemned in 1050. He opposed Paschasius who took the 'realist' doctrine a long step further towards transubstantiation. The last opponent of this trend was Berengar of Tours in the eleventh century. His denials of 'realism' provoked further definitions (for example, by Lanfranc who opposed him). Finally, transubstantiation was adopted at the Fourth Lateran Council in 1215 . . . Theories were developed that through the offering of Christ himself under the forms of bread and wine in the sacrifice of the mass, atonement was made for both living and dead. This in turn led to the later medieval proliferation of masses for the dead.*[1076]

In regard to the controversy between Berengar and Lanfranc, Professor Robert Clouse tells us:

> *Discussion revolved around the meaning of the words of consecration in the mass: 'This is my body, this is my blood.' Berengar held that a real and true change takes place in these elements, but that the change is spiritual and that the bread and wine remain of the same substance. Lanfranc and other theologians debated with him, believing that the underlying substance of the bread and wine was changed to Christ's blood and body, while the 'accidents' (touch, taste, sight and smell) of the bread and wine remained the same. During a long and bitter controversy (1045-80) the term 'transubstantiation' emerged and took on Lanfranc's definition. Berengar was condemned and forced to disown his views.*[1077]

According to the Catholic writer Felician Foy, transubstantiation was not adopted as an official dogma of the Church until the Council of Rome in 1079 and the Lateran Council of 1215, and then only after overcoming substantial disagreements in the ninth century and the vehement objection of a Catholic bishop, Berengarius in the eleventh century in France.[1078] In 1246 the feast of "Corpus Christi" (the body of Christ) was instituted, which involved carrying the Eucharist through the streets for adoration.[1079]

All the Reformers, including Martin Luther, rejected the concept of repetitive sacrifices of Jesus Christ for sin in the Mass:

> *At the same time the abominable error was condemned according to which it was taught that our Lord Christ had by his death made satisfaction only for original sin, and had instituted the Mass as a sacrifice for other sins. This transformed the Mass into a sacrifice for the living and the dead, a sacrifice by means of which sin was taken away and God was reconciled. There upon followed a debate at to whether one Mass held for many people merited as much as a special Mass held for an individual. Out of this grew the countless multiplication of Masses, by the performance of which men expected to get everything needed from God. Meanwhile faith in Christ and true service of God were forgotten . . . . [T]he Scriptures show in many places that there is no sacrifice for original sin, or for any other sin, except the one death of Christ. For it is written in the Epistle to the Hebrews that Christ offered himself once and by this offering made satisfaction for all sin.*[1080]

John Calvin and the "Reformed" churches regarded transubstantiation as superstition:

> *For neither did godly antiquity believe, neither do we believe, that the body of Christ can be eaten corporeally and essentially, with a bodily mouth.*[1081]

> *In this sacrament Christ is not offered up to his Father, nor any real sacrifice made at all for remission of sins of the quick or dead, but only a commemoration of that one offering up of himself, by himself, upon the cross, once for all, and a spiritual oblation of all possible praise unto God for the same; so that the Popish sacrifice of the Mass, they call it, is most abominably injurious to Christ's one only sacrifice, the alone propitiation for the sins of the elect.*[1082]

For Calvin, "[T]he body of Christ is in the heavens, at the right hand of the Father," the eating of the bread and drinking of the wine was "spiritually" partaking of Christ, for the "Spirit giveth life," and when Christ taught that we must "eat" him, he immediately afterward explained to his disciples that "the words that I speak to you are spirit and life" (John 6:63).[1083] Therefore, by taking Christ's words into our hearts we partake of the bread of life. Furthermore, Jesus' "bread of life" sermon as recorded in John 6 was separated in time and location from the Last Supper—the bread and wine were not offered to those present on the occasion of the "bread of life sermon," so Jesus could not have been referring to partaking of the communion bread and wine when he taught in the bread of life sermon that his disciples must 'eat" him. Although the accounts of the Last Supper by Matthew and Mark say that Jesus said, "Take eat, this is my body,"[1084] the account in Luke and Paul's letter to the Corinthians says, "This do in remembrance of me."[1085] The Reformer John Oecolampadius insisted that the scriptures teach that the body of Christ has ascended into heaven and did not come down piecemeal for every Mass.[1086] Another Reformer, Andrew Carlstadt, interpreted Christ's instruction, "This do in remembrance of me," as indicating that the bread and wine were "merely reminders, not even symbols, let alone channels to God."[1087]

The Calvinists believed the Catholic practice had led to many abuses, such as:

> *Private masses, or receiving his sacrament by a priest, or any other, alone; as likewise the denial of the cup to the people [offering only the wafer to the worshippers], worshipping the elements, the lifting them up, or carrying them about for adoration [such as on Corpus Christi], and the reserving them for any pretended religious uses, are all contrary to the nature of this sacrament, and to the institution of Christ.*[1088]

John Calvin argued forcefully that the sacrifice of Christ had been done "once for all"[1089] and that no actual sacrifice of Christ took place in the Mass:

> *That doctrine which maintains a change of the substance of the bread and wine into the substance of Christ's body*

(commonly called transubstantiation) by consecration of a priest, or by any other way, is repugnant, not to Scripture alone, but even to common-sense and reason; overthroweth the nature of the sacrament; and hath been, and is the cause of manifold superstitions, yea, of gross idolatries.[1090]

Luther struggled with this issue, but, eventually, maintained the doctrine of the "real presence" and the "ubiquity" or capacity for "multi-presence" of Jesus' glorified flesh,[1091] but taught that Christ's body was present in the Eucharist "along with" the bread and wine, by "consubstantiation," viz., the body and blood of Christ coexisted with the substance of the bread and wine[1092]— not by transubstantiation."[1093] The Reformers allowed the communicant to take both the wafer and the wine with his own hands, to take communion without previous confession, and to hear the worship services in his own language.[1094] Masses for the dead were discontinued.

The Catholic Church did not accept any of the Reformer's criticisms, but have maintained all of the foregoing practices to the present day. Currently, *The Rites of the Catholic Church* states:

In turn, Eucharistic reservation, which became customary in order to permit the reception of communion, led to the practice of adoring this sacrament and offering to it the worship which is due to God. This cult of adoration is based upon valid and solid principles. Moreover, some of the public and communal forms of this worship were instituted by the Church itself.[1095]

No one therefore may doubt 'that all the faithful show this holy sacrament the veneration and adoration that is due to God himself, as has always been the practice recognized in the Catholic Church . . .'[1096]

The current *Catechism of the Catholic Church* says:

At the heart of the Eucharistic celebration are the bread and the wine that, by the words of Christ and the invocation of the Holy Spirit, become Christ's Body and Blood . . . The signs of bread and wine become, in a way surpassing understanding, the Body and Blood of Christ . . .[1097]

In the most blessed sacrament of the Eucharist . . . the whole Christ is truly, really, and substantially contained.[1098]

When the Church celebrates the Eucharist, she commemorates Christ's Passover, and it is made present: the sacrifice offered for all on the cross remains ever present.[1099]

Christ is present whole and entire in each of the species and whole and entire in each of their parts, in such a way that the breaking of the bread does not divide Christ.[1100]

In the liturgy of the Mass we express our faith in the real presence of Christ under the species of bread and wine by, among other ways, genuflecting or bowing deeply as a sign of adoration of the Lord. 'The Catholic Church has always offered and still offers to the sacrament of the Eucharist the cult of adoration, not only during Mass, but also outside of it, reserving the consecrated hosts with the utmost care, exposing them to the solemn veneration of the faithful, and carrying them in procession.'[1101]

The Catholic Catechism quotes St John Damascene and Thomas Acquinas:

You ask how the bread becomes the Body of Christ, and the wine . . . the Blood of Christ. I shall tell you: the Holy Spirit comes upon them and accomplishes what surpasses every word and thought . . . Let it be enough for you to understand that it is by the Holy Spirit, just as it was of the Holy Virgin and by the Holy Spirit that the Lord, through and in himself, took flesh.[1102]

That in this sacrament are the true Body of Christ and his true Blood is something that 'cannot be apprehended by the senses, but only by faith, which relies on divine authority.'[1103]

The Catechism says:

The Eucharistic sacrifice is also offered for the faithful departed who 'have died in Christ but are not yet fully purified [in purgatory], so that they may be able to enter into the light and peace of Christ.'[1104]

The Catholic Church further teaches:

> *[T]he Eucharist . . . wipes away venial sins . . . The Eucharist is not ordered to the forgiveness of mortal sins—that is proper to the sacrament of Reconciliation [penance].*[1105]

> *Anyone who is aware of having committed a mortal sin must not receive Holy Communion, even if he experiences deep contrition, without having first received sacramental absolution, unless he has a grave reason for receiving Communion and there is no possibility of going to confession. Children must go to the sacrament of Penance before receiving Holy Communion for the first time.*[1106]

Pastors in the Catholic churches are to see to it that the churches are open everyday "so that the faithful may easily pray in the presence of the blessed sacrament."[1107] The holy Eucharist is to be reserved in an immovable and solid tabernacle. It must be opaque and locked in such a way as to provide every possible security against the danger of desecration.[1108]

When the priest conducts Mass, he genuflects before the host, takes and raises it, and says, "This is the Lamb of God who takes away the sins of the world."[1109] The priest may "apply Mass, i.e., say it for someone's intention, for anyone, living or dead."[1110] Furthermore, "A priest who celebrates Mass may take an offering to apply the Mass according to a definite intention."[1111] Even marriages and funerals are to be performed within the Mass ritual[1112] and, "The celebration of the Eucharist as viaticum, food for the passage through death to eternal life, is the sacrament proper for the dying Christian."[1113] Currently, *The Rites of the Catholic Church* states:

> *The original and primary reason for the reservation of the Eucharist outside Mass is the administration of Viaticum: the distribution of Holy Communion and the adoration of our Lord Jesus Christ present in the Blessed Sacrament are derivative. For in fact the reservation of the sacred species for the benefit of the sick led to the admirable practice of adoring this heavenly food reserved in our churches. This practice of adoration is essentially proper and rational because faith in the real presence of our Lord spontaneously evokesa public and external manifestation of that faith.*[1114]

Under Catholic doctrine, only members of the Catholic Church may partake of the Eucharist.[1115] The faithful are required to partake of communion at least once each year during the Easter season.[1116]

Modern practice in other churches varies. The Eastern Orthodox Church only administers communion four times a year, Seventh Day Adventists—the same, Jehovah's Witnesses once a year, and Quakers not at all.[1117]

When Joseph Smith sought direction from Jesus Christ on this issue he was told that partaking of the elements of communion, called the "sacrament," was symbolic. The members of the Church were to eat and drink of Christ "spiritually" in accordance with Paul's instruction to the Corinthians:

> *Moreover, brethren, I would not that ye should be ignorant, how that all our fathers were under the cloud, and all passed through the sea; And were all baptized unto Moses in the cloud and in the sea; And did all eat the same spiritual meat; And did all drink the same spiritual drink; for they drank of that Spiritual Rock that followed them: and that Rock was Christ.*[1118]

He found that when Jesus had visited the American continent he had taught them:

> *He that eateth this bread eateth of my body to his soul; and he that drinketh this wine drinketh of my blood to his soul; and his soul shall never hunger nor thirst but shall be filled.*[1119]

> *And this shall ye do in remembrance of my body, which I have shown unto you. And it shall be a testimony unto the Father that ye do always remember me. And if ye always remember me ye shall have my Spirit to be with you...[and in regard to the wine] And this shall ye do to those who repent and are baptized in my name; and ye shall do it in remembrance of my blood, which I have shed for you, that ye may witness unto the Father that ye do always remember me. And if ye do always remember me ye shall have my Spirit to be with you.*[1120]

In regard to the use of wine, Jesus told him:

[I]t mattereth not what ye shall eat or what ye shall drink when ye partake of the sacrament, if it so be that ye do it with an eye single to my glory—remembering unto the Father my body which was laid down for you, and my blood which was shed for the remission of your sins.[1121]

As a consequence, bread and water are taken each Sunday "in remembrance of" the body and blood of Christ with the promise that, by so doing worthily, "His Spirit will be with us."[1122] *The Book of Mormon* also teaches that those who are unworthy as a result of serious sin should not partake of the sacrament, and if the priesthood officiators know someone is unworthy, they should not administer the sacrament to him or her, but they should not deny them admission to the worship meetings of the Church if they are earnestly seeking the truth.[1123]

6. GRACE AND WORKS.

One of the most important doctrinal differences developed by Martin Luther was in regard to the relationship of grace and works. *The Bible* is full of references to the importance of works—see, for example, Revelations 20:12, where John saw the dead, small and great stand before God and the dead were judged "according to their works," Paul's teachings to the Corinthians, "For we must all appear before the judgment seat of Christ; that every one may receive the things done in the body, according to that he hath done, whether it be good or bad,"[1124] and James' teaching, "But wilt thou know, O vain man, that faith without works is dead."[1125] But in Luther's time he was very anxious that the majority of Christians were practicing an outward form of ceremonialism, but did not have real faith in, and an understanding of, the role of Jesus Christ as their Savior:

[F]aith in Christ is to be esteemed far above all works. On this account St. Paul contended mightily against the law of Moses and against human tradition so that we should learn that we do not become good in God's sight by our works but that it is only through faith in Christ that we obtain grace for Christ's sake. This teaching has been almost completely

extinguished by those who have taught that grace is to be earned by prescribed fasts, distinctions among foods, vestments, etc.[1126]

As a monk, Luther had tried rigorous discipline and had become convinced that he could never do enough to save himself, and, no matter how hard he tried, he could not always avoid sins, either of commission or omission. He had true Augustinian guilt. Paul had told the Ephesians, "For by grace you are saved through faith; and that not of yourselves: it is the gift of God; not of works, lest any man should boast." [1127] He discovered in reading Paul's epistle to the Romans that "the just shall live by faith"[1128]—this became Luther's doctrine of "justification by faith," which enabled men to release their guilt and experience joy in the atonement of Jesus Christ for their sins. This became one of Luther's most ardent teachings and was designed to down-play the importance of a person's own merit and to increase the recognition that no salvation was possible without the atonement (grace) of Jesus Christ. Philip Melanchthon, in the *Augsburg Confession*, the most influential of the Lutheran creeds, wrote:

It is also taught among us that we cannot obtain forgiveness of sin and righteousness before God by our own merits, works or satisfactions, but that we receive forgiveness of sin and become righteous before God by grace, for Christ's sake, through faith, when we believe that Christ suffered for us and that for his sake our sin is forgiven and righteousness and eternal life are given to us. [1129]

It is also taught among us that such faith should produce good fruits and good works and that we must do all such good works as God has commanded, but we should do them for God's sake and not place our trust in them as if thereby to merit favor before God.[1130]

Luther quoted Ambrose, the early Catholic bishop:

It is ordained of God that whoever believes in Christ shall be saved, and he shall have forgiveness of sins, not through works but through faith alone, without merit[1131]

Where Luther found contradictory teachings, for example, in James ("faith without works is dead"[1132]), he down-played or disregarded them, characterizing James as an "epistle of straw."[1133] He is once reported to have said he would give his "doctor's beret" if anyone could reconcile the teachings of Paul and James on the subject of grace and works.[1134] Luther became almost fanatic about the issue, "The Gospel preaches nothing of the merit of works; he that says the Gospel requires works for salvation, I say flat and plain he is a liar."[1135] "Astoundingly, Luther was willing to call the Sermon on the Mount 'the devil's masterpiece' since its emphasis on works seemed incompatible with Luther's understanding of grace."[1136] Luther characterized as "childish and useless works rosaries, the cult of saints, monasticism, pilgrimages, appointed fasts, holy days, brotherhoods, etc."[1137] The Calvinists argued that it was no use pretending to good works because the scriptures teach, "For all have sinned and come short of the glory of God."[1138]

> *Wherefore we should seem to bring in and set up Judaism again if we should multiply ceremonies or rites in the Church according to the manner of the Jewish Church.*[1139]

As the Reformers systematically eliminated ceremonies, including sacraments and sacramentals that they argued were not based on scripture, the Catholic Church saw the doctrine of justification by faith as nothing more than expecting salvation by a mere verbal confession that Jesus was the Christ. As a result, they reemphasized the importance of "works" to man's salvation, citing such scriptures as Jesus', Paul's and John's sayings:

> *Not every one that saith unto me, Lord, Lord shall enter the kingdom of heaven; but he that doeth the will of my Father which is in heaven.*[1140]

> *For the Son of man, shall come in the glory of his Father with his angels; and then he shall reward every man according to his works.*[1141]

> *And why call ye me, Lord, Lord, and do not the things which I say?*[1142]

> *[In the judgment day God] will render to every man according to his deeds.*[1143]

> *Be not deceived; God is not mocked: for whatsoever a man soweth, that shall he also reap.*[1144]

> *Little children, let no man deceive you: he that doeth righteousness is righteous, even as he is righteous.*[1145]

The Catholics asked how Jesus' commandment, "Be ye therefore perfect as your Father in heaven is perfect"[1146] could have any meaning if our works and effort were of no account. Luther was forced to concede that works had some relevance: "Good works do not make a man good, but a good man does good works."[1147] And that "Faith is a living, restless thing. It cannot be inoperative. We are not saved by works; but if there are no works, there must be something amiss with faith."[1148]

Today, the Catholic Church teaches that "grace is necessary for salvation," but maintains the "principal means of grace are the sacraments (especially the Eucharist), prayer and good works."[1149]

The doctrine of The Church of Jesus Christ, as expressed in *The Book of Mormon* and the revelations Joseph Smith received from Jesus Christ, was that this was a false dichotomy. Both "grace" and "works" are important to salvation. One terse scripture in *The Book of Mormon* expressed the relationship as follows:

> *For we labor diligently to write, to persuade our children, and also our brethren, to believe in Christ, and to be reconciled to God; for we know that it is by grace we are saved, after all we can do.*[1150]

This was understood to mean that we need to be diligent in performing the commandments of Jesus Christ, but, in the end, all men will sin and then, for those who have accepted Christ and are sincerely trying to follow his teachings, the "grace" of the atonement of Jesus Christ will pay the price of punishment for such sins. The third "Article of Faith" of the Church also refers to both of these principles: "We believe that through the Atonement of Christ, all mankind may be saved, by obedience to the laws and ordinances of the

Gospel."[1151] In regard to ordinances, such as baptism and confirmation, the Lord told Joseph Smith:

> *Wherefore he that prayeth, whose spirit is contrite, the same is accepted of me, if he obey mine ordinances. He that speaketh, whose spirit is contrite, whose language is meek and edifieth, the same is of God if he obey mine ordinances.*[1152]

It was useless to argue that either grace or works was not important. C.S. Lewis commented on the Catholic-Protestant debate on this issue by saying:

> *Christians have often disputed as to whether what leads the Christian home is good actions, or faith in Christ. I have no right really to speak on such a difficult question but it does seem to me like asking which blade in a pair of scissors is most necessary . . . The Bible really seems to clinch the matter when it puts the two things into one amazing sentence. The first half is, 'Work out your own salvation with fear and trembling'—which looks as if everything depended on us and our good actions: but the second half goes on, 'For it is God who worketh in you'—which looks as if God did everything and we nothing.*[1153]

This is consistent with Paul's teachings to Titus:

> *[T]o be ready to every good work . . . But after the kindness and love of God our Saviour towards man appeared, not by works of righteousness which we have done, but according to his mercy he saved us, by the washing of regeneration, and renewing of the Holy Ghost . . . that being justified by his grace we should be made heirs according to the hope of eternal life . . . I will that thou affirm constantly that they which believed in God might be careful to maintain good works. Those things are good and profitable unto men.*[1154]

Professor Dummelow attributed the different emphases on faith and works in Paul's teaching simply to the fact that Paul was addressing different groups, and for one, more emphasis on faith was necessary, while for another, more emphasis on works was necessary.

Eastern Orthodox Christians also emphasize a unity of faith and works.[1155]

7. ELECTION AND PREDESTINATION.

Related to the foregoing subject—the role of works in our salvation—the Reformers, who emphasized grace, also taught election or predestination. Ironically, the earliest Christian advocate of election and predestination was Augustine, the most influential Catholic scholar until Thomas Acquinas. Augustine concluded that there was a "fixed number of the elect."[1156]

> *I have said all this about those who have been predestined to the kingdom of God, whose number is so fixed that no one can be added to it, or taken from it . . . The number of the elect is fixed, not to be increased or diminished.*[1157]

He maintained that the elect are saved by "irresistible grace."[1158] However, the Catholic Church, at the Council of Orange, convened by Pope Gregory in 592 A.D., rejected predestination and in its conclusion, proclaimed that 'all men, after having received grace by baptism, can with the cooperation of God, accomplish that which is necessary for the salvation of their souls.'[1159]

Dante, in his exposition of Christian doctrine in the 1300's, says:

> *The greatest gift which God in His bounty bestowed in creating, and the most conformed to His own goodness, and that which he prizes most, was the freedom of the will, with which the creatures that have intelligence, they all and they alone, were and are endowed.*[1160]

Martin Luther, as an Augustinian monk, emphasized the importance of the grace of God as a gift to justify men's salvation. Luther taught:

> *[M]an possesses some measure of freedom of the will which enables him to live an outwardly honorable life and to make choices among the things that reason comprehends. But without the grace, help and activity of the Holy Spirit man is not capable of making himself acceptable to God, of fearing God and believing God with his whole heart, or of expelling inborn evil lusts from his heart.*[1161]

When Erasmus, the Enlightenment scholar, challenged Luther in regard to God's electing some persons for salvation and damning others, Luther argued that we can tell it's the work of God because it does not make sense to man:

> *Common sense and natural reason are highly offended that God by his mere will deserts, hardens, and damns, as if he delighted in sins and in such eternal torments, he who is said to be of such mercy and goodness. Such a concept of God appears wicked, cruel and intolerable, and by it many men have been revolted in all ages. I myself was once offended to the very depth of the abyss of desperation, so that I wished I had never been created. There is no use trying to get away from this by ingenious distinctions. Natural reason, however, much it is offended, must admit the consequences of the omniscience and omnipotence of God.*
>
> *If it is difficult to believe in God's mercy and goodnesswhen he damns those who do not deserve it, we must recall that if God's justice could be recognized as just by human comprehension, it would not be divine. Since God is true and one, he is utterly incomprehensible and inaccessible to human reason.*[1162]

John Calvin, in his study of the scriptures, agreed with Luther that grace was far more important than works, and found in *The Bible* a doctrine that he described as "election," and that others have characterized as predestination. In Calvin's reading of the epistles of Paul he thought he had detected that God had "elected" certain persons to salvation and others to hell at God's pleasure. Moreover, no one could know during this life what their destiny would be, so we should seek to do good in case we are one of those elected to heaven. "Calvin claimed that even before the creation, God chose some of his creatures for salvation and others for destruction."[1163] In the *Second Helvetic Confession*, Heinrich Bullinger, the successor to Ulrich Zwingli in Zurich, Switzerland set forth the belief of the "Reformed" churches:

> *God has from the beginning freely, and of his pure grace, without any respect of men, predestinated or elected the saints, whom he will save in Christ, according to the saying of the apostle, "He chose us in him before the foundation of the world"(Eph. 1:4) . . .*[1164]

In *The Westminster Confession of Faith* the authors wrote:

By the decree of God, for the manifestation of his glory, some men and angels are predestinated unto everlasting life, and others foreordained to everlasting death. These angels and men, thus predestinated and foreordained, are particularly and unchangeably designed; and their number is so certain and definite that it can not be either increased or diminished.[1165]

Those that were predestined to everlasting life were chosen "without any foresight of faith or good works or perseverance in either of them," that this was according to the "unsearchable counsel" of God's will "whereby he extended or withholdeth mercy as he pleaseth," and that such persons, even if they commit sins, "can never fall from the state of justification:"[1166]

They whom God hath accepted in his Beloved, effectually called and sanctified by his Spirit, can neither totally nor finally fall away from the state of grace; but shall certainly persevere therein to the end, and be eternally saved. The perseverance of the saints depends, not upon their own free-will, but upon the immutability of the decree of election, flowing from the free and unchangeable love of God the Father . . .[1167]

Since election appeared to deny that man has free will or that his works are of any importance, and characterizes God as being arbitrary, if not unjust, the Catholic Church rejected Calvin's position. The scriptures often give hope to all men and women who seek salvation:

God will render to every man according to his deeds: to them who by patient continuance in well doing seek for glory and honour and immortality, eternal life: But unto them who are contentious and do not obey the truth, but obey unrighteousness, indignation and wrath, tribulation and anguish, upon every soul of man that doeth evil . . . . For there is no respect of persons with God.[1168]

Christ became the author of eternal salvation to all them that obey him.[1169]

[We should pray for kings and all men] for this is good and acceptable in the sight of God our Savior, who will have all men to be saved, and to come unto the knowledge of the truth.[1170]

The Catholics concluded that any acceptance of predestination would have the result that men would become indifferent to learning and practicing the commandments of God or trying to make this life better for themselves and others. Father McSorley summarizes the modern position of the Catholic Church as follows:

The church teaches that man needs the grace of God to begin, to continue, and to persevere in the way of salvation, but that man on his part, must co-operate with grace. Salvation, therefore, depends upon both divine grace and human free will; and it is heretical to exaggerate either of these elements to exclude the other. At one extreme, Pelagius overemphasized the human will and minimized divine grace. Predestinarians [Augustinians] exaggerated grace and minimized the will.[1171]

Catholics teach that men have freedom of choice:

God created man a rational being, conferring on him the dignity of a person who can initiate and control his own actions . . . Freedom is the power, rooted in reason and will, to act or not to act, to do this or that, and so to perform deliberate actions on one's own responsibility. By free will one shapes one's own life. Human freedom is a force for growth and maturity in truth and goodness; it attains its perfection when directed toward God . . .[1172]

The more one does what is good, the freer one becomes. There is no true freedom except in the service of what is good and just. The choice to disobey and do evil is an abuse of freedom and leads to 'the slavery of sin.' Freedom makes man responsible for his acts to the extent they are voluntary.[1173]

Although it may seem contradictory to the doctrine of original sin, the Catholic Catechism teaches:

> *God predestines no one to go to hell; for this, a willful turning away from God (a mortal sin) is necessary, and persistence in it until the end.*[1174]

> *By free will, he [man] is capable of directing himself toward his true good. He finds his perfection 'in seeking and loving what is true and good.'*[1175]

C.S.Lewis thought that God's knowledge was not foreknowledge, but present knowledge based on God being outside of time:

> *You never suppose that your actions at this moment were any less free because God knows what you are doing. Well, he knows your tomorrow's actions in just the same way—because He is already in tomorrow and can simply watch you.*[1176]

Under the Catholic practice adults who receive baptism sign the "Book of the Elect" when they are baptized.[1177] At that time:

> *The Church makes its 'election,' that is the choice and admission of those catechumens who have the dispositions that make them fit to take part, at the next major celebration, in the sacraments of initiation. This step is called election because the acceptance made by the Church is founded on the election by God, in whose name the Church acts.*[1178]

A more modern day variation of the doctrine of predestination is that preached by the Jehovah's Witnesses, that only 144,000 will be saved.[1179]

The Lord provided to Joseph Smith divine insight on this issue. Due in part to translation errors, the references in *The Bible* to election were ambiguous, confusing and conflicting. Joseph was taught that men and women were created as spirit children of God long before this earth was organized and births began here. Living in heaven with God, those spirits were instructed and progressed in knowledge. When such progress had reached its limits in the spirit form, God announced that an earth would be created where each spirit would receive a body and would learn to overcome the temptations of sin. Based on God's knowledge of each spirit child's progress in the spirit world, God "foreordained" certain persons to be leaders and play key roles in the history of the earth. These included the prophets and, the most important, Jesus Christ. Despite such foreordination, each person would retain their free agency, would have the ability to choose good and evil and would be accountable for their sins. He also foresaw, based on his knowledge of our personalities and progress in the pre-earth school that certain spirits would likely choose evil when they came to earth and experienced temptation. Nevertheless, they were to be placed under no impediment, they would be encouraged by the righteous, and they could receive all the promised blessings if they would choose righteousness. In addition, to fulfill certain promises that God would make to certain righteous persons such as Abraham, a number of righteous spirits would be born through certain lineages, for example, Jesus and the House of Israel through the lineage of Abraham. It thus became clear that the "election" being referred to by Paul in some of his epistles was in fulfillment of these promises of lineage. In *The Book of Mormon* there is an account of the Zoramites, who prayed:

> *[W]e believe that thou hast elected us to be thy holy children . . . and thou has elected us we shall be saved, whilst all around us are elected to be cast by thy wrath down to hell . . . .*[1180]

The prophet Alma declared that "such wickedness among this people doth pain my soul."[1181]

A scribe records that Joseph Smith spoke on the subject of election, and:

> *Read the 9th chapter of Romans, from which it was evident that the election there spoken of was pertaining to the flesh, and had reference to the seed of Abraham, according to the promise God made to Abraham saying, 'In thee, and in thy seed, all the families of the earth shall be blessed.' To them belonged the adoption and the covenants, etc. Paul said, when he saw their unbelief, 'I wish myself accursed'—according to the flesh—not according to the spirit. Why did God say to Pharaoh, 'For this cause have I raised thee up?' Because Pharaoh was a fit instrument—a wicked man, and had committed acts of cruelty of the most atrocious nature.*

> *The election of the promised seed still continues, and in the last day, they shall have the Priesthood restored unto them, and they shall be the 'saviors on Mount Zion,' the ministers of our God: if it were not for the remnant which was left, then men might now be as Sodom and Gomorrah. The whole of the chapter had reference to the Priesthood and the house of Israel; and unconditional election of individual to eternal life was not taught by the Apostles, God did not elect or predestinate, that all those who would be saved, should be saved in Christ Jesus, and through obedience to the Gospel; but he passes over no man's sins, but visits them with correction, and if His children will not repent of their sins He will discard them.*[1182]

Joseph further learned that whatever "election" or opportunity to know and live the gospel one might receive in this life, that such persons must make their election "sure," as Peter had taught:

> *Wherefore, the rather, brethren, give diligence to make your calling and election sure: for if ye do these things ye shall never fall.*[1183]

This would be accomplished by righteous living and receiving the sealing ordinances of the temple.[1184] Jesus taught Joseph Smith that those who are faithful in obtaining the Priesthood of Aaron and the Priesthood of Melchizedek and magnifying their calling are sanctified by the Spirit and "become the elect of God."[1185]

Joseph further taught that God did not predestine anyone to wickedness. One of the changes in the translation of *The Bible* that Jesus Christ directed Joseph Smith to make was where the text indicated in the Old Testament, "God hardened Pharaoh's heart," to "Pharaoh hardened his heart against God," which makes clear that each of us are constantly exercising our free will to choose good or evil, and that we cannot shift the responsibility for such choices to God.

8. MARRIAGE AND FAMILY.

For many of the Reformers the primary concern in regard to Catholic doctrine on marriage and family was the celibacy of priests, monks and nuns. Luther was a celibate priest, had been a monk for 19 years, and believed he should honor his vow not to marry. According to Professor Bainton:

> *Yet even St. Thomas Acquinas himself declared the taking of the cowl to be a second baptism, restoring the sinner to the state of innocence which he enjoyed when first baptized. The opinion was popular that if the monk should sin thereafter, he was peculiarly privileged because in his case repentance would bring restoration to the state of innocence. Monasticism was the way par excellence to heaven.*[1186]

But the Reformers cited such scriptures as Paul's statement to Timothy:

> *Now the Spirit speaketh expressly, that in the latter times some shall depart from the faith, giving heed to seducing spirits, and doctrines of devils, speaking lies in hypocrisy having their conscience seared with a hot iron, forbidding to marry . . . .*[1187]

To Timothy that bishops "must be the husband of one wife,"[1188] to Titus that the elders in the Church should be "the husband of one wife"[1189] and to the Corinthians, "Nevertheless neither is the man without the woman, neither the woman without the man, in the Lord."[1190] They could find no support for monasticism or the vow of chastity, particularly as creating a status of superior spirituality. Instead, they found that God created Eve as a companion for Adam because "it is not good that the man should be alone,"[1191] and commanded Adam to "cleave unto his wife"[1192] and "to be fruitful and multiply." [1193] Finally, they pointed out that the early Church historian Eusebius had taught that all the apostles, including Peter and Philip were married and had families.[1194] History was clear that, although there had been a local council in Elvira Spain as early as 306 A.D. enjoining celibacy at a time when the clergy included both unmarried men and married men,[1195] the Catholic Church never declared the marriage of priests unlawful until the Second Lateran Council in 1139.[1196] The report of the Council of Nicaea held in 325 A.D. states, "On the question of clerical celibacy the Council inclined to require continence of married priests; but Paphnutius, Bishop of Upper Thebes, persuaded his peers to leave unchanged the prevailing custom, which forbade marriage after ordination, but permitted a priest to cohabit with a wife whom he had married before ordination." [1197] The Eastern Orthodox Church allowed marriage for bishops before ordination and deacons and priests could marry at any time.[1198] According to the historian Will Durant,

> *In the ninth and tenth centuries the marriage of priests was customary in England, Gaul and north Italy. Pope Hadrian II (867-72) himself had been a married man; and Bishop Raherius of Verona (tenth century) reported that practically all priests in his diocese were married. By the beginning of the eleventh century celibacy in the secular clergy was exceptional.*[1199]

The Reformers pointed to the many scandals arising from celibacy, including illegitimate children of popes and priests.

> *Celibacy of the clergy introduced two great abuses. Many so-called celibate clergy in fact lived with women who were not their wives (called subintroductae), a practice repeatedly condemned by church councils and writers. Jerome was particularly biting about such disgraceful behavior. Also, enthusiastic men were tempted to desert their wives in order to follow the celibate life. A Roman law of 420 expressly forbade this.*[1200]

Zwingli said, "I know of no greater scandal than the prohibition of lawful marriage to priests, while they are permitted, on payment of a fine, to have concubines. Shame!"[1201]

Based on these considerations, all of the Reformers including Luther eventually married. As Professor Bainton states it, Luther's earliest writings are "unguarded in creating the impression that the sole object of marriage is to serve as a remedy for sin;" however, after Luther's own marriage his emphasis shifted to portraying marriage as a "school for character."[1202] Luther also thought that the father should "check up on the children at least once a week."[1203] In the *Augsburg Confession* the Lutherans stated:

> *It can be demonstrated from history and the writings of the Fathers that it was customary for priests and deacons to marry in the Christian church of former times . . . It was only four hundred years ago that the priests in Germany were compelled by force to take the vows of celibacy. At that time there was such serious and strong resistance that an arch-bishop of Mayence [Mainz] who had published the new papal decree was almost killed during an uprising of the entire body of priests.*[1204]

The Lutherans concluded Christians may marry "without sin." In regard to monasticism they wrote:

> *In the days of St. Augustine the monastic life was voluntary. Later when true discipline and doctrine had become corrupted, monastic vows were invented, and the attempt was made to restore discipline by means of these vows as if in a well-conceived prison. It was claimed that monastic vows were equal to Baptism, and that by monastic life one could earn forgiveness of sin and justification before God . . . They also claimed that more merit could be obtained by monastic life than by all other states of life instituted by God . . .*[1205]

Professor Bainton summarized Luther:

> *Monastic vows rest on the false assumption that there is a special calling, a vocation, to which superior Christians are invited to observe the counsels of perfection while ordinary Christians fulfill only the commands; but there simply is no special religious vocation, declared Luther, since the call of God comes to each man at the common tasks.*[1206]

The Reformed churches taught that marriage or celibacy was equally acceptable to God. Those "who have the gift of chastity" may serve God in that "calling" as long as they feel themselves endowed with the "heavenly gift," but they should not "lift themselves up above others."[1207] In regard to communities takings vows of chastity they wrote:

We, therefore, knowing certainly that monks and the orders or sects of them, are instituted neither by Christ nor by his apostles, we teach that they are so far from being profitable that they are pernicious and hurtful unto the Church of God.[1208]

No man may vow to do anything forbidden in the Word of God, or what would hinder any duty therein commanded, or which is not in his own power, and for the performance whereof he hath no promise or ability from God. In which respect, popish monastical vows of perpetual single life, professed poverty, and regular obedience, are so far from being degrees of higher perfection, that they are superstitious and sinful snares, in which no Christian may entangle himself.[1209]

The Lutherans "condemned" "those who teach that Christian perfection requires the forsaking of house and home, wife and child."[1210] As a result, in general, neither celibacy nor monasticism is practiced in modern Protestant churches.

Currently, both continence and celibacy are required for Roman Catholic clergy (except married deacons) based on Matthew 19:12 and Paul's teachings in I Corinthians 7:32-35.[1211] The Catholic Church does recognize that marriage is a desirable state—in the sacrament of the marriage ceremony the priest says, "Father, by your plan man and woman are united, and married life has been established as the one blessing that was not forfeited by original sin or washed away in the flood."[1212] Those being married recite, "I take you for my lawful wife [husband], to have and to hold from this day forward, for better, for worse, for richer for poorer, in sickness and in health, until death do us part."[1213] But the Church also esteems those who forego marriage for the "sake of the kingdom of God," i.e., taking Holy Orders. According to the Roman Catholic scholars Jacques Dupuis and Josef Neuner:

Till the third century, bishops and priests were mostly married. As a result of the growing awareness of a close bond between priesthood and celibacy, by the fourth century the unmarried clergy became the majority; by then too, ordained ministers were forbidden to enter the married state. Celibacy, however, was not imposed as a rule, but continence in marriage was gradually required from the married clergy of the Western Church. The first document which witnesses to this is found in the Council of Elvira, Spain (c. 300-03)(cf. DS 119). In the sixth century continence became a clear obligation for the clergy of the Western Church. Recent popes have reaffirmed that, though there is no bond of necessity between ministry and celibacy, as is made clear by the practice of the Eastern Church, there exists nevertheless a clear harmony between the two which recommends that the long tradition of the Western Church be preserved.[1214]

The Catechism says:

Some forego marriage in order to care for their parents or brothers or sisters, to give themselves more completely to a profession, or to serve other honorable ends. They can contribute greatly to the good of the human family.[1215]

Parents should welcome and respect with joy and thanksgiving the Lord's call to one of their children to follow him in virginity for the sake of the Kingdom in the consecrated life or in priestly ministry.[1216]

In regard to divorce and children, the Roman Catholic Church teaches that divorce is not permitted, that marriage between two baptized persons, even of different faiths, is a sacrament and "cannot be dissolved by any human power or for any reason, save death."[1217] "The matrimonial union of man and woman is indissoluble: God himself has determined it: 'what therefore God has joined together, let no man put asunder.'"[1218] This contract is to "live together till death."[1219] If divorced persons remarry they are then "in a situation of public and permanent adultery" and cannot receive Eucharistic communion as long as this situation persists.[1220] Only if certain conditions existed at the time of the commencement of the marriage can it be annulled by the Church. The pope can also dissolve marriages (1) between two non-baptized persons if one of the persons is thereafter baptized, (2) the marriage was never consummated, or (3) between a baptized person and a non-baptized person if one of the parties either becomes a Catholic or wishes to marry a Catholic.[1221] Despite the indissolubility of marriage in this life and the Church's teaching that from a valid marriage arises a bond between the spouses which by its very nature is "perpetual,"[1222] "Virginity for the sake of the kingdom of heaven is an unfolding of baptismal grace…a sign which also recalls that marriage is a reality of this present age which is passing away."[1223] As to children, no artificial contraception is permitted—only natural rhythm birth control is acceptable.[1224] Abortion is grounds for automatic excommunication.[1225]

The Reformers allowed for divorce, for example, as taught by Jesus, for adultery, and modern Protestant churches allow for divorce for various reasons, and for contraception and abortion. The Eastern Orthodox Church also permits divorce in certain circumstances, and re-marriage after divorce.[1226]

Joseph Smith was never instructed by Christ to implement any monastic practices, perhaps for some of the reasons discussed in Part I, Section 11, "Non-Attachment or Love." The Lord commanded the Church members to marry. Joseph was instructed that Paul's teachings in I Corinthians 7 extolling the single life applied only to those who were called to full time missionary service for the Church and during such time only. Any marriage made before a person is baptized into the Church should be held sacred and fulfilled.[1227] Bishops in the Church can perform marriage ceremonies between members and non-members of the Church, however as discussed hereafter in Section 14, "Temple Worship," Joseph was taught that marriage could be more than "until death do you part." Through the "sealing" power of the priesthood, members of the Church who wished to unite for "time and all eternity" could do so, and these same opportunities would apply to all those who had lived in former ages of the earth. Joseph taught:

> *Except a man and his wife enter into an everlasting covenant and be married for eternity, while in this probation, by the power and authority of the Holy Priesthood, they will cease to increase when they die; that is, they will not have any children after the resurrection. But those who are married by the power and authority of the priesthood in this life, and*

> *continue without committing the sin against the Holy Ghost, will continue to increase and have children in the celestial glory.*[1228]

Joseph learned that Christ's statement that there would be no marriage or giving in marriage after this life [1229] pertained only to those who are wicked (such as the Pharisees to whom Jesus spoke) and who do not comply with the requirements of the sealing ordinances. The Church teaches that all those who are physically and mentally able should marry and have children. All those who live righteously and desire to be married will have the opportunity in the Millennium if they have not had that opportunity in this life. Those whose children have died will have the opportunity in the Millennium of raising the children to adulthood. Through raising children we best understand how much our Heavenly Father loves us as his children and in sacrificing for them we learn true selflessness.

Divorce is permitted, although discouraged. For temple marriages, the principle of free will or "agency" continues to apply and no person "sealed" to another person will be forced to continue to be married to such person against their will, either in this life or after the resurrection. For those who chose not to marry, or did not comply with the requirements of the sealing ordinances when given the opportunity, they would remain "separate and single" throughout all eternity. Birth control is permitted, although all healthy couples are encouraged to have children. Abortion is permitted in case of grave danger to the life of the mother or rape or incest. To strengthen the family, they are to gather once a week for "Family Home Evening" for spiritual discussion and recreation.

9. MARY, SAINTS AND RELICS.

In Catholic practice prayers can be addressed to either the Father, Jesus Christ, or the Holy Ghost[1230] (in the "Trinity" they are one person), and both the Father and the Son are addressed as "Lord."[1231] St Augustine said, and the current Catholic Catechism says, that Christians pray to "Jesus as our God"[1232] and to the Holy Spirit.[1233] In addition, in Catholic doctrine prayers to, and adoration of, Mary, the mother of Jesus—in particular, the Ave Maria[1234]—and prayers to, and veneration of, the martyrs and canonized saints, is permitted and encouraged. These are also accorded anniversaries and commemorative services.[1235] As stated in *The Penguin Dictionary of Saints*:

> *Cultus, Cult (from Lat., colere, 'to honor') As regards the saints, cultus is the reverence evinced by individuals for a particular saint; but more especially it is the totality of the veneration, and its expression in public religious acts, given to a saint, constituting his 'public cultus', local or universal . . . . A common manifestation of cultus of a saint is prayer addressed to him or her; this is more exactly described as prayer to God through a saint . . .*[1236]

The Church did distinguish between the worship given to God and the "veneration" given to saints. This veneration ("dulia" in Greek) includes "honoring the saints and seeking their intercession with God."[1237] The term "hyperdulia" is applied to veneration of Mary and "latria" for the veneration of God.[1238]

According to Professor Gasque:

> *The martyrdom of Polycarp, whose execution was recorded so lovingly by a disciple, was celebrated annually by his church at Smyrna. This celebration became the pattern for the practice of venerating the martyr's remains and commemorating their death. Later the belief developed that prayers addressed to God through the martyrs were especially effective.*[1239]

Initially, the process of canonization of "saints" was local by bishops. The first saint canonized by Rome was St. Ulrich by Pope John XV in 993 A.D.,[1240] and in the twelfth century, Pope Alexander III reserved all canonizations to Rome.[1241] According to Durant, "The Church arranged an ecclesiastical calendar in which every day celebrated a saint; but the year did not find room for the 25,000 saints that had been canonized by the tenth century."[1242] The "Roman Martyrology" was first officially approved by the Catholic Church in 1584 and has been added to since then. It lists 4,500 names.[1243] The Bollandists, a society of Catholic Jesuits, has compiled the "Acts of the Saints" (Acta Sanctorum) in 67 volumes and it is still in progress.[1244] This "hagiographical" literature has been admitted by

Catholic scholars to consist of a mixture of biography, "myth, folklore, legend and romantic and edifying fiction."[1245] The decisions regarding "sainthood" have not always been consistent. For example, in 1431 the Catholic Church burned Joan of Arc at the stake for heresy, but in 1920 she was canonized as a saint.

Caroline Marshall has written:

> *In the Middle Ages, popular religion concentrated on the least abstract expressions of faith. Particularly popular were veneration of the saints, especially the Virgin Mary, emphasis on the relics and their shrines, pilgrimages, and heroic efforts to recapture the Holy Land.*[1246]

Ronald Finucane says:

> *The cult of the Virgin became very popular in later medieval Christianity. Shrine after shrine was dedicated to her throughout Europe. The use of the rosary, the 'Hail, Mary', the feast of the Virgin became increasingly common.*[1247]

A Dominican preacher who lived between 1428-1475 in northern France successfully propagated the devotion of the rosary—a series of prayers to Mary, counted on a string of beads.[1248]

In regard to Mary specifically, the Catholic Donald Attwater states:

> *In the Roman Catholic church it is an article of faith that God preserved Mary from the taint of 'original sin' from the first moment of her conception in her mother's womb (her 'immaculate conception'); and also, without denying her natural death, that at the end of her earthly life he took her to Heaven in both soul and body (her 'assumption'). The second of these beliefs is commonly held also by the Christians of the ancient churches of the East.*[1249]

The Franciscan Catholic Felician Foy summarized:

> *She was conceived without original sin (her Immaculate Conception) through the application to her of the merits of her Son before His redemptive death and resurrection. She was full of grace and sinless throughout her life. She was a virgin before, in and after the birth of Jesus . . . At his resurrection, Jesus bequeathed her to all peoples as spiritual mother.*[1250]

Louis De Montfort, who was born in 1673 and canonized as a saint by the Roman Catholic Church in 1947, wrote *True Devotion to Mary*, *The Secret of the Rosary* and *The Secret of Mary*.[1251] In the *True Devotion to Mary*, he prescribed a number of practices, including the recitation of the Rosary prayer to include 15 decades of the "hail Marys," every morning saying "sixty or a hundred times, Ave Maria, Virgo Fidelis" (Hail Mary, Faithful Virgin)," and carrying a picture or image of her with the person.[1252] He advocated saying the following prayer:

> *Hail Mary, beloved Daughter of the Eternal Father, admirable Mother of the Son, faithful Spouse of the Holy Ghost, august Temple of the most Holy Trinity! Hail, sovereign princess, to whom all owe subjection in Heaven and on earth! Hail, sure refuge of sinners, Our Lady of Mercy, who has never refused any request. All sinful though I am, I cast myself at thy feet and beseech thee to obtain from Jesus, thy beloved Son, contrition and pardon for all my sins, as well as the gift of divine wisdom. I consecrate myself entirely to thee and all that I have. I choose thee today for my Mother and Mistress. Treat me, then, as the least of thy children and the most obedient of thy servants. Listen, my princess, listen to the sighs of a heart that desires to love and serve thee faithfully. Let it never be said that all of all those who have had recourse to thee, I was the first to be abandoned. O my hope, O my life, O my faithful and Immaculate Virgin Mary, defend me, nourish me, hear me, teach me and save me. Amen.*[1253]

During the review of his writings in 1853 for beatification as a saint, the Catholic Church determined that his writings were exempt from all errors and Pope Leo XIII granted a plenary indulgence for all persons who practice Montfort's *True Devotion to Mary*.[1254]

Today, "Catholics pray to God through Mary because they believe she is a powerful intercessor and that, in keeping with what Christ said on Calvary, 'Behold thy mother!', she is the mother of all mankind."[1255]

Currently, when someone is baptized into the Catholic Church, the "Litany of the Saints" is led by the cantors which includes a request to the following saints that they pray for those receiving baptism:

> *Mary, Saint Michael, Gabriel, Raphael, Holy Angels of God, Abraham, Moses, Elijah, Saint John the Baptist, Saint Joseph, Saint Peter and Saint Paul, Saint Andrew, Saint John, Saint James, Saint Thomas, Saint Matthew, Saint Luke, Saint Mark, Saint Barnabas, Saint Mary Magdalene, Saint Stephen, Saint Ignatius, Saint Polycarp, Saint Justin, Saint Lawrence, Saint Cyprian, Saint Boniface, Saint Thomas Becket, Saint John Fisher, Saint Thomas More, Saint Paul Miki, Saint Isaac Jogues, Saint John de Brebeuf, Saint Peter Chanel, Saint Charles Lwanga, Saint Perpetua, Saint Felicity, Saint Agnes, Saint Maria Goretti, Saint Leo, Saint Gregory, Saint Ambrose, Saint Jerome, Saint Augustine, Saint Athanasius, Saint Basil, Saint John Chrysostom, Saint Martin, Saint Patrick, Saint Cyril, Saint Methodius, Saint Charles Borromeo, Saint Francis de Sales, Saint Pius, Saint Anthony, Saint Benedict, Saint Bernard, Saint Francis, Saint Dominic, Saint Thomas Acquinas, Saint Ignatius Loyola, Saint Francis Xavier, Saint Vincent de Paul, Saint John Vianney, Saint John Bosco, Saint Catherine, Saint Teresa, Saint Rose, Saint Louis, Saint Monica, Saint Elizabeth 'all holy men and women,' and others may be added, such as the patron saint of the place.*[1256]

Bringing the baptized infants to the altar of Mary is the custom in the Catholic Church.[1257] When a penitent seeks absolution for his or her sins, after confession of the sins to "almighty God" he or she is to "ask blessed Mary, ever virgin, all the angels and saints" to "pray for me to the Lord our God."[1258]

The Reformers could find nothing in *The Bible* that justified any adoration, prayers to, worship of, or intercession by, Mary or the saints and felt that directing any adoration to anyone except God the Father through the mediation of Jesus Christ was blasphemous. The Calvinists stated:

> *Let all the prayers of the faithful be poured forth to God alone, through the mediation of Christ only, out of a true faith and pure love. As for invocation of saints, or using them as*

intercessors to entreat for us, the priesthood of our Lord Christ and true religion will not permit us.[1259]

They further held that only Jesus Christ was sinless throughout his life and that it was doubtful that Mary continued as a virgin because *The Bible* expressly refers to Jesus' birth as Mary's "first-born" son,[1260] refers to normal matrimonial relations between Mary and Joseph after his birth,[1261] and expressly refers to Jesus' brothers and sisters in several places, including by their names.[1262] (The Catholic Church teaches that Jesus' "brethren" were "sons of Joseph by a former wife" or "cousins" of Jesus).[1263]

Some are of the opinion that the doctrine of the Trinity contributed to the popularity of the cult of the saints—when the Church taught that God the Father and Jesus Christ were the same person, there was no mediator to soften the harsh judgments of God that they feared, so they turned to Mary and the saints. Ramon Smullin says:

Jesus intercedes with the Father in our behalf. When the people heard all three Persons were in the same substance, they searched for another intercessor. This is when people began to pray to saints and to rely upon the works of these dead people (in the mass and in indulgences) to cleanse them from their sins instead of Jesus Christ.[1264]

Others claimed that the adoration of Mary was taken over and substituted for the worship of Diana, the Roman goddess. Professor Richard Todd writes:

The veneration of the Virgin Mary was probably stimulated by parallels to pagan religion. Some scholars believe that the worship of [the Greek goddess] Artemis (Diana) was transferred to Mary.[1265]

However, it is more likely that the doctrine that original sin was entailed upon children was the principal cause. When the Church began to teach the doctrine of original sin it became clear that Mary, as a mortal woman would have passed that sin to her son, Jesus Christ, but this was inconsistent with the Church's teaching that Jesus Christ was sinless throughout his life and baptism was received by him merely as an example, not because he needed forgiveness of sins. The only way out was to promulgate the doctrine that Mary was also born sinless—this is known as the Immaculate Conception, and refers to the birth of Mary, not Jesus. All this led the Reformers to accuse Catholics of engaging in "Mariolatry." Luther said:

> *[I]t cannot be proved from the Scriptures that we are to invoke saints or seek help from them. 'For there is one mediator between God and men, Christ Jesus'(I Timothy 2:5), who is the only saviour, the only highpriest, advocate, and intercessor before God (Romans 8:34) . . . 'If anyone sins we have an advocate before the Father, Jesus Christ the righteous'(I John 2:1)*[1266]

The "Reformed" Christian churches taught:

> *Religious worship is to be given to God, the Father, Son and Holy Ghost; and to him alone: not to angels, saints, or any other creature: and since the fall [of Adam and Eve], not without a Mediator; nor in the mediation of any other but of Christ alone.*[1267]

Consequently, no Protestant Church today prays to, venerates, or worships Mary or any of the other canonized saints. The veneration of Mary by Catholics has continued, however, and in 1854 Pope Pius IX proclaimed the dogma of the "Immaculate Conception" of Mary, making her the only person besides Christ who was born without original sin.[1268] He said:

> *[T]he doctrine which affirms that the Blessed Virgin Mary has been preserved and freed from all contamination of original sin from the first instant of her conception by a grace and special privilege of the all-powerful Lord and in view of the merits of Christ, the Savior of mankind, is a doctrine revealed from God, and that for this motive, all the faithful must believe with firmness and constancy.*[1269]

The current *Catechism of the Catholic Church* further says:

> *Mary benefited first of all and uniquely from Christ's victoryover sin: she was preserved from all stain of original sin and by a special grace of God committed no sin of any kind during her whole earthly life.*[1270]

By the grace of God Mary remained free of every personal sin her whole life long.[1271]

In 1950 Pope Pius XII declared the dogma of the "Assumption of Mary,"[1272] i.e., that "The Immaculate Mother of God, the ever Virgin Mary, having completed the course of her earthly life, was assumed body and soul into heavenly glory."[1273] She was "exalted by the lord as Queen over all things [the Queen of Heaven or Queen of All Saints]" and by her prayers "will deliver our souls from death."[1274]

Therefore, the Blessed Virgin is invoked in the Church under the titles of Advocate, Helper, Benefactress, and Mediatrix.[1275] *The liturgical feasts dedicated to the Mother of God and Marian prayer, such as the rosary, an 'epitome of the whole Gospel,' express this devotion to the Virgin Mary.*[1276] *From the Church he [the Christian] learns the example of Holiness and recognizes its model and source in the all-holy Virgin Mary . . .*[1277]

The Eastern Orthodox Church honors Mary "most" among the saints, believes she was born in original sin, but was cleansed at the time the angel announced her motherhood, believes she committed no actual sin during her life, but does not believe that she was assumed bodily into heaven."[1278]

While formerly each of the saints had their "feast day" on the calendar, in 1969 the Roman Catholic Church drastically reduced on its General Calendar the number of days on which commemoration of a saint is appointed or allowed.[1279] Today, the Church "recommends the veneration of the Blessed Mother and the cult of the saints."[1280] It proposes the saints as "models and intercessors."[1281]

Their intercession is their most exalted service to God's plan. We can and should ask them to intercede for us and for the whole world.[1282]

The veneration of relics was directly related to the veneration of saints. The Roman Catholic Professor of Theology, Franz Zaver von Funk has said:

Whereas the veneration of images was opposed in both East and West, that of the saints was everywhere popular. New

> *feasts were established in their honor...their remains, or even fragments of them, were everywhere in great demand and though at first their relics were religiously preserved in the churches, it soon became customary to carry them about in procession, to bear them in battle, and to dispose of them in exchange for alms destined for the building of churches.*[1283]

According to Professor Barker, "Since the Seventh General Council (787), the bishops were forbidden to consecrate new churches which possessed no relics."[1284] Similarly, the Church taught that veneration of the relics of the righteous, such as the apostles or martyrs, collected in many Christian churches could reduce a person's time in purgatory. The True Cross on which Christ had been crucified was alleged to have been discovered by the Roman Emperor Constantine's mother in 326 A.D.[1285] In Luther's own castle church at Wittenburg, Germany his political prince, Frederick the Wise, elector of Saxony, had collected many relics.

> *The collection had as its nucleus a genuine thorn from the crown of Christ, certified to have pierced the Savior's brow. Frederick so built up the collection from this inherited treasure that the catalogue illustrated by Lucas Cranach in 1509 listed 5,005 articles, to which were attached indulgences calculated to reduce purgatory by 1,443 years. The collection included one tooth of St. Jerome, of St. Chrysostom four pieces, of St.Bernard, six, and of St. Augustine four; of Our Lady four hairs, three pieces of her cloak, four from her girdle, and seven from the veil sprinkled with the blood of Christ. The relics of Christ included one piece from his swaddling clothes, thirteen from his crib, one wisp of straw, one piece of the gold brought by the Wise Men and three of the myrrh, one strand of Jesus' beard, one of the nails driven into his hands, one piece of bread eaten at the Last Supper, one piece of stone on which Jesus stood to ascend into heaven, and one twig of Moses' burning bush. By 1520 the collection had mounted to 19,013 holy bones. Those who viewed these relics on the designated day and made the stipulated contributions might receive from the pope indulgences for the reduction of purgatory, either for themselves or others, to the*

extent of 1,902,202 years and 270 days. These were the treasures made available on the day of All Saints.[1286]

James Harvey Robinson in *An Introduction to the History of Western Europe* says:

Princes rivaled each other in collecting the relics of saints . . . In the time of Luther, Fredrick the Wise . . . had accumulated no less than five thousand of the sacred objects. In a catalogue of them, we find the rod of Moses, a bit of the burning bush, thread spun by the virgin, etc. The elector of Mayence possessed even a larger collection, which included forty-two whole bodies of saints and some of the earth from a field near Damascus out of which God was supposed to have created man.[1287]

According to Professor Bainton:

Popes frequently specified how much benefit could be derived from viewing such holy bones. Every relic of the saints in Halle, for example, was endowed by Pope Leo X with an indulgence for the reduction of purgatory by four thousand years. The greatest storehouse for such treasures was Rome. Here in the single crypt of St. Callistus forty popes were buried and 76,000 martyrs. Rome had a piece of Moses' burning bush and three hundred particles of the Holy Innocents. Rome had the portrait of Christ on the napkin of St. Veronica. Rome had the chains of St. Paul and the scissors with which Emperor Domitian clipped the hair of St. John. The walls of Rome near the Appian gate showed the white spots left by the stones which turned to snowballs when hurled by the mob against St. Peter before his time had come. A church in Rome had the crucifix which leaned over to talk to St. Brigitta. Another had a coin paid to Judas for betraying our Lord. Its value had greatly increased, for now it was able to confer an indulgence of fourteen hundred years. The amount of the indulgences to be obtained between the Lateran and St. Peter's was greater than that afforded by a pilgrimage to the Holy Land. Still another church in Rome possessed the twelve-foot beam on which Judas hanged himself. This, however, was not strictly a relic and doubt was permitted as to its authenticity. In front of the Lateran were the Scala Sancta, twenty eight stairs, supposedly those which had once stood in front of Pilate's palace. He who crawled up them on hands and knees repeating a Pater Noster for each one, could thereby release a soul from purgatory. Above all, Rome had the entire bodies of St. Peter and St. Paul. They had been divided to distribute the benefits among the churches. The heads were in the Lateran, and one half of the body of each had been deposited in their respective churches.[1288]

Saint Louis of France (1214-1270) spent an enormous amount of money buying many relics, including the Crown of Thorns and a part of the True Cross from the Latin emperor of Constantinople. For them he built the largest reliquary ever made—the Sainte-Chapelle in Paris.[1289] The historian Will Durant says:

A church in St. Omer claimed to have bits of the True Cross, of the lance that had pierced Christ, of His cradle and His tomb, of the manna that had rained from heaven, of Aaron's rod, of the altar on which St. Peter had said Mass, of the hair, cowl, hair shirt and tonsure shavings of Thomas a Becket, and of the original stone tablets upon which the Ten Commandments had been traced by the very finger of God. The Cathedral of Amiens enshrined the head of St. John the Baptist in a silver cup. The abbey of St. Denis housed the crown of thorns and the body of Dionysius the Areopagite. Each of three scattered churches in France professed to have a complete corpse of Mary Magdalen; and five churches in France that they held the one authentic relic of Christ's circumcision. Exeter Cathedral showed parts of the candle that the angel of the Lord used to light the tomb of Jesus, and fragments of the bush from which God spoke to Moses. Westminster Abbey had some of Christ's blood, and a piece of marble bearing the imprint of His foot. A monastery at Durham displayed one of St. Lawrence's joints, the coals that had burned him, the charger on which the head of the Baptist had been presented to Herod, the Virgin's shirt, and a rock marked with drops of her milk. The churches of

Constantinople, before 1204, were especially rich in relics; they had the lance that had pierced Christ and was still red with His blood, the rod that had scourged Him, many pieces of the True Cross enshrined in gold, the 'sop of bread' given to Judas at the Last Supper, some hairs of the Lord's beard, the left arm of John the Baptist . . . . All relics were credited with supernatural powers, and a hundred thousand tales were told of their miracles. Men and women eagerly sought even the slightest relic, or relic of a relic, to wear as a magic talisman—a thread from a saint's robe, some dust from a reliquary, a drop of oil from a sanctuary lamp in the shrine. Monasteries vied and disputed with one another in gathering relics and exhibiting them to generous worshipers, for the possession of famous relics made the fortune of an abbey or a church . . . So profitable a business enlisted many practitioners; thousands of spurious relics were sold to churches and individuals; and monasteries were tempted to 'discover' new relics when in need of funds. The culmination of abuse was the dismemberment of dead saints so that several places might enjoy their patronage and power.[1290]

Luther exclaimed:

What lies there are about relics! One claims to have a feather from the wing of the angel Gabriel, and the Bishop of Mainz has a flame from Moses' burning bush. And how does it happen that eighteen apostles are buried in Germany when Christ had only twelve?[1291]

Luther was concerned that the buying and selling of these relics by political leaders and churches was deceiving the common people. Luther protested vehemently and sought to teach that men should avoid sin and not rely on relics to avoid the pains of hell.

Today, the Catholic Church teaches that the altars on which the Eucharistic sacrifice is celebrated "should contain a relic of a martyr or other saint."[1292] They further teach:

First class relics are parts of the bodies of saints and instruments of their penance and death; second-class relics are objects which had some contact with their persons. Catholic doctrine condemns the view that relics are not worthy of veneration.[1293]

The members of The Church of Jesus Christ of Latter-day Saints pray exclusively to God the Father in the name of Jesus Christ and do not venerate any saints or relics.

10. THE TRINITY.

The concept of the Trinity—three Gods—the Father, the Son and the Holy Ghost in one "person"—was a long time in being formulated. The earliest purported formulation, the "Apostles Creed"—supposedly composed by the Apostles on the tenth day after Christ's ascension into heaven—was shown by Lorenzo Valla to not actually have been formulated until the sixth or seventh century A.D.[1294] The initial official promulgation of the doctrine of the "Trinity" was at the Council of Nicaea in 325 A.D. It was based on Athanasius' arguments, on behalf of the "pope" [bishop] of Alexandria, Egypt, that the scriptures declare, "I and my Father are one,"[1295] "[T]he Father is in me and I in him,"[1296] and "[H]e that hath seen me hath seen the Father."[1297] The Creed of Nicaea was debated for 50 years before it became the consensus of the Church.[1298] In fact, following Nicaea, the bishops of the Eastern Church met in Antioch in 341 A.D. and formulated their creed that the Father, Son and Spirit are "three as persons" but one "in agreement" or harmony of will.[1299] After that, in the Western church the doctrine was not complete until the fifth century.[1300] In the Middle Ages, Acquinas wrote, "It is impossible to attain the knowledge of the Trinity by natural reason."[1301] In Dante's *The Divine Comedy* he writes, "Foolish is he who hopes our reason may compass the infinite course taken by One Substance in Three Persons." [1302] Today, the *Catechism of the Catholic Church* says:

The Trinity is a mystery of faith in the strict sense, one of the 'mysteries that are hidden in God, which can never be known unless they are revealed by God.'[1303]

The Catholic Church admits that the concept of the Trinity is not wholly Biblical:

> *In order to articulate the dogma of the Trinity, the Church had to develop its own terminology with the help of certain notions of philosophical origin: 'substance,' 'person' or 'hypostasis,' 'relation' and so on. In doing this, she did not submit the faith to human wisdom, but gave a new and unprecedented meaning to these terms, which from then on would be used to signify an ineffable mystery, 'infinitely beyond all that we can humanly understand.'*[1304]

The true formulators of this concept of God was Origen, a Greek convert to Christianity (b.185 d. 254 A.D.), and the Christian school in Alexandria, Egypt. Origen, who was steeped in the philosophy of Plato and had studied with the Neoplatonists, tried to reconcile the teachings of the Christians with the one, unknowable, spirit accepted as God by the philosophical Greeks.[1305] By teaching that God the Father was a spirit who had been incarnated in Jesus Christ (i.e., they were the same "person"), Origen believed that the Greek philosophy and Christianity could be reconciled and missionary work among the Greeks would be easier for Christians. Earlier, Philo, a Jew who was a contemporary of Jesus, also contributed to the synthesis by trying to reconcile Judaism's monotheism with the single, immaterial spirit God of Plato.[1306] Augustine, around 400 A.D. battled against the pagan philosophies, but he believed that Plato's philosophy was compatible with Christianity. "It is evident that none come nearer to us than the Platonists," he wrote.[1307]

The German and Swiss Reformers did not seriously question the doctrine of the Trinity. By that time this doctrine was well settled in Catholic theology after having been the subject of innumerable debates in the early councils of the Christian churches. Since none of the Reformers claimed to have any direct experience with God they accepted the current interpretation. This was despite the fact, as noted by S.G.F Brandon, "Judaism, Islam and Christianity claim to be monotheistic but the title of Christianity is disputed by the other two on the grounds that the doctrine of the trinity is tritheism."[1308] In Switzerland, a "Unitarian," Michael Servetus was put to death by John Calvin for heresy. In Poland and Hungary such men as Faustus Socinus, and in England, Joseph Priestly, established Unitarianism. In the United States William Ellery Channing, the minister of the Congregational Church in Boston promoted it, and the Harvard Divinity School became the center of Unitarian thought.[1309] According to Dr. Ian Sellers:

> *Unitarianism rejects the idea of the Trinity. It questions the divinity of Christ and of the Holy Spirit in favor of the oneness of God.*[1310]

Such deeply religious thinkers as John Milton and Sir Isaac Newton both concluded that the doctrine of the Trinity was not the doctrine of *The Bible*—that Christ, though the Son of God, was not equal in time or power with God the Father.[1311]

For Joseph Smith it was not a matter of reasoning or trying to interpret scripture. When he determined to ask God which of all the churches were true he had no preconceived notion of God except that taught by the Roman Catholic and Protestant churches of his day. When God the Father and Jesus Christ appeared to him at the same time he understood that they were distinct persons and that both had the form of men. It was only later, after obtaining such knowledge from direct experience, that he and other students of the scripture compared what Joseph Smith saw to what the scriptures taught. As described in Part I, both the Old and New Testaments, are filled with references to seeing God, God possessing human-like qualities and God the Father speaking to Jesus Christ. Indeed, every Jewish and Christian theologian of any consequence has felt compelled to "explain away" these clear references by "spiritualizing" them or arguing that these references are merely "allegorical." Once Joseph had such knowledge by direct experience he did not have to accept the then-current interpretations in the creeds such as the "homousia" and same-substance doctrines. Jesus himself had referred to "the Father" and "your heavenly Father' fourteen times in the Sermon on the Mount.[1312] At Jesus' baptism and again on the Mount of Transfiguration, the apostles heard the Father's voice declaring out of heaven that Jesus was his beloved son—clearly demonstrating that they were different persons.[1313] When Jesus prayed to his Father at the Last Supper in the presence of his Twelve Apostles he said:

Holy Father, keep through thine own name those whom thou has given me, that they may be one, as we are . . . Neither pray I for these alone, but for them also which shall believe on me through their word; That they all may be one, as thou, Father art in me, and I in thee, that they also may be one in us: that the world may believe that thou hast sent me.[1314]

Jesus was clearly not expecting the apostles and other believers to inhabit or assume the same physical bodies or become the same "person." The "oneness" that Christ was referring to was a unity of purpose, a shared will to pursue righteousness. From this it was clear that the unity the Father had with Christ was not a physical unity—that they were not the same "person." In fact to invoke the law of witnesses,[1315] Jesus expressly stated that his Father and he were two separate persons.[1316]

In addition, Joseph saw clearly in the 24th chapter of Luke that Christ had a physical body after the resurrection, that he kept it while he ministered unto his apostles for 40 days, and he had it when he ascended into heaven. Consequently, if Christ had a body in heaven and God the Father was merely a spirit, the unity of the Trinity was incomplete. Currently, Catholic doctrine teaches that Christ has a body in heaven and the Father does not, but the unity of the Trinity is an "incomprehensible mystery."[1317] However, in the New Testament, when Stephen was stoned, he looked into heaven and saw God the Father, with Jesus Christ standing on his right hand, as separate persons.[1318] Joseph's doctrine was also able to maintain the proper relationship between the Son as the mediator, advocate or intercessor on behalf of humans and the Father. Paul speaks to the Romans of Christ risen again, who is at the "right hand of God, who also maketh intercession for us," and of Christ the "one mediator between God and men," while John speaks of Christ as our "advocate with the Father."[1319] Jesus Christ clearly taught that he was subordinate to the Father in many passages of scripture:

[Prayer should be made to] "Our Father which art in heaven" [not to Jesus].[1320]

Why callest thou me good? There is none good but one, that is, God."[1321]

But of that day [his Second Coming] and that hour knoweth no man, no, not the angels which are in heaven, neither the Son, but the Father."[1322]

[And when he prayed in the Garden of Gethsemane] "Father, all things are possible unto thee; take away this cup from me: nevertheless not what I will, but what thou wilt."[1323]

The Son can do nothing of himself.[1324]

And this is life eternal, that they may know thee, and Jesus Christ whom thou hast sent.[1325]

Joseph Priestly in *A History of the Corruption of Christianity* held:

Notwithstanding the supposed derivation of the Son from the Father, and therefore their being of the same substance, most of the early Christian writers thought the text 'I and my Father are one' (John 10:30) was to be understood as a unity or harmony of disposition only. Thus Tertullian observes the expression is 'unum'—one thing—not one person; and he explains it to mean unity, likeness, conjunction, and of the love that the Father bore the Son. Origen says, let him consider the text, 'All that believed were of one (unum) heart and of one (unum) soul,' and then he will understand this, 'I and my Father are one. '(unum). Novation says, 'One thing (unum) being in the neuter gender, signifies an agreement of society, not a unity of person,' and explains it by this passage in Paul: 'he that planteth and he that watereth are both one' (unum).[1326]

Early Christian "Fathers" thought that those who were teaching that the Father and the Son were one person were teaching false doctrine; for example, Hippolytus says against Noetus:

If, again, he alleges his own word when he said, 'I and the Father are one, let him [Noetus] attend to the fact, and understand that he did not say, 'I and the Father am one, but are one.' For the word are (esmen) is not said of one person, but it refers to two persons and one power. He has himself made clear when he spake to the Father concerning his disciples, 'The glory which Thou gavest me I have given them, that they may be made perfect in one; that the world may know that Thou has sent me. What have the Noetians to say to these things? Are all one body in respect of substance, or is it that we become one in the power and disposition of unity of mind.' . . . A man, therefore, even though he will it not, is compelled to acknowledge God the Father Almighty, and Christ Jesus the Son of God, who being God, became man, to whom also the Father made all things subject, himself excepted, and the Holy Spirit; and that these therefore, are three.[1327]

Jesus clearly distinguished between the separate persons when he said:

But when the Comforter is come, whom I will send unto you from the Father, even the Spirit of truth, which proceedeth from the Father, he shall testify of me.[1328]

Another ambiguity that Joseph Smith was able to clarify through the writings of the early American prophets in *The Book of Mormon* and the revelations he received directly from Jesus Christ was that Jesus Christ was the same as Jehovah, the God of the Old Testament as taught by Paul in I Corinthians 10:1-4. Catholic doctrine is that it was God the Father who was the God of the Old Testament and who was born as Jesus Christ.[1329] According to the Catholic Catechism this idea comes from Christ's statements during his ministry to the Jews that he (Jesus) was Abraham's and David's God.[1330] Instead of concluding from these scriptures that Jesus Christ was the God of the Old Testament (Jehovah) before his birth in mortal life, Catholics concluded that God the Father and Jesus Christ were the same "person." Joseph learned that God the Father had created his spirit children, that Jehovah was the first of those children,[1331] and that Jehovah had progressed outstandingly well in the pre-mortal school, sufficiently so that he had acquired the title of "God." God the Father, known in scripture as Elohim, and Jehovah planned the creation of the world and Jehovah carried it out.[1332] For example, the book of Genesis, in describing the creation of the earth, states, "And God said, Let us make man in our image, after our likeness . . . ,"[1333] further, "[T]hen your eyes shall be opened, and ye shall be as gods, knowing good and evil," [1334] finally, "And the Lord God said, Behold, Adam is become as one of us, to know good and evil . . ."[1335] Joseph learned that the plural persons referred to the participation of Jehovah with God the Father in such creation. He also learned that prior to birth spirits have the shape and form of humans, so that Jehovah, even before his birth in mortality as Jesus Christ, was recognizable to those who saw him.[1336] After the creation of the earth by Jehovah under the direction of God the Father, most of the administration of the affairs of the earth and men was delegated to Jehovah. Consequently, the God of Abraham, Isaac, Jacob, Moses and the Jews was Jehovah (or Yahweh in Hebrew) and was a spirit God in the form of a man, but God the Father had a body. When Jehovah as a spirit personage was born in a mortal body he was known as Jesus (Joshua in Hebrew) the "Christ" ("messiah" in Hebrew, "anointed one" in Greek). These revelations to Joseph enabled him to reconcile conflicting scriptures and more clearly understand the meaning of the word "God" as applied to God the Father (Elohim) and Jehovah (Jesus Christ) at different times. These revelations explained inconsistencies raised by such *Bible* scholars as Professor Dummelow:

> *There are two distinct and independent accounts of the Creation, one in Genesis 1-2:4, the other in Genesis 2:4-25 . . . Again in one set of passages, of which Genesis 1-2:4 is a type, the Almighty is called God (Hebrew Elohim), while in another set, of which Genesis 2:4-26 is an example, He is designated Lord (Hebrew Jehovah).*[1337]

Joseph learned that one of the accounts referred to the planning and spiritual creation and the other account was the physical execution of the plan.[1338] These revelations also explained the confusing language of John 1:1-15, and the references to the "Word"—Jesus Christ in his pre-mortal state, known as Jehovah and the God of the Old Testament—who was with God the Father and was made flesh as the only begotten of the Father (Elohim).

11. PRE-EXISTENCE.

One of the things Joseph Smith came to understand was that each man and woman was created and existed as a spirit child of God long before he or was born into mortality. This turned out to be consistent with many scriptures in *The Bible* that had largely been overlooked or ignored by other Christian churches. For example, "the word of the Lord " came to Jeremiah saying:

> *Before I formed thee in the belly I knew thee; and before thou camest forth out of the womb I sanctified thee, and I ordained thee a prophet unto the nations.*[1339]

In one of the books in the Catholic *Bible*, the Wisdom of Solomon, it says, "I was, indeed, a child well-endowed, having had a noble soul fall my lot; or rather being noble I entered an undefiled body."[1340] Jude speaks of our pre-mortal existence as our "first estate."[1341] (See also the many references cited in Part I, "God as Our Father," that men were created as spirit children of God). Although in one place in the Roman Catholic funeral the priest may say on behalf of the deceased, "You knew me, Lord, before I was born," [1342] the current Catholic Catechism does not appear to expressly address the issue for all men,[1343] but does teach that Jesus Christ was created by God in a spirit form and he existed long before his birth in the flesh.[1344]

One of the important insights this knowledge provides is an explanation for the different personalities that children have, even when raised in the same family, and their different talents and capabilities. A knowledge of the pre-existence allows us to understand that the progress in that school or "estate" was different for each spirit and that their capabilities came with their spirit born in their bodies. It also allows us to understand that when we were informed about the plan to create the earth, "all the sons of God shouted for joy,"[1345] because this would permit our further progress to become more like God by receiving a body and learning to overcome sin. We learn that we exercised our free will to come to the earth and that we did "ask to be born." We learn that some of God's spirit children rebelled against the plan, that their leader was Satan or Lucifer, and that they were cast out of heaven or the presence of God—these are the spirits that tempt and try to persuade mortals to disobey the commandments of God. We can understand the very important concept that, as mortals, we have power over all those spirits who do not have bodies, and that such spirits can exercise no power over us unless and until we turn away from our conscience and the commandments of God.

12. NAME OF THE CHURCH.

Despite the reference in *The Bible* to the believers in Antioch as being the first "Christians,"[1346] from *The Book of Mormon*, Joseph Smith learned that the ancient believers in Christ on the American continent were also called Christians[1347] and their church was called The Church of Jesus Christ.[1348] When Jesus Christ commanded Joseph to organize a new church he gave express commandment that the name of the church "in the last days" should be "The Church of Jesus Christ of Latter-day Saints."[1349] This apparently came as somewhat of a surprise to Joseph, in particular the addition of the phrase "Latter-day Saints." In Joseph's day, the commonly understood meaning of a "saint" was the canonized saints of the Catholic Church. However, the meaning of the name specified by the Lord soon became clear. In many passages of the New Testament, in particular the letters of Paul addressed to the churches and their members, the word "saint" was used as a reference to all the believers in Christ, not to some special minority of super-righteous persons. The Reformed Protestant churches had a similar belief:

> *Forasmuch as God from the beginning would have men to be saved, and to come to the knowledge of the truth (I Tim. 2:4), therefore it is necessary that there should always have been, and should be at this day, and to the end of the world, a Church, that is, a company of the faithful called and gathered out of the world; a communion of all saints . . . terming the faithful upon the earth saints (I Cor. 4:1) . . .*[1350]

Donald Attwater, the author of *The Penguin Dictionary of Saints*, states:

> *St. Paul, for instance, addresses himself to the saints in Achaia, at Ephesus, at Philippi, at Colossae: and by 'saints' he means all the members, the faithful of the Christian*

> *communities in those places, God's holy people, the New Israel.*[1351]

Professor Dummelow says, "All believers in Christ are 'saints' (Romans 1:7, 15:26, 16:15, I Corinthians 1:2, 6:1, 14:33, etc.)"[1352]

As the members of Christ's church were known as "saints" in the former days or the New Testament period, the members of Christ's Church on the earth prior to his Second Coming would be known as "latter-day" saints. The Catholic Church teaches the "Apostles Creed"—which refers to the Christian church as the "communion of the saints." "What is the Church if not the assembly of all the saints? The communion of the saints is the Church."[1353] The Catholic Church also says:

> *To this end catechesis for confirmation should strive to awaken a sense of belonging to the Church of Jesus Christ, the universal Church as well as the parish community.*[1354]

> *The Church, then, is 'the holy People of God,' and her members are called 'saints.'*[1355]

13. CONTINUING REVELATION.

Another thing the Catholic Church and the Reformers apparently agreed on was that revelation had ended with the life of Jesus Christ, or at least with the death of the last of the original twelve apostles. Although Jews, Muslims, and Roman Catholic and Protestant Christians all accepted the authority of the prophets of the Old Testament to receive revelation from God, the idea was that these prophets wrote all the thing we were intended to know in *The Bible* and prophesied of Christ, and Christ, in his personage, embodied the fulfillment of all revelation. For example, the current *Catechism of the Catholic Church* says:

> *The Christian economy, therefore, since it is the new and definitive Covenant, will never pass away; and no new public revelation is to be expected before the glorious manifestation of our Lord Jesus Christ.*[1356]

The Catechism quotes St. John of the Cross:

In giving us his Son, his only Word (for he possesses no other), he spoke everything to us at once in this sole Word—and he has no more to say . . . because what he spoke before to the prophets in parts, he has now spoken all at once by giving the All Who is His Son. Any person questioning God or desiring some vision or revelation would be guilty of not only foolish behavior but also of offending him, by not fixing his eyes entirely upon Christ and by living with the desire for some other novelty. [1357]

In regard to prophets, the Catholic Church teaches, "John [the Baptist] surpasses all the prophets, of whom he is the last."[1358] "In him, the Holy Spirit concludes his speaking through the prophets."[1359]

For the Protestants the end of revelation made the [H]oly scriptures to be most necessary, those former ways of God's revealing his will unto his people being now ceased.[1360] *The whole counsel of God, concerning all things necessary for his own glory, man's salvation, faith, and life, is either expressly set down in Scripture, or by good and necessary consequence may be deduced from Scripture: unto which nothing at any time is to be added, whether by new revelations of the Spirit, or traditions of men.*[1361]

According to the Catholic Felician Foy, "Prophecy disappeared after the New Testament times."[1362] The Catholic scholar Joseph McSorley says:

The apostolic deposit of faith is capable of development, of unfolding. What is obscure may be made clear; what is implicit may be made explicit; but no new revelation is ever added.[1363]

In regard to the Old Testament and the Apocrypha, Professor Dummelow says:

According to the theory of the Jewish Church, direct revelation ceased with the prophets; hence no books were admitted into the Old Testament canon which were known to have been produced after the time of Ezra and the Great Synagogue.[1364]

In the Vatican Council I in 1870 the Roman Catholic Church declared:

> *The Holy Ghost is not promised to the successors of Peter [the bishops of Rome—the popes] in order that through his revelation they might manifest new doctrine; but that through his assistance they might religiously guard and faithfully expound the revelation handed down by the Apostles, or the 'Deposit of Faith.'*[1365]

Even though the Protestants and Catholics did not agree even on what writings should be included in the canon of scripture as sacred—the Catholics accepting the Apocrypha consisting of 15 books—and the Protestants rejecting it,[1366] the passage of scripture at the end of the current edition of *The Bible* in Revelation was interpreted to mean that no further revelation could be added to *The Bible*:

> *For I testify to every man that heareth the words of the prophecy of this book, If any man shall add unto these things, God shall add unto him the plagues that are written in this book: And if any man shall take away from the words of the book of this prophecy, God shall take away his part out of the book of life, and out of the holy city, and from the things which are written in this book.*[1367]

But Biblical scholarship demonstrates that the arrangement of the order of the books of *The Bible* in the New Testament was according to length and importance, was not chronological, and that the books were written in a different order than they appear in our *Bible*s today. For example, the consensus of all *Bible* scholars, Christian and Protestant, is that the Book of Revelation was written before the Gospel of John and other books so that its arrangement at the end of the collection of books of the New Testament does not mean that nothing could be added to *The Bible*, but that nothing could be added to the Book of Revelation. Indeed, Moses himself had written in the Old Testament that nothing could be added to the words he commanded to the Israelites.[1368] Furthermore, even after Jesus Christ, who was supposed to be the end of all revelation, the first congregation of Christians at Antioch included "prophets"[1369] and Judas and Silas were also "prophets."[1370] Amos had said, "Surely the Lord God will do nothing but he revealeth his secret unto his servants the prophets."[1371] Joseph Smith repeatedly quoted Revelation 19:10, that "[T]he testimony of Jesus is the spirit of prophecy"; consequently, all those who enjoy the testimony of Jesus will have the spirit of prophecy.[1372]

More importantly, however, the question arises as to why revelation would end? Certainly, by reading the writings of the Old Testament prophets it is abundantly clear that their ministry and writings were not limited to prophesying of Jesus Christ. Not only did they prophesy of many things that were not fulfilled before or at the time of Christ, including prophecies about his Second Coming, they also gave many specific warnings to the people of their specific time period regarding particular problems. In regard to the prophecies in *The Bible* Joseph Smith said:

> *They speak plainly of great things that shall be accomplished in the last days—such as preaching the everlasting Gospel to all nations; the gathering of the elect from the four winds of heaven; the building up of Zion and Jerusalem, or the ingathering of the remnants of Jacob, and the planting them in the lands of their fathers' inheritance; the necessary preparations to meet the Savior at his second coming, with all the Saints to dwell with them in the millennial reign. And now who with The Bible in his hand, can suppose that these great and marvelous works can be accomplished by the Church without more revelations from the Lord?*[1373]

Joseph Smith wrote in the ninth Article of Faith of the Church:

> *We believe all that God has revealed, all that He does now reveal, and we believe that He will yet reveal many great and important things pertaining to the Kingdom of God.*[1374]

Joseph taught that continuing revelation is the principle that explains apparent contradictions in God's commands:

> *That which is wrong under once circumstance, may be, and often is, right under another. God said, 'Thou shalt not kill;' [Exodus 20:13] at another time he said 'Thou shalt utterly*

destroy.'[I Samuel 15:3]. This is the principle on which the government of God is conducted—by revelation adapted to circumstances in which the children of the kingdom are placed. Whatever God requires is right, no matter what it is, although we may not see the reason thereof till long after the events transpire.[1375]

Hugh B. Brown[1376] has asked the questions this way: (1) perhaps God has lost the power to communicate with us. But, this is inconsistent with the omnipotence and unchangeableness of God taught in the scriptures; (2) perhaps revelation has ceased because we no longer need God's help. Most people would agree that the problems of war, destruction and evil are such that we need God's help, guidance and warnings as much as we ever have in the course of the history of the world. (3) perhaps, God no longer loves us. Again, the scriptures repeatedly testify of God's love for us, his spirit children, and that our progress individually and collectively is his supreme concern. Joseph Smith learned that there was much that needed to be done to prepare the earth for the Second Coming of Jesus Christ, including the gathering of Israel—the Jews to Palestine, the rest to Zion—the restoration of temple worship, etc. Joseph learned that he had been "foreordained" by God in the pre-existence to do this work and that as long as he obeyed the commandments of God he would be given divine power to accomplish it. It could not, however, be accomplished without imparting the knowledge of God to Joseph by revelation, both in the form of previously written books that would be brought to light (*The Book of Mormon* and *The Book of Abraham*) and by revelations Joseph would receive himself (*The Doctrine and Covenants* and *The Book of Moses*). Joseph learned that there were prophecies in *The Bible* that would be fulfilled by the coming forth of *The Book of Mormon*, such as Ezekiel 37:15-16 and Isaiah 29.

In fact, the Catholic Church has always recognized that "revelation" was continuing in the form of spiritual manifestations of the Holy Ghost, and that personal revelation from God was necessary in order for each individual to receive the witness that Jesus was the Christ. One of the "charisms"—gifts or graces of God given to persons for the good of others and the Church—includes "prophecy."

[1377] The current Catechism states, "God can reveal the future to his prophets or to other saints."[1378] Many spiritual manifestations, such as appearances of Mary, were accepted by the Cathlolic Church as authentic. The Franciscan Felician Foy lists 70 such appearances in his book, *A Concise Guide to the Catholic Church.*[1379] According to Foy, Christ appeared to Margaret Mary Alacoque in a "private revelation" in 1675 and taught her the devotion of the "Sacred Heart" of Jesus and promised to bless every place where a picture of his heart was set up and honored, and to give the "grace of final penitence" to those who receive communion on the first Friday of nine consecutive months."[1380] Another instance was the appearance of Christ to Catherine of Sienna in response to her prayers when Christ replaced her heart with his own.[1381] Another was the appearance of Mary to St. Dominic, the founder of the Dominican order, to whom she gave the rosary.[1382] As such, communication with heaven was occurring. The Catholic doctrine, however, classifies these as "private" revelations and teaches that there is no more "public" revelation since the time of Christ. Even when the pope is deciding matters of "faith and morals" under the authority of papal infallibility, the pope is not receiving any new revelation, he is merely interpreting the "deposit of faith" in a correct manner. According to *The Catholic Encyclopedia*:

> *All subsequent revelations conferred by God are known as private revelations, for this reason that they are not directed to the whole Church, but are for the good of the individual members alone.*[1383]

The Reformers were more interested in the "gifts of the Spirit"[1384] and some, like the three "prophets" who visited Luther, and George Fox, the founder of the Quakers, decided that the Spirit was able to teach all things, and that *The Bible* was secondary, if not irrelevant. The Quakers believe in continuing revelation from God through the "Inner Light" in every man.[1385] Many of the Reformers commented that the gifts of the Spirit seemed to be much more prevalent in the writings of the early Christian Church and that the loss of these gifts was further evidence of the apostasy and corruption of the Catholic Church. Joseph Smith learned that his time period—shortly after the establishment of the first country with religious freedom

(America)—would be the time for the restitution of all things and the beginning of the dispensation of the fullness of times when the restored gospel would be preached to all the earth prior to the Second Coming of Jesus Christ. This work of preaching the restored gospel was not completed by the time of the death of Joseph Smith and successor prophets and apostles have continued that work up to this day through continuing revelation.

14. LIFE AFTER DEATH.

According to the Unitarians, "heaven and hell are myths."[1386]

The Jehovah's Witnesses say:

> *Hell is the grave, a place of rest in hope of resurrection, not a place of torment. Hell is one of Satan's lies.*[1387]

However, the Catholic and other Protestant churches generally teach that after death each person will be assigned to heaven—"Abraham's bosom"—or hell.[1388] The Calvinists summarized:

> *For we believe that the faithful, after bodily death, do go directly unto Christ, and, therefore, do not stand in need of helps or prayers for the dead, or any other such duty of them that are alive. In like manner, we believe that the unbelievers are cast headlong into hell, from whence there is no return opened to the wicked by any offices of those who live.*[1389]

There is some difference in the timing in this assignment to heaven or hell. As discussed above, Catholics allow those who have sinned, but not "gravely" or "mortally"—the so-called "venial " sins—to enter into heaven after a period of suffering in "purgatory." Cyprian had cited Matthew 5:26 and I Corinthians 3:11-15 as support for the concept of purgatory. Augustine had concluded that the existence of purgatory was "probable."[1390] In 592 A.D. at the Council of Orange Pope Gregory made belief in purgatory obligatory.[1391] Today, the Catechism states:

> *As for certain lesser faults, we must believe that, before the Final Judgment, there is a purifying fire. He who is Truth says that whoever utters blasphemy against the Holy Spirit will be pardoned neither in this age nor in the age to come.*

From this sentence we understand that certain offenses can be forgiven in this age, but certain others in the age to come . . . . [Those who are purified after death] may attain the beatific vision of God.[1392]

For those who die in mortal (grave) sin "the punishment of hell begins immediately after death and lasts forever."[1393] Augustine taught, "That hell which is also called a lake of fire and brimstone will be material fire and will torment the bodies of the damned."[1394] Those who are judged worthy of heaven will enter it immediately or "through a purification."[1395] Entering into the presence of God is the divine "beatitude" and, with the angels, contemplating God is to bring to the saved the greatest of satisfactions and happiness. A "particular" judgment will be made at the time of each person's death and a "final" judgment at the time of the end of the world and the general resurrection.[1396] Protestants, finding no support for the concept of purgatory in *The Bible*, believe that the assignment to heaven or hell is made immediately at the time of death. One thing the Catholics and Protestants agreed on was that the vast majority of the human race would go to hell. This came in part from the statements in *The Bible*, "[S]trait is the gate and narrow is the way, which leadeth unto life, and few there be that findeth it,"[1397] "many are called but few are chosen,"[1398] and "He that believeth and is baptized shall be saved; but he that believeth not shall be damned."[1399] Will Durant says:

Most Christians believed that all Moslems—and most Moslems (Mohammed excepted)—believed that all Christians would go to hell; and it was generally believed that all 'heathen' were damned . . . Pope Gregory IX condemned as heresy Raymond Lully's hope that 'God hath such love for his people that almost all men will be saved, since if more were damned than saved, Christ's mercy would be without great love.' No other prominent churchman allowed himself to believe—or say—that the saved would outnumber the damned. Berthold of Regnesburg, one of the most famous and popular preachers of the thirteenth century, reckoned the proportion of the damned to the saved as a hundred thousand to one. St Thomas Acquinas thought that

> *'in this also doth God's mercy chiefly appear, that He raiseth a few to that salvation wherefrom very many fail.'*[1400]

The Catholic Church does not believe in any Millennial reign of Christ on the earth for a thousand years—they assert that such belief is based on an "erroneous interpretation of Revelations 20:4-6," without explanation as to what is erroneous about it.[1401]

When Joseph Smith sought information on this subject, the revelations he received were very enlightening. He and Sidney Rigdon were reading in John 5:28-29 as follows:

> *Marvel not at this: for the hour is coming in which all that are in the graves shall hear his voice, and shall come forth; they that have done good, unto the resurrection of life; and they that have done evil, unto the resurrection of damnation.*

Joseph says it appeared "that if God rewarded everyone according to the deeds done in the body, the term 'Heaven,' as intended for the Saints' eternal home, must include more kingdoms than one."[1402] Perhaps he was thinking of Jesus' words to his apostles, "In my Father's house are many mansions: if it were not so, I would have told you; I go to prepare a place for you."[1403] After discussing this and pondering it for some time, he and Sidney Rigdon made it a matter of prayer. Joseph and Sidney, in the presence of about 12 other men, received a vision of the future and the eternal worlds, now recorded as Section 76 of *The Doctrine and Covenants*. Later he received another revelation, *The Doctrine and Covenants* Section 88. Together, Joseph and the Church members were able to ascertain the following:

- Prior to the death of Jesus Christ the souls of all those who died were separated into those who were righteous and those who were "wicked," which included those who had not heard the gospel of Jesus Christ.[1404] However, after Christ's death and before his resurrection he initiated the preaching of the gospel in the spirit world.[1405] This preaching has continued to the present day and will continue until the Second Coming of Jesus Christ in order that every person will have the opportunity to accept or reject the gospel.[1406]

- The resurrection of the dead will be to one of three glories, in accordance with the words of Paul in I Corinthians 15:39-42, compared in brightness and glory to the sun, the moon and the stars.
- The highest of the three glories or heavens, termed the "celestial" was the place that Paul referred to when he says that he knew a man that was caught up to the "third heaven" in II Corinthians 12:2.
- Those who obtain the highest or third heaven will be those who "received the testimony of Jesus, and believed on his name and were baptized after the manner of his burial, being buried in the water in his name . . . and receive the Holy Spirit by the laying on of the hands of him who is ordained and sealed unto this power; and who overcome by faith and are sealed by the Holy Spirit of promise, which the Father sheds forth upon all those who are just and true."[1407] It will also include those who had no opportunity to hear the gospel of Jesus Christ during their mortal life, but heard it and accepted it in the spirit world prior to Christ's Second Coming.[1408] All the foregoing will dwell in the presence of the Father and the Son forever.[1409] They will be resurrected in the "morning" of the first resurrection.[1410]
- Within the highest or third heaven, there are three divisions. The highest of these is termed "exaltation." This is the "strait" gate that is achieved by "few."[1411] Those who qualify for the two higher of these sub-divisions are those that enter into the temple ordinances. Husbands and wives who are "sealed" by priesthood authority will have the power to live together in a marriage relationship for "all eternity." They will also be the only ones among those resurrected who will continue to have the power of procreation.[1412]
- They who are "honorable men of the earth who were blinded by the craftiness of men" who did not qualify under the foregoing requirements in their mortal life will inherit the second glory, the "terrestrial."[1413] They consist of those who heard but did not accept the gospel of Jesus Christ in their mortal life, but accepted it later in the spirit world, and those who accepted the

gospel of Jesus Christ in their mortal life, but were "not valiant in the testimony of Jesus." They receive the "presence" of the Son, but "not of the fullness of the Father." They are resurrected in the "afternoon" of the first resurrection.[1414]

- Those in the foregoing two groups will reign with Christ on the earth after his Second Coming for a Millennial period of 1,000 years in accordance with Revelations 20:4, 6 and I Thessalonians 4:16.
- The third group, those who will inherit the "telestial " kingdom, are those who "received not the gospel of Christ, neither the testimony of Jesus" either in their mortal life or in the spirit world. These are "thrust down to hell," but this is further explained that they suffer for their own sins for the period of the Millennium while Christ and those of the two other glories live together as resurrected beings. At the end of this period they are resurrected in accordance with Revelations 20:5 and inherit the "telestial" glory. They are then entitled to the Holy Spirit and the ministering of angels, but not the presence of the Father or the Son.[1415]
- During the Millennial period Satan will be "bound" and will have no power to tempt or influence the righteous. At the end of that time period he will be released to make a final war against the righteous, but the "saints" will prevail (see Revelations 20:2, 7-10, Doctrine and Covenants 88:110).
- There is a fourth group who accept the gospel of Jesus Christ during their mortal life, receive the Holy Spirit, and who know and partake of the power of Jesus Christ, but permit themselves to be overcome by the power of the devil. These, the sons of Perdition (another name for Satan), commit the unpardonable sin referred to by Jesus and are resurrected, but they suffer for their own sins, receive no forgiveness and are consigned to be with Satan and his angels forever.[1416]

These revelations answer many questions about the justice of God and the Final Judgment. From this we learn that the missionary work inaugurated by Jesus Christ in the spirit world during the three days between his mortal death and resurrection continues in the spirit world.[1417] We learn that little children or others who die without hearing the true, uncorrupted gospel of Jesus Christ will have the opportunity to hear it in the spirit world and receive all the blessings that those who received it in this world were promised. We also see that those who reject the true gospel of Jesus Christ in their mortal life but accept it in the spirit world do not inherit the same glory as those who accept it in mortal life; however, those who accept the true gospel in mortal life but are not diligent in its practice will lose the highest glory, and if they engage in serious sin and do not repent, will go to the lowest—telestial—glory. We understand that the word "salvation" has different meanings as used in different scriptures.[1418] We can also see that "purgatory" as a place for punishment for sins applies only to those who do not accept the true form of Christianity in this life or, later, in the spirit world, and ends after the Millenium.

15. TEMPLE WORSHIP

In the Old Testament, the Israelites recorded their construction of the Temple of Solomon[1419] and, later, the Temple of Zerubbabel.[1420] Even prior thereto they had a portable temple, called the "tabernacle" that Moses and the Israelites carried with them when they wandered in the desert for 40 years after leaving Egypt.[1421] God gave Moses and his brother Aaron, Aaron's sons, and the tribe of Levi detailed instructions regarding the ceremonies and rituals to be performed in these temples. In particular, sacrifices of animals were to be made in the morning and evening each day. These rituals were performed as long as the Israelites had a temple. Christ was presented before God in his infancy at the temple,[1422] he attended the temple and taught the Elders when only 12 years old,[1423] he cleansed the temple, calling it his "Father's house,"[1424] and he often taught in the temple courts, such as when he observed the offering of the widow's mite.[1425] The Temple of Zerubbabel, the "second temple" was partially burned, repaired by Herod, and then was destroyed by the Roman armies in 70 A.D. After that time, Jews continued to meet in synagogues in which to pray and worship as a community, but the morning prayer of the Orthodox Jew is still, "May the holy Temple speedily be rebuilt [in Jerusalem] in our days, that we may bring before thee our daily offering,"[1426] and the prophecy that they will do so is one of the signs of the Second Coming of Jesus Christ.[1427] The Roman Catholic Church says:

> *The Temple [of Zerubbabel] prefigures his own mystery. When he [Jesus] announces its destruction, it is as a manifestation of his own execution and of the entry into a new age in the history of salvation, when his Body would be the definitive Temple.*[1428]

When Joseph Smith translated *The Book of Mormon* he learned that the ancient American people also had temples, patterned after those among the Jews and observing the same ceremonies and rituals.[1429] Joseph also learned that all of the animal sacrifices in these temples were intended as a symbol of the death that Jesus Christ—"the Lamb of God"— would experience when he surrendered his life as a sacrifice for the sins of all those who would accept him and keep his commandments. Joseph was told that as a part of the "restitution of all things" temples were to be built again. But, because sacrifice by the shedding of blood ended with the death of Jesus Christ as a method of worship, the rituals of the new temples would be different. Joseph was commanded to build a house "of prayer, a house of fasting, a house of faith, a house of learning, a house of glory, a house of order, a house of God."[1430] Jesus Christ told him:

> *I will manifest myself to my people in mercy in this house. Yea, I will appear unto my servants, and speak unto them with mine own voice, if my people will keep my commandments, and do not pollute this holy house.*[1431]

At that time and subsequently, Jesus Christ did appear to various people in the temples of the Church. Jesus Christ told Joseph that those who come to the temple would be "endowed" with power from on high and blessings would be poured out upon them.[1432] Jesus also explained that because he had initiated the preaching of the gospel in the spirit world within the three day period between his death and resurrection,[1433] the temples would be for the purpose of providing the necessary ordinances, such as baptism, for those who were accepting the gospel in the spirit world, but, no longer having a body until the resurrection, were unable to be baptized for themselves. These vicarious ordinances made it possible to fulfill the requirement of Jesus that all those who enter his kingdom must be baptized and receive the laying on of hands for the Holy Spirit. This was also consistent with the practice of the early Christian Church:

> *Else what shall they do which are baptized for the dead, if the dead rise not at all? Why are they then baptized for the dead?*[1434]

Church members could do family history research and perform these ordinances of salvation and exaltation for their families. Missing information would become known in the Millenium. Joseph further learned that the highest or "celestial " glory (see the previous Section) is divided into three divisions and that temple ordinances were necessary to qualify for the higher two of the three divisions. Church members could enter into the temple and renew their covenants with the Lord at baptism to keep his commandments and, in addition, the "sealing" ordinances of the priesthood uniting husbands, wives and families for all eternity (subject to their individual compliance with the commandments of Jesus Christ) would be performed there. Later, Joseph said:

> *The question is frequently asked, 'Can we not be saved without going through with all those ordinances?' I would answer, No, not the fullness of salvation.*[1435]

Joseph learned that many temples were to be built prior to the Second Coming of Jesus Christ and the temple work for the performance of these ordinances would continue even after the first resurrection and through the Millennium. By that time, all those who desired and qualified for the blessings associated with these ordinances would receive them.

Joseph said:

> *[T]he Church is not fully organized in its proper order, and cannot be, until the Temple is completed, where places will be provided for the administration of the ordinances of the Priesthood.*[1436]

After the Millenium and the Final Judgment the need for temples will no longer exist, as seen by the Apostle John.[1437]

16. CHURCH GOVERNMENT.

In the Old Testament times, the prophet or seer was the head of the believers in God with whom God communicated directly by personal appearance, vision or inspiration. The prophet Amos declared, "Surely the Lord God will do nothing, but he revealeth his secret unto his servants the prophets."[1438] In later times, particularly beginning in the inter-testament time period, the Jews were governed by the Sanhedrin, composed of 70 rabbis headed by the High Priest. In the time of Jesus Christ, he was head of the Christian believers, although he ordained twelve apostles[1439] and appointed "other seventy" to preach the gospel.[1440] These church leaders continued after the ascension of Jesus Christ and governed the church along with bishops (pastors),[1441] elders,[1442] evangelists,[1443] teachers[1444] and deacons.[1445] As the gospel was taken to other countries, it appears that it was typical for the apostles to establish churches with these local leaders. Paul declared that the Christian church was built upon the "foundation of the apostles and prophets, Jesus Christ himself being the chief corner stone."[1446]

As discussed in Section 2 above, the Roman Catholic Church increasingly took the position that the bishop of Rome was pre-eminent over any other bishops, particularly as conflict and competition with the Eastern Orthodox bishops increased. Eventually, the Roman Catholic Church declared the bishop of Rome (the "pope") infallible.

The Reformers generally rejected the government of their churches by bishops ("episcopal" government). Having a great disdain for consolidating the power of government in one person, particularly in light of the numerous corrupt popes they decried, they generally established government by councils of elders ("presbyterian" government). The problem, of course, was that local councils of congregations could disagree with one another on doctrine or practice and there was no uniformity. This conflicted with Jesus' prayer to be one,[1447] and Paul's teachings that there should be one faith and one baptism.[1448] National and international councils were established to bring some uniformity to the churches.

Today, the Roman Catholic Church, the Eastern Orthodox

Church, the Anglican Communion, and its American counterpart, the Protestant Episcopal Church, have episcopal governments. The bishop of Rome, the Pope, centrally controls the doctrine and practices of the Roman Catholic Church and authorizes ordination of all bishops. The Patriarch of Constantinople being "first among equals" is generally regarded as the spiritual leader of world Orthodoxy. The Archbishop of Canterbury is regarded as the world leader of Anglicans and Episcopalians, although he does not have the authority of the Roman Catholic pope and merely presides over a general convention of delegates from national conventions.[1449] The Baptists, Congregationalists, Disciples of Christ, Jehovah's Witnesses, Lutherans, Presbyterians, Quakers, Seventh-day Adventists and Unitarians have councils of elders or directors who govern the churches.[1450] The Methodists are somewhat of a hybrid with local congregations governed by bishops and with periodic councils of the bishops.[1451] In certain groups, like the Baptists, Congregationalists, Disciples of Christ. Lutherans, and the Unitarians, the local congregation is supreme (the local church is a "law unto itself" and the "freedom of the congregation is inviolable"); in other groups, like the Jehovah's Witnesses, Presbyterians, and Seventh-day Adventists, local congregations are subject to higher, regional, national or international conferences, conventions or boards of directors.[1452]

When The Church of Jesus Christ of Latter-day Saints was initially organized, Jesus Christ instructed that Joseph Smith should be received by the members as a "prophet, an apostle of Jesus Christ, an elder of the Church,"[1453] Oliver Cowdery was to be the "second elder" of the Church, and Jesus said:

> *Wherefore, meaning the church, thou shall give heed unto all his words and commandments which he shall give unto you as he receiveth them, walking in all holiness before me; For his word ye shall receive, as if from mine own mouth, in all patience and faith. For by doing these things the gates of hell shall not prevail against you; yea, and the Lord God will disperse the powers of darkness from before you, and cause the heavens to shake for your good, and his name's glory.*[1454]

As the Church grew Jesus Christ gave further instructions

regarding the organization and government of the Church. He told the Church that three High Priests, consisting of the president of the Church and his counselors (the First Presidency), should be established.[1455] (Students of *The Bible* may recall that Peter was joined by James and John in an administrative presidency of the original apostles. Jesus had exclusively involved these three in some of the most important spiritual experiences of his ministry, including his Transfiguration on the Mount—where God the Father's voice testified of Christ's divinity and Elijah and Moses appeared[1456]—when Christ led them privately to the room where the daughter of Jairus was restored to life,[1457] and when they were allowed to observe from close range his suffering in the Garden of Gethsemane.[1458]) Further, Twelve Apostles, who would also be "prophets, seers and revelators" should officiate under the direction of the First Presidency,[1459] and finally, a quorum of Seventy to act under the direction of the Twelve Apostles[1460] should be established as the governing bodies of the Church. Other officers, such as a presiding and local bishops, elders, priests, teachers, deacons, women's organization presidencies, youth and children's organizations and presidencies were established, acting under the direction and authority of the governing bodies of the Church. Joseph Smith wrote:

> *We believe in the same organization that existed in the Primitive Church [the Church of the New Testament period], namely, apostles, prophets, pastors, teachers, evangelists, and so forth.*[1461]

Joseph taught, "It is also the privilege of any officer in this Church to obtain revelations, so far as relates to his particular call and duty in the Church,"[1462] but Joseph also taught, "[I]t is contrary to the economy of God for any member of the Church, or any one, to receive instruction for those in authority higher than themselves"[1463]—therefore, only the First Presidency would receive revelation applicable to the whole Church.[1464] In this way, the doctrine of the Church would be uniform throughout the Church worldwide. The calling and ordaining of all such officers, general and local, including the president of the Church, is subject to the approval or ratification of all the members of the Church.[1465] This principle is known as the law of "common consent."

17. CHURCH FINANCES.

Today, the Roman Catholic Church operates by contributions from its members and its extensive income generating assets.

The customary offertory collection at Sunday Mass, which includes parish envelopes, is the ordinary way the faithful support their local church. The diocese and its various agencies are supported in large part by a system of parish assessments. The diocesan bishop can levy a moderate tax on all of the public juridic persons in the diocese. The tax is to be proportionate to the income of the juridic person.

The Holy See [Rome] receives a major portion of its financial support from 'Peter's Pence,' the offerings which the bishops send each year to the pope from their dioceses. These funds, given in proportion to the resources of the diocesan church, enable the Holy See to serve the universal church[1466].

Historically, Church finance has evolved. According to Professor Todd:

Churches had begun to acquire property by the third century, but it was the extraordinary growth of church wealth in the fourth century that changed the pattern of church support. After Constantine, endowments, supplemented by government subsidies, provided the major income, although voluntary offerings always remained an important part of church income. Earlier on the bishop allocated these revenues, which resulted in abuses. By the end of the fifth century the church at Rome had devised a system by which all income from rents and offerings was divided into four parts—for bishop, clergy, the poor, and for repair and lighting of the churches. Elsewhere the distribution varied.[1467]

Will Durant says:

The widest stream of income was the tithe: after Charlemagne all secular lands in Latin Christendom were required by state law to pay a tenth of their gross produce or income, in kind or money, to the local church. After the tenth century every parish had to remit a part of its tithes to the bishop of the diocese. Under the influence of feudal ideas the tithes of a parish could be enfeoffed, mortgaged, bequeathed, or sold like any other property or revenue, so that by the twelfth century a financial web had been woven in which the local church and its priest were rather the collectors than the consumers of its tithes. The priest was expected to 'curse for his tithes,' as the English put it—to excommunicate those who shirked or falsified their returns . . . The basic revenue of the Church was from her own lands. These she had received through gift or bequest, through purchase or defaulted mortgage or through reclamation of waste lands by monastic or other ecclesiastical groups. In the feudal system each owner or tenant was expected to leave something to the Church at death; those who did not were suspected of heresy, and might be refused burial in consecrated ground. Since only a few of the laity could write, a priest was usually called in to draft the wills; Pope Alexander III decreed in 1170 that no one could make a valid will except in the presence of a priest; any secular notary who drew up a will except under these conditions was to be excommunicated; and the Church had exclusive jurisdiction over the probate of wills. Gifts or legacies to the Church were held to be the most dependable means of telescoping the pains of purgatory . . . Some monasteries, by 'confraternities' gave their benefactors a share in the merits or purgatorial deductions earned by the prayers and good works of the monks . . . As the property of the Church was inalienable, and, before 1200, was normally free from secular taxation, it grew from century to century. It was not unusual for a cathedral, a monastery, or a nunnery to own several thousand manors, including a dozen towns or even a great city or two. The bishop of Langres owned the whole county; the abbey of St. Martin of Tours ruled over 20,000 serfs; the bishop of Bologna held 2000 manors, so did the abbey of Lorsch, the abbey of Las Huelgas in Spain, held sixty-four townships. In Castile, about 1200 the Church owned a quarter of the soil; in England a fifth; in Germany a third; in Livonia one half . . . It has been calculated that the total income of the papal see about 1250 was greater than the combined revenues of all the secular sovereigns of Europe.

From England in 1252 the papacy received a sum thrice the revenue of the crown.[1468]

With centuries of gifts, bequests and landholdings, the Roman Catholic church accumulated enormous resources. Prior to Luther's time, the Catholic Church regularly appointed clergy to various positions in return for "gifts" to the Church. These appointments were valuable because they brought the appointee the income from the benefices, including real estate rentals, crops and livestock, and the Church members' contributions. The Roman Catholic James Coriden said:

The reservation of appointments to church benefices was perhaps the most offensive exercise of the fullness of the jurisdictional authority. However, an even greater abuse was the practice of 'pluralism,' that is, the simultaneous possession of several benefices by the same person. Some cardinals of the papal curia held more than fifteen offices at the same time. They were ecclesiastical positions, with incomes, all over Europe. Their holders never visited the places, to say nothing of fulfilling the sacred duties attached to the offices. They coveted the income. They might hire a substitute to perform the local ministries if they were keen of conscience. (One extreme example: As late as 1556, Cardinal Allesandro Farnese, grandson of Pope Paul III, possessed ten Episcopal sees, twenty-six monasteries, and 133 other benefices—canonries, parishes and chaplaincies.)[1469]

Prior to the Reformation, generally clergy were paid by their political ruler. James Coriden states, "In the feudal period the parish became 'privatized,' that is, owned by the local lord who entrusted its care and its income to a priest, as his job and sustenance."[1470] Professor Barker comments on the financial issues as follows:

In opposing masses for the dead, and indulgences, Luther deprived the Lutheran Church of an important source of revenue, and it became necessary to find some other means of assuring church support. Luther thought it the duty of the state to support the church by taxation. In principle, in addition to subordinating the church to the state, this did not differ from a compulsory tithing and, though effective in raising funds, it did not, because it was not voluntary, further Christian growth of character, and was without spiritual value.[1471]

One of the Reformers, Thomas Muntzer, was unusual in deciding that the pastor should not be supported by the congregation, but should support himself by working.[1472] After the Reformation, the rise of nationalism resulted in many political rulers seizing Catholic Church property. According to James Coriden this was dealt with as a compromise:

For example, the concordat with Napoleon allowed the French ruler to name bishops, but assured that the state would pay the salaries of the clergy in compensation for confiscated church property. This pact was the prototype for several subsequent agreements in the nineteenth century.[1473]

Another source of revenue was "chantries:"

Another way the pious laymen tried to reassure himself of his chances of salvation was by establishing a private chantry. During the fourteenth and fifteenth centuries more and more of these chantries were endowed. The idea was simple enough: a wealthy individual or family, even a guild, provided a sum of money for a priest to sing a mass periodically and, in 'perpetual chantries,' forever, for the soul of the benefactor. Sometimes special chantry altars were built—private chapels licensed by the local church authority. It was an easy way for a poor priest to make a bit of money, and was one of the things the more conscientious reformers disliked.[1474]

Ultimately, the Reformation began over the sale of indulgences as a method to finance the building of St Peter's Cathedral in Rome.

Today, as one of the "precepts" of the Catholic Church, "The faithful also have the duty of providing for the material needs of the Church, each according to his abilities."[1475] Catholic clergy are guaranteed a "decent remuneration" for their support by the Church[1476] Bishops of each province set the amount charged for Mass stipends and "stole fees,"—the offerings on the occasion of sacramental ministrations such as baptisms, weddings and funerals.[1477]

> *The minister should ask nothing for the administration of the sacraments beyond the offerings defined by the competent authority, always being careful that the needy are not being deprived of the help of the sacraments because of their poverty. The competent authority determines these 'offerings' in accordance with the principle that the Christian people ought to contribute to the support of the Church's ministers. 'The laborer deserves his food.'*[1478]

Priests "may take an offering" to "apply" the benefits of the Mass, for example, for the dead or any other person specified by the donor.[1479] The Franciscan Catholic Feliciano Foy also notes that tithing is mentioned 46 times in *The Bible* and states that it has "aroused new attention in recent years in the United States."[1480]

Protestant clergy are supported by the revenues of their churches, usually primarily from the collections of their own church.

In some European countries the government assesses a "church tax," which is then distributed to the various churches in accordance with the denomination indicated by the taxpayer. For example, Germany assesses 8%, Finland, 1.3% and Sweden, 2%. In Spain taxpayers can earmark .1% of their tax go to the Catholic Church or to programs for the socially needy; in Italy the taxpayer can earmark .8% of his or her taxes for the Catholic or other churches. In Belgium there are no special taxes but the government pays the wages of the clergy and maintains church buildings.[1481] As far as the author is aware, no Asian country assesses any taxes or provides any financial support to any religion except for the upkeep of public temples. In certain Middle Eastern countries governments financially support the Muslim faith by assessing the "zakat." The property on which the tax is assessed and the amount due is complicated but, "In practice, the most common measure is 2.5 percent of the amount of cash an individual holds in savings or investment for a year"—in other words, it is assessed on assets, not on income.[1482]

The Lord commanded Joseph Smith that The Church of Jesus Christ of Latter-day Saints should operate by voluntary contribution of a tithe of each member's annual income as was done in Biblical times.[1483] No charge was to be made or "contributions" accepted for the performance of any ordinance, including baptisms, confirmations, blessings of children, marriages, funerals or temple ordinances. Jesus Christ commanded that certain rich persons and certain poor persons should all repent:

> *Woe unto you rich men, that will not give your substance to the poor, for you riches will canker your souls; and this shall be your lamentation in the day of visitation and of judgment, and of indignation . . . Woe unto you poor men, whose hearts are not broken, whose spirits are not contrite, and whose bellies are not satisfied, and whose hands are not stayed from laying hold on other men's goods, whose eyes are full of greediness; and who will not labor with your own hands.*[1484]

Due to the growth in numbers of The Church of Jesus Christ and the tithes faithfully paid by its members, the Church has been able to build many new meetinghouses and temples. Those Church leaders that devote their full time to the work of the Church receive modest salaries, but most Church leaders, including local bishops who serve part time while holding secular employment, and the missionaries of the Church, receive no income from the Church.

There are other differences between The Church of Jesus Christ of Latter-day Saints and the other Christian churches. Some of them are relatively minor. There are also a large number of overlapping beliefs, mostly in the area of virtuous conduct. But the doctrines discussed above are of substantial importance to the faith of many persons who are seeking the "fullness" of Christian truth.

CONCLUSION

Is it that difficult to find the truth? The real answer is that it depends on how hard you look for it and how willing you are to accept it when you find it. Although the number of religions and sects is overwhelming, God did not intend that everyone would have to attend a religious seminary or study for years to know the truth. While there is no question that the reward for doing so is worth the effort, God's love for us and His power makes it possible for Him to guide us individually to experiences, people and scriptures through which we can find the truth. We lived together with Him for a long period of time before being born on this earth. Each of us has been given the light of Christ to teach us fundamental morality and to guide us to more truth.[1485] As a result, those who are sincerely seeking truth are able to find it and recognize it when they see it. Jesus Christ told Joseph Smith:

> *For there are many yet on the earth among all sects, parties, and denominations, who are blinded by the subtle craftiness of men, whereby they lie in wait to deceive, and who are only kept from the truth because they know not where to find it.*[1486]

However, many people really do not want to find the truth. They realize that to do so will require effort; furthermore, they are concerned that if they find something that has rules, commandments or constraints, it will interfere with the way they want to live their lives. In addition, there are many who because of strong nationalistic or patriotic loyalties, social pressure, or loyalty to family, friends or race, will not embrace truth, no matter how plainly it is presented to them.

Jesus Christ gave a very important parable in Matthew Chapter 13—the parable of the sower. The sower sows the seed, which Jesus explained to his apostles is the true word of God. Some of the seeds fall in hard places and the birds of the air eat them before they can begin to sprout. Other seeds fall in rocky places and begin to sprout, but when the sun comes out the roots are not deep, and for lack of moisture and strength, the plant dies. The third group of seeds falls in good soil and begins to grow, but eventually the weeds choke them out. The fourth group sprouts, gets its roots down, and eventually bears fruit, some 30 fold, some 60 fold and some 100 fold. Jesus explained that the soil is like the hearts of men who hear the gospel. Some hearts are hard and shut it out, saying or believing that they already know about religion, or that all religions are false, or that no religion is any better than any other religion. Another group accepts the gospel in the beginning, but they do not continue to pray, study the scriptures, attend church and give charitable service—as a result, when some adversity comes into their life, they lose their faith in God, questioning whether He really exists or whether He is aware of and loves them. The third group also accepts the gospel initially, but the weeds represent their friends and other influences that mock them for their beliefs and challenge their gospel lifestyle. Soon, peer pressure and the desire for the things of man more than the things of God drag them into inactivity and loss of faith. Only the fourth group—those who continue in the practice of the gospel, strengthening themselves, and getting their roots down, including making new friends that share their goals—are the ones that feel and see the fruits of their choice. Even then, many become impatient because they do not see the fruit as quickly as they want.

Within Christianity, Jesus told those who heard him if they would do the things he told them they would know of a surety whether his teachings were his own or whether they came from God.[1487] This is still a great promise for those who want to know about the truthfulness of Christianity. Similarly, when God initiated the restoration of the Christian Church he knew that very few people would believe Joseph Smith, an uneducated farm boy. But God provided Joseph with a new witness for Christianity and The Church of Jesus Christ of Latter-day Saints in the form of *The Book of Mormon* and the revelations given to Joseph that any person can read and evaluate for themselves. *The Book of Mormon* contains a promise near the end as follows:

Behold, I would exhort you that when ye shall read these things, if it be wisdom in God that ye should read them, that ye would remember how merciful the Lord hath been unto the children of men, from the creation of Adam even down until the time that ye shall receive these things, and ponder it in your heart. And when ye shall receive these things, I would exhort you that ye would ask God, the Eternal Father, in the name of Christ, if these things are not true; and if ye shall ask with a sincere heart, with real intent, having faith in Christ, he will manifest the truth of it unto you, by the power of the Holy Ghost. And by the power of the Holy Ghost ye may know the truth of all things.[1488]

In other words, read *The Book of Mormon* and pray about it. I think I would add that you must ask with a willingness to accept and obey the gospel of Jesus Christ and the teachings of The Church of Jesus Christ of Latter-day Saints; otherwise, your prayer is nothing more than idle curiosity and there is no real desire to know. The extent of our effort often depends on whether we have faith that God exists, that He loves us and that He will hear and answer our prayers. If we are proud and think that we know better than God how to make a good life for ourselves or what will truly make us happy, we will be unsuccessful in gaining the blessing of this knowledge. As Jesus described it, the gospel is like a pearl of great price—when a man has found it and recognizes its true value, he will go and sell all that he has to buy it[1489]—in other words, sacrifice time, money, worldly honors, and even his lifestyle, habits, addictions and sins conflicting with the gospel.

It is not the purpose of the author or The Church of Jesus Christ of Latter-day Saints to condemn other churches or their sincere believers. Joseph Smith said:

We don't ask any people to throw away the good they have got; we only ask them to come and get more.[1490]

The inquiry is frequently made of me, 'Wherein do you differ from others in your religious views?' In reality and in essence we do not differ so far in our religious views but that we could all drink into one principle of love. One of the grand fundamental principles of 'Mormonism' is to receive truth, let it come from whence it may . . . . Christians should cease wrangling and contending with each other and cultivate the principles of union and friendship in their midst.[1491]

His successor, Brigham Young, said:

The truth and sound doctrine possessed by the sectarian world, and they have a great deal, all belongs to this Church. As for their morality, many of them are, morally, just as good as we are. All that is good, lovely and praiseworthy belongs to this Church and Kingdom. 'Mormonism' includes all truth.[1492]

A later apostle of the Church, James Talmage, said:

The Church today has no fight with any other religious organization. It is not in intolerant conflict with Catholics or Protestants. It is not in conflict with men of any denomination. It's adversary is sin. The object of its attack is evil.[1493]

The purpose of The Church of Jesus Christ of Latter-day Saints is to add to the measure of truth that many people already have. Joseph Smith said, "Truth is 'Mormonism.' God is the author of it."[1494]

It is easy to accept that people are good, while believing the religions they practice contain false teachings. But it is also important to recognize that all people act in accordance with their beliefs. It is undeniable that false beliefs result in needless suffering, both for the believer and those with whom they interact. There is no ultimate happiness or salvation in following false doctrines. Finally, it is important to recognize that "[H]e that doeth righteousness is righteous,"[1495] and not rationalize that we are good because of our subjective belief that we are a "good person," unless we learn and keep the commandments of Jesus Christ. The apostle John said, "He that doeth truth [not merely believes] cometh to the light . . ."[1496]

I pray that the foregoing opinions have been communicated in a spirit of respect, with a proper balance between being indifferent about so important a subject and a fanaticism that would be contrary to the commandment, "Therefore, all things whatsoever ye would that men should do to you, do ye even so to them." As Blaise Pascal said, "Knowing about God is far from loving Him." Similarly, Brigham Young, the second prophet of The Church of Jesus Christ of Latter-day Saints, taught:

> *Do you think that people will obey the truth because it is true, unless they love it? No, they will not. Truth is obeyed when it is loved. Strict obedience to the truth will alone enable people to dwell in the presence of the Almighty.*[1497]

By reading the scriptures and serving God in accordance with the teachings of the restored gospel of Jesus Christ we can come to know God the Father and His Son through the testimony of the Holy Spirit to our own spirit, which testimony brings a conviction and peace to the soul greater than any logic or reason. I have felt that spirit many times since obeying the restored gospel and I pray that you may also know the "peace that passeth all understanding"[1498] by gaining that testimony. Then you will also understand the words of Alma the prophet:

> *Behold I testify unto you that I do know that these things whereof I have spoken are true. And how do ye suppose that I know of their surety? Behold I say unto you that they are made known unto me by the Holy Spirit of God. Behold, I have fasted and prayed many days that I might know these things of myself. And I do know of myself that they are true; for the Lord God hath made them manifest unto me by the Holy Spirit; and this is the spirit of revelation which is in me.*[1499]

And, you will be able to do as Peter counseled:

> *Be ready always to give an answer to every man that asketh you a reason of the hope that is in you with meekness and fear.*[1500]

Tom Johnson
Chicago, 2003

BIBLIOGRAPHY

A Commentary on the Holy Bible (J.R. Dummelow)(New York, New York: MacMillan Publishing Co.1909).

A Comprehensive History of the Church of Jesus Christ of Latter-day Saints (Brigham H. Roberts)(Salt Lake City, Utah: Deseret Book 1930)(6 Vols.).

A Concise Guide to the Catholic Church (Felician A. Foy)(Huntington, Indiana: Our Sunday Visitor Publishing Co. 1986)(nihil obstat).

A History of the Popes (Nicolas Cheetham)(New York, New York: Dorset Press 1982).

A Marvelous Work and a Wonder (LeGrand Richards)(Salt Lake City, Utah: Deseret Book 1958).

A Sourcebook in Indian Philosophy (S. Radhakrishnan & C. Moore)(Princeton, New Jersey: Princeton University Press 1957).

An Introduction to Canon Law (James Coriden)(New York, New York: Paulist Press 1991)(nihil obstat)

Apostasy from the Divine Church (James L. Barker)(Salt Lake City, Utah: Bookcraft 1960).

As Translated Correctly (Mark E. Petersen)(Salt Lake City, Utah: Deseret Book 1966).

Bartlett's Familiar Quotations (Sixteenth Edition)(Justin Kaplan, General Editor)(Boston, Massachusetts: Little, Brown & Company 1992).

Benet's Readers Encyclopedia (Third Edition)(New York, New York: Harper & Row Publishers, Inc. 1987).

Best Loved Stories of the LDS People, Vol. 1 (Jack M. Lyon, Linda Ririe Gundry, Jay A. Parry)(Salt Lake, City: Deseret Book 1997).

Book of Prayers (Sephardic)(David DeSola Pool)(New York, New York: Union of Sephardic Congregations 1946).

Catechism of the Catholic Church (New York, New York: Doubleday 1995).

Christian Religions: A Comparative Chart, Vols. 1, 2 (Rex Bennett)(Comparative Chart 1985).

Concept of God in Islam (Chicago, Illinois: The Institute of Islamic Information and Education [no date]).

Concluding Unscientific Postscript (Soren Kierkegaard)(Princeton, New Jersey: Princeton University Press 1941).

Creeds of the Churches (John H. Leith)(Louisville, Kentucky: John Knox Press 1982).

Discourses of Brigham Young (John A. Widtsoe)(Salt Lake City, Utah: Deseret Book 1954).

Eerdman's Handbook to the History of Christianity (Tim Dowley, Organizing Editor)(Grand Rapids, Michigan: Wm. B. Eerdmans Publishing Co. 1977).

Eerdman's Handbook to the World's Religions (Pat Alexander, Organizing Editor) (Grand Rapids, Michigan: Wm.B. Eerdmans Publishing Co. 1994).

Essays (Ralph Waldo Emerson)(New York, New York: Everyman's Library 1971)

Great Books of the Western World (Second Edition)(Mortimer J. Adler, Editor in Chief) (Chicago, Illinois: Enclyclopedia Britannica 1990)(60 Vols.) Volumes cited are the following:

Volume 1—Syntopicon (A-L)
Volume 2—Syntopicon (M-Z)
Volume 7—Aristotle
Volume 11—Epictetus
Volume 17—Thomas Acquinas
Volume 19—Dante Alighieri
Volume 20—John Calvin
Volume 23—Michel Montaigne
Volume 28—Rene Descartes
Volume 30—Blaise Pascal
Volume 32—Isaac Newton
Volume 34—Jonathan Swift
Volume 34—Voltaire [Francois-Marie Arouet].
Volume 39—Immanuel Kant
Volume 49—Charles Darwin

Here I Stand: A Life of Martin Luther (Roland H. Bainton)(New York, New York: Mentor Books 1977).

History of the Church of Jesus Christ of Latter-day Saints (Salt Lake City, Utah: Deseret Book 1951)(7 Vols.)

How to Think About God (Mortimer J. Adler)(New York, New York: Collier Books 1980).

Japanese Things (Basil Chamberlain)(Rutland, Vermont: Charles E. Tuttle Co. 1971).

Jesus the Christ (James E. Talmage)(Salt Lake City, Utah: Deseret Book 1915).

Joseph Smith's Kirtland (Karl R. Anderson)(Salt Lake City, Utah: Deseret Book 1996).

Lectures on Faith (Salt Lake City, Utah: Deseret Book 1985).

Let No Man Deceive You (Bruce D. Richardson)(Sandy, Utah: Camden Court Publishers 1998).

Life After Death (Chicago, Illinois: The Institute of Islamic Information and Education [no date]).

Luther and His Times: The Reformation from a New Perspective (Ernest Schweibert)(St. Louis, Missouri: Concordia Publishing House 1950).

Martin Luther: A Biographical Study (John M. Todd)(Newman Press 1964)

Medieval Church Treasuries (Margaret English Frazer)(New York, New York: Metropolitan Museum of New York 1986).

Offenders for a Word (Daniel Peterson & Stephen Ricks)(Salt Lake City, Utah: Aspen Books 1992).

Philosophical Dictionary (Voltaire)[Edited and translated by Theodore Besterman](London, England: Penguin Books Ltd. 1972).

Philosophy of Religion (Mel Thompson)(Chicago, Illinois: NTC Contemporary Publishing 1997).

Prophethood in Islam (Chicago, Illinois: The Institute of Islamic Information and Education [no date]).

Proslogion (Anselm)[Translated by Thomas Williams](Indianapolis, Indiana: Hackett Publishing Company, Inc 1995)

Readings in the Philosophy of Religion (Benedict A.

Brody)(Englewood Cliffs, New Jersey: Prentice Hall 1992)

Religions in America (Leo Rosten)(New York, New York: Simon & Schuster 1953)

Religions in Japan (William K. Bunce)(Rutland, Vermont: Charles E. Tuttle Company 1955).

Signs and Symbols in Christian Art (George Ferguson)(Oxford, England: Oxford University Press 1954).

Tao Te Ching (Lao Tzu [Translated by D.C. Lau])(London, England: Penguin Books 1963).

Teachings of the Prophet Joseph Smith (Joseph Fielding Smith)(Salt Lake City, Utah: Deseret Book Company 1976).

The Abolition of Man (C.S. Lewis)(New York, New York: Touchstone Books 1947).

The Analects [of Confucius] (Translated by D.C. Lau)(London, England: Penguin Books 1979).

The Book of Mormon (Salt Lake City, Utah: The Church of Jesus Christ of Latter-day Saints 1981)

The Book of Pontiffs (Lieber Pontificalis)(Raymond Davis)(Liverpool, England: Liverpool University Press 1989).

The Book of Virtues (William J. Bennett)(New York, New York: Simon & Schuster 1993).

The Case for Christianity (C.S. Lewis)(New York, New York: Collier Books 1989).

The Christian Faith in the Doctrinal Documents of the Catholic Church (J.Dupuis & Josef Neuner)(New York, New York: Alba House 1996).

The Complete Book of Jewish Observance (Leo Trepp)(New York, New York: Behrman House 1980).

The Difference of Man and the Difference It Makes (Mortimer J. Adler)(New York, NewNew York, New York: Holt, Rinehart & Winston 1967)

The Doctrine and Covenants (Salt Lake City, Utah: The Church of Jesus Christ of Latter-day Saints 1982).

The Father is Not the Son: Godhead or Trinity (Ramon D. Smullin)(Sandy, Utah: Camden Court Publishers 1998).

The Great Apostasy (James E. Talmage)(Salt Lake City, Utah: Deseret

Book 1968).

The Guide for the Perplexed (Moses Maimonides [Translated by M. Friedlander](New York, New York: Dover Books 1956).

The History of the Church from Christ to Constantine (Eusebius [G.A. Williamson, Translator])(London, England: Penguin Books 1965).

The Holy Bible (King James [Authorized] Version)(Salt Lake City, Utah: The Church of Jesus Christ of Latter-day Saints 1979)(including Joseph Smith translation in footnotes and appendices].

The Incredible Human Machine (Video)(National Geographic 1993).

The Koran (Translated by N.J. Dawood)(New York, New York: Mentor Books 1974)

The Lessons of History (Will & Ariel Durant)(New York, New York: Simon & Schuster 1968).

The Living Talmud (Judah Goldin)(New York, New York: Mentor Books 1957).

The Mishnah (Herbert Danby)(London, England: Oxford Press 1933).

The Original Illustrated Sherlock Holmes (Arthur Conan Doyle)(Secacus, New Jersey: Castle [no date]).

The Pearl of Great Price (Salt Lake City, Utah: The Church of Jesus Christ of Latter-day Saints 1982).

The Penguin Dictionary of Saints (Donald Attwater)(London, England: Penguin Books 1965).

The Philosophical Basis of Mormonism (James E. Talmage)(Salt Lake City, Utah: 1915).

The Religions of Man (Huston Smith)(New York, New York: Harper Perennial 1986).

The Rites of the Catholic Church (Second Vatican Ecumenical Council, Commission on English in the Liturgy)(New York, New York: Pueblo Publishing Co. 1990).

The Story of Civilization (Will & Ariel Durant)(New York, New York: Simon & Schuster)(11 Vols.) Volumes cited as follows:

Volume I—Our Oriental Heritage (1935)

Volume III—Caesar and Christ (1944)

Volume IV—The Age of Faith (1950)

Volume V—The Renaissance (1953)

Volume VI—The Reformation (1957)
Volume VII—The Age of Reason Begins (1961)
Volume VIII—The Age of Louis XIV (1963)
Volume IX—The Age of Voltaire (1965)
Volume X—Rousseau and Revolution (1967)
Volume XI—The Age of Napoleon (1975)

The Teaching of Buddha (Tokyo, Japan: Buddhism Missionary Foundation 1982).

The Varieties of Religious Experience (William James)(New York, New York: Mentor Books 1958).

The Wonder of God's Creation (Video) (Moody *Bible* Institute of Science 1992).

The Works of Josephus (William Whiston)(Peabody, Massachusetts: Hendrickson Publishers 1987).

The Works of Robert G. Ingersoll (Clinton Farwell)(New York, New York: The Dresden Publishing Co.1902).

The Works of Thomas Jefferson (H.A. Washington)(New York, New York: Townsend Mac Coun 1884).

Totem and Taboo (Sigmund Freud) (New York, New York: W.W. Norton & Company 1950).

True Devotion to Mary (St. Louis de Montfort [Translated by Fr. Frederick Faber])(Rockford, Illinois: Tan Books 1941).

Truth in Religion (Mortimer J. Adler)(New York, New York: Collier Books 1990).

Understanding Islam (Thomas W. Lippman)(New York, New York: Mentor Books 1990).

Voltaire: Candide, Zadig and Selected Stories (Translated by Donald M. Frame)(New York, New York: Signet Classic 1961).

Why I Am Not a Christian (Bertrand Russell)(New York, New York: Simon & Schuster 1957).

ENDNOTES

1 Cf. “Where do we come from; what is our origin? Where are we going; what is our end?,” *Catechism of the Catholic Church*, par. 282; “Know whence thou comest, wither thou art going, and before Whom thou art destined to give an accounting,” Rabbi Akabya ben Mahalalel, Sayings of the Fathers 3:1, quoted in *Book of Prayers*, p. 242.

2 *Syntopicon*, Vol. 2, p. 696, *Great Books of the Western World.*

3 *Syntopicon* Vol.1, p. 433, *Great Books of the Western World.*

4 John 17:3.

5 *The Doctrine and Covenants* 14:7.

6 *Totem and Taboo*, Part 4, Sub-part (6), p. 182.

7 “Friedrich Nietzsche” in *Benet’s Reader’s Encyclopedia*, p. 694.

8 Introduction to the Critique of the Hegelian Philosophy of Right, *Bartlett’s Familiar Quotations*, p. 481.

9 *Pensees*, Section XIV, No. 895, *Great Books of the Western World*, Vol. 30.

10 The Adventure of the Naval Treaty, *The Original Illustrated Sherlock Holmes*, p. 313.

11 Genesis, Chapter 1.

12 Genesis 2:9.

13 Isaiah 45:12.

14 Isaiah 6: 3.

15 *Discourses*, Book 1, Chapter 16, *Great Books of the Western World*, Vol. 11.

16 Entry for January 5, 1856, *Bartlett’s Familiar Quotations*, p. 477.

17 Essays, p. 81.

18 Psalms 19:1

19 Romans 1:19-20.

20 Acts 14:17.

21 *Here I Stand: A Life of Martin Luther*, p. 231.

22 Job 12:7-9.

23 Job 36:26-41:34.

24 Job 37:14.

25 Alma 30:44.

26 *History of the Church of Jesus Christ of Latter-day Saints*, Vol. 1, p. 13-14.
27 *The Wonders of God's Creation.*
28 Trees (1913), *Bartlett's Familiar Quotations*, p. 661-62.
29 Antigone, Ode I, line 333, *Bartlett's Familiar Quotations*, p. 66.
30 *The Wonders of God's Creation*; The Incredible Human Machine.
31 Moses 6:63, *The Pearl of Great Price.*
32 Mosiah 2:20-21, *The Book of Mormon*; see also *The Doctrine and Covenants* 63:3.
33 *How to Think About God*, p. 156; see also, *The Difference of Man and the Difference it Makes*; Genesis 1:26.
34 The Origin of Species, chapter XV (last paragraph), *Great Books of the Western World*, Vo. 49.
35 The Laws, 10th Book, *Great Books of the Western World*, Vol. 6.
36 Physics, Book VIII, Sections 5, 6, 10; Metaphysics, Book XII, Sections 6, 7, 8, *Great Books of the Western World*, Vol. 7.
37 *Proslogion*, Chapter 2.
38 Part I, Q2, Art.1, *Great Books of the Western World*, Vol. 17.
39 Ibid., Q2, Art. 2.
40 Part I, Q3, Art. 3.
41 Meditations on the First Philosophy, *Great Books of the Western World*, Vol. 28.
42 "General Scholium', Mathematical Principles of Natural Philosophy, *Great Books of the Western World*, Vol. 32.
43 *A Commentary on the Holy Bible*, p. xcix.
44 *Catechism of the Catholic Church*, par. 32
45 Vatican Council I, Dei Filius 2:DS 3004, 30026 quoted in, *Catechism of the Catholic Church.*, par. 36.
46 *The Guide for the Perplexed*, p. 369-71.
47 *Philosophy of Religion*, p. 96-97.
48 Summa Theologica, Part I, Q1, Art. 1, *Great Books of the Western World*, Vol. 17.
49 Job 11:7-9.
50 p. 156.
51 *Catechism of the Catholic Church*, par. 50.
52 *Creeds of the Churches*, p. 193.
53 John 1:18. Joseph Smith stated that the translation was faulty and should have read, "No man hath seen God at any time, except he hath borne record of the Son."

54 John 6:46.
55 Colossians 1:15; 1 Timothy 1:17; Hebrews 11:27.
56 Genesis 2:16-17; 3:18-19.
57 Moses 7:4, *The Pearl of Great Price*; cf. Genesis 3:22-24.
58 Genesis 12:6.
59 Genesis 15:1.
60 Genesis 17:1, 22.
61 Genesis 18:1, 22, 33.
62 Abraham 3:1, *The Pearl of Great Price.*
63 Genesis 33:20, 30.
64 Exodus 33:11.
65 Numbers 12:8.
66 Exodus 24:9-11.
67 1 Kings 3:5, 9:2, 11:9.
68 Isaiah 6:1-5.
69 Matthew 5:8.
70 Matthew 3:13-17.
71 Matthew 17:5.
72 Acts 7:55-56; see also Hebrew 1:3.
73 1 John 3:2.
74 1 Corinthians 13:12.
75 Exodus 31:18; Deuteronomy 9:10.
76 Exodus 33:23; Psalms 117:16.
77 Exodus 33:23; 1 Peter 3:12; Revelations 22:4.
78 Matthew 4:4.
79 Philippians 2:6.
80 Ezekiel 1:26-28.
81 Isaiah 30:27.
82 1 Peter 3:12; Psalms 33:16.
83 Job 40:41.
84 Philippians 3:21.
85 1 Nephi 1:8.
86 2 Nephi 11:3.
87 Alma 19:13.
88 Ether 3:13-15.
89 Joseph Smith History 1:17, *The Pearl of Great Price.*
90 *The Doctrine and Covenants* 76:2-23.
91 Lyman Wight, Harvey Whitlock, John Murdock, Zebedee Coltrin, as recorded in, *Joseph Smith's Kirtland*, p. 107-110.

92 Matthew 11:27.

93 1 Corinthians 2:11.

94 Institutes of Christian Religion, Part First, Chapter VII, par. 4, *Great Books of the Western World*, Vol. 20.

95 *Lectures on Faith*, Lecture VI, p. 67-68.

96 *Lectures on Faith*, Lecture II, p. 37.

97 Institutes of the Christian Religion, Part First, Chapter III, *Great Books of the Western World*, Vol. 20.

98 *Pensees*, Section IV, No. 278, *Great Books of the Western World*, Vol. 30.

99 General Introduction, p. xxv-xxvi, 353-355, *A Sourcebook in Indian Philosophy*.

100 *Emile*, p. 254, quoted in *The Story of Civilization*, Vol. 11, p. 181.

101 The Critique of Practical Reason, *Great Books of the Western World*, Vol. 39.

102 *The Case for Christianity*, p. 7.

103 *The Case for Christianity*, p. 20.

104 *Catechism of the Catholic Church*, par. 46.

105 *Catechism of the Catholic Church*, par. 1706.

106 *Catechism of the Catholic Church*, pars. 1776-77; see also par. 1860.

107 "What I Believe," in *Why I Am Not a Christian*, p. 74.

108 *Catechism of the Catholic Church*, par. 2072.

109 Romans 2:14-15.

110 2 Corinthians 4:2.

111 1 Timothy 4:2.

112 Ephesians 4:17-19.

113 Titus 1:15.

114 Moroni 7:16, *The Book of Mormon*.

115 *The Doctrine and Covenants* 84:46.

116 *Philosophy of Religion*, p. 6.

117 Philippians 4:7.

118 *The Varieties of Religious Experience*, p. 198-99.

119 *The Varieties of Religious Experience*, p. 215-17.

120 *Pensees*, Section III, No. 233, *Great Books of the Western World*, Vol. 30.

121 "The Will to Believe," in *Readings in the Philosophy of Religion*, p. 42, 44, 46.

122 *The Varieties of Religious Experience*, Lecture III, p. 59.

123 Ibid., Lecture II, p. 57.

[124] Ibid., Lecture XX, p. 389.
[125] *Concluding Unscientific Postscript*, p. 90
[126] Alma 32:27-28, 37-42, *The Book of Mormon.*
[127] *A Commentary on the Holy Bible*, p.civ.
[128] "What I Believe" in, *Why I Am Not a Christian*, p. 50.
[129] Essays, Of Atheism (1625), *Barlett's Familiar Quotations*, p. 159.
[130] Carlos P. Romulo, I Saw the Fall of the Philippines (1942), *Bartlett's Familiar Quotations*, p. 711.
[131] *The Varieties of Religious Experience*, p. 45.
[132] *The Case for Christianity*, p. 32.
[133] Hippolyte Taine, *The French Revolution*, Vol. 2, p. 3-4, quoted in, *The Story of Civilization*, Vol 11, p. 254.
[134] *Pensees*, Section IV, No. 357; see also Section III, No. 194, *Great Books of the Western World*, Vol. 30.
[135] *Pensees*, Section VII, No. 430, Id.
[136] *Lectures on Faith*, Lecture II.
[137] *Teachings of the Prophet Joseph Smith*, p. 137.
[138] Alma 38:15, 37:47, 42:31, *The Book of Mormon.*
[139] *Catechism of the Catholic Church*, par. 2128.
[140] *Catechism of the Catholic Church*, par. 1791.
[141] *How to Think About God*, p. 79.
[142] Id., p. 157.
[143] Hebrews 11:6.
[144] *Understanding Islam*, p. 1.
[145] *The Religions of Man*, p. 313.
[146] Sura 59:22-24, quoted in, *Concept of God in Islam.*
[147] *The Complete Book of Jewish Observance*, p. 93.
[148] *Book of Prayers* (Sephardic), p. 177.
[149] *The Living Talmud*, p. 80.
[150] Jeremiah 9:23-24.
[151] 1 Samuel 15:1-3; see the discussion in Part III, Section 13.
[152] *A Sourcebook in Indian Philosophy*, p. 4-15.
[153] *The Story of Civilization*, Vol. 1, p. 404.
[154] *A Sourcebook in Indian Philosophy*, xxvii, p. 21.
[155] Id., p. xx.; see also, "Darshana" in *Benet's Reader's Encyclopedia*, p. 239.
[156] *A Sourcebook in Indian Philosophy*, General Introduction, p. xxii.
[157] Id., p. xxvii.
[158] Id., p. 356.

159 Id., p. 17.
160 *The Story of Civilization*, Vol. 1, p. 403.
161 *The Religions of Man*, p. 36, 51, 95, 98; see also, *The Story of Civilization*, Vol. 1, p. 507.
162 "Trimurti" in *Benet's Reader's Encyclopedia*, p. 994.
163 *The Religions of Man*, p. 97-99; see also, *A Sourcebook in Indian Philosophy*, p. 506-08.
164 *The Religions of Man*, p. 136.
165 *The Complete Book of Jewish Observance*, p. 317.
166 *Religions in Japan*, p. 85.
167 *The Teaching of Buddha*, p. 42.
168 Id., p. 48.
169 Id., p. 52.
170 Id., p. 66.
171 Id., p. 352.
172 *The Lessons of History*, p. 49.
173 *The Religions of Man*, p. 186.
174 Id.
175 *Eerdman's Handbook to the World's Religions*, p. 197, 204.
176 *The Religions of Man*, p. 269-70.
177 *The Analects*, pars. 8, 9, p. 73.
178 *The Analects*, Book IV, pars. 8, 9, p. 73; Book XVI, par. 7, p. 140.
179 Id., Book VI, par. 6, p. 82.
180 Id., Book III, par. 13, p. 69; Book VI, pars. 6, 84, p. 82, 84; Book VIII, par. 21, p. 95;
181 *The Religions of Man.*, p. 234.
182 *Religions in Japan*, p. 99.
183 *Religions in Japan*, p. 125.
184 *The Story of Civilization*, Vol. 1, p. 832.
185 *Eerdman's Handbook to the History of Christianity*, p. 158; *Catechism of the Catholic Church*, pars. 242, 253; see also, *Creeds of the Churches*, p. 30.
186 *Catechism of the Catholic Church*, pars. 184 (Appendix), 194, 196; *Creeds of the Churches*, p. 24.
187 Confession of Dositheus (1672), *Creeds of the Churches*, p. 486.
188 Sermo 52, 6, 16: PL 38:360 and Sermo 117, 3,5:PL 38, 663, quoted in, *Catechism of the Catholic Church*, par. 230.
189 Saint John of Damascus, De Fide Orthodoxa, Book 1, Chapter 9, based on Saint Gregory of Nazianzus, Oration 38, *Bartlett's Familiar*

Quotations, p. 120.

190 Quoted in, *The Story of Civilization*, Vol. VI, p. 804.

191 Quoted in, *The Varieties of Religious Experience*, Lecture XVIII, p. 335.

192 p. 116.

193 *Catechism of the Catholic Church*, par. 2112.

194 *Catechism of the Catholic Church*, par. 370.

195 Chapter II, Article 1, *Creeds of the Churches*, p. 197.

196 Article I, *Creeds of the Churches*, p. 266-67.

197 The Works of Robert G. Ingersoll, Vol 2:361, quoted in, *Let No Man Deceive You*, p. 59.

198 *The Living Talmud*, p. 140.

199 "What is a Jew," in *Religions in America*, p. 106; *Christian Religions: A Comparative Chart*, Vol. 2.

200 *Summa Theologica*, Part I, Q.3, Article 1, *Great Books of the Western World*, Vol. 17.

201 *Teachings of the Prophet Joseph Smith*, p. 345.

202 Id., p. 18.

203 Brigham Young, the second prophet of the Church added: "Immaterial substance—it is like the center of a being everywhere and his circumference nowhere, or like being seated on the top of a topless throne. These are self-confounding expressions, and there is no meaning to any of them." *Discourses of Brigham Young*, p. 49.

204 *The Doctrine and Covenants* 130:22.

205 *Teachings of the Prophet Joseph Smith*, p. 345.

206 *Joseph Smith History* 1:17.

207 Genesis 2:8, 3:8.

208 Genesis 11:5, 18:21.

209 Genesis 7:16.

210 Genesis 1:26; Genesis 5:1-3.

211 James 3:9.

212 Summa Theologica, Part I, Q.2, Article 2, fn. 5, *Great Books of the Western World*, Vol. 17.

213 Histoire Critique de Manichee et du Manicheisme, Vol. 1, p. 85, quoted in Joseph Priestly, Disquisitions Relating to Matter and Spirit, p. 184-85, quoted in, *The Father is Not the Son: Godhead or Trinity*, p. 63.

214 *Offenders for a Word*, p. 74.

215 *The Story of Civilization*, Vol. VIII, p. 238.

216 *Philosophical Dictionary*, p. 219.
217 *Lectures on Faith*, Lecture III, p. 38.
218 Acts 15:18; Isaiah 46:9-10.
219 Hebrews 11:3; Genesis 1:1, Isaiah 14:24, 27.
220 Psalm 89:14, Isaiah 45:21, Zephaniah 3:5, Zechariah 9:9: Acts 10:34-35.
221 Psalm 89:14, Deuteronomy 32:4, Psalm 9:7, Psalm 9:16; Psalm 103:6-8.
222 Psalm 89:14, Exodus 34:6, Nehemiah 9:17; Psalm 103:6-8, Psalm 103:17-18.
223 Psalm 89:14, Exodus 34:6, Deuteronomy 32:4, Psalm 31:5; Numbers 23:19
224 1 John 4:8.
225 *Lectures on Faith*, Lecture IV, p. 55.
226 Malachi 3:6, James 1:17; Hebrews 1:10-12.
227 Numbers 16:22.
228 Deuteronomy 14:1.
229 Psalms 82:6.
230 Malachi 2:10.
231 Yoma 85b, quoted in, *The Complete Book of Jewish Observance*, p. 94.
232 Id., p. 41.
233 *Book of Prayers*, p. 222.
234 *The Complete Book of Jewish Observance*, p. 92.
235 Matthew 6:9.
236 Matthew 5:48.
237 Matthew 5:16, 45, 48, 6:1, 4, 6, 8, 9, 14, 15, 18, 26, 32, 7:11.
238 Luke 15:11-32.
239 Acts 17:22-31.
240 Hebrews 12:9.
241 Romans 8:16.
242 Ephesians 4:4-6.
243 "The Scripture Way of Salvation" (1765), quoted in, *Creeds of the Churches*, p. 365.
244 p. lxxix.
245 *Catechism of the Catholic Church*, par. 366.
246 *The Rites of the Catholic Church*, p. 422, 613.
247 *Catechism of the Catholic Church*, pars. 1, 460, 1214, 1243, 1250, 1265, 1709.

[248] *The Doctrine and Covenants* 76:24.

[249] John 1:11-13; Mosiah 5:7, *The Book of Mormon*.

[250] John 18:37-38.

[251] Collected Papers, Vol. 5, p. 211, quoted in, *Bartlett's Familiar Quotations*, p. 538.

[252] *The Doctrine and Covenants* 93:24.

[253] *Truth in Religion*, p. 64-65.

[254] Id., p. 135-36.

[255] *Syntopicon*, "Good and Evil," Vol 1, p. 475, *Great Books of the Western World.*

[256] *Syntopicon*, "Truth," Vol. 2, p. 730, *Great Books of the Western World.*

[257] *The Varieties of Religious Experience*, p. 31.

[258] Id., p. 326.

[259] Id., p. 323.

[260] Id., p. 324.

[261] *The Doctrine and Covenants* 50:2-3.

[262] "Ye shall know them [false prophets] by their fruits." Matthew 7:15-16.

[263] *The Varieties of Religious Experience*, p. 291.

[264] "Has Religion Made Useful Contributions to Civilization," in *Why I Am Not A Christian*, p. 30-31.

[265] "Can Religion Cure Our Troubles," in *Why I Am Not A Christian*, p. 196-97.'

[266] Hebrews 11:1; Lecture 1, *Lectures on Faith*, p. 1.

[267] *A Sourcebook in Indian Philosophy*, p. 250-51, 261-62.

[268] *The Varieties of Religious Experience*, p. 368.

[269] *Truth in Religion*, p. 3-6.

[270] Id., p. 25.

[271] Id., p. 15.

[272] John 8:31-32.

[273] *The Doctrine and Covenants* 93:30.

[274] Preface, in *Why I Am Not a Christian*, p. v.

[275] *Gulliver's Travels*, Part I, A Voyage to Lilliput, p. 22, *Great Books of the Western World*, Vol. 34.

[276] *Philosophical Dictionary*, p. 213.

[277] Ephesians 4:5-6.

[278] *Catechism of the Catholic Church*, par. 2105.

[279] *The Koran* 3:19, 81 (p. 409).

280 *The Doctrine and Covenants* 1:30.
281 *The Teaching of Buddha*, p. 558.
282 *A Sourcebook in Indian Philosophy*, p. 273.
283 *The Religions of Man*, p. 451; Religions in America, p. 92, 154.
284 *A Sourcebook in Indian Philosophy*, General Introduction, p. xx, xxii, 350.
285 *The Koran*, 30:31 (p. 194).
286 *Understanding Islam*, p. 136-65.
287 *The Complete Book of Jewish Observance*, p. 9-12; *The Living Talmud*, p. 35.
288 *Religions in Japan*, p. 177-79.
289 International Bulletin of Missionary Research, Vol. 27, No. 1, January 2003, p. 25 (Overseas Ministries Study Center (New Haven, Connecticut).
290 Matthew 7:13-14.
291 Religion: A Humanist Interpretation (Routledge 1966), p. 215, quoted in, *Philosophy of Religion*, p. 75-76.
292 Diogenes Laertius, Lives of Eminent Philosophers, Book V, section 21, quoted in *Bartlett's Familiar Quotations*, p. 77.
293 *The Analects* 12: 2; 15:24.
294 *Lao Tzu, Tao Te Ching*, Book II, Chapter LXIII, verse 148 (p. 124).
295 Quoted in, *Truth in Religion*, p. 87.
296 Id.
297 Mishnah, Shabbat 31a, quoted in, *The Living Talmud*, p. 102).
298 Matthew 7:12.
299 *Truth in Religion*, p. 87.
300 Appendix, p. 93-109.
301 Alma 29:7-8.
302 *The Koran*, 16:36 (p. 306). See also, 10:47 (An apostle is sent to every nation)(p. 68); 13:7 (Every nation has its mentor) (p. 143); 17:71 (p. 239); 16:88 (p. 310).
303 *Discourses of Brigham Young*, p. 10.
304 "What is a Jew," in Religions in America, p. 105.
305 The Anatomy of Melancholy, Democritus to the Reader, Part II, Section 2, Member 2, Sub-section 1, *Bartlett's Familiar Quotations*, p. 235.
306 *Mere Christianity*, p. 12.
307 *Catechism of the Catholic Church*, par. 2104.
308 1 Peter 3:15.

309 Essays, *The Over-Soul*, p. 156-57.
310 *The Doctrine and Covenants* 123:12.
311 John 7:14-17.
312 *History of the Church of Jesus Christ of Latter-day Saints*, Vol. 5, p. 340.
313 Matthew 7:7-11.
314 John 16:13.
315 The Autocrat of the Breakfast Table, Chapter 4, *Bartlett's Familiar Quotations*, p. 447.
316 *Mere Christianity*, p. 136.
317 *The Doctrine and Covenants* 9:8-9.
318 *Teachings of the Prophet Joseph Smith*, p. 223.
319 John 14:17.
320 2 Timothy 3:7.
321 Philippians 4:8; *Catechism of the Catholic Church*, par. 1803.
322 *The Pearl of Great Price*, p. 60-61.
323 Matthew 22:35-40; Mark 12:30-31.
324 Deuteronomy 6:5.
325 Leviticus 19:18.
326 Exodus 20:1-17, Deuteronomy 5:6-21.
327 *Discourses of Brigham Young*, p. 5.
328 *Why I Am Not A Christian*, p. 62.
329 Quoted in, The Book of Virtues, p. 794.
330 Jules Bertant, Napoleion in His Own Words, p. 112-13, quoted in, *The Story of Civilization*, Vol. 11,p. 154.
331 *The Analects*, p.1.
332 *Tao Te Ching*, Introduction, p. 13.
333 Id., p. 74, fn.
334 *The Analects*, Book VII, par. 25 (p. 89).
335 Id., par. 21 (p. 88).
336 Id., Book XIII, par. 18 (p. 121).
337 *The Story of Civilization*, Vol. 1, p. 431.
338 *The Teaching of Buddha*, p. 328-30.
339 (The Westminster Press 1981), p. 41, quoted in, *The Father is Not the Son*, p. 75.
340 *Catechism of the Catholic Church*, par. 285.
341 *Catechism of the Catholic Church*, par. 285.
342 A Concise Guide to the Catholic Church, p. 141.
343 *A Sourcebook in Indian Philosophy*, p. 17.

344 *Japanese Things*, p. 419.
345 *Book of Prayers*, p. 65.
346 Quoted in, *Barlett's Familiar Quotations*, p. 271.
347 *Apology for Raimond de Sebonde*, *Great Books of the Western World*, Vol. 23, p. 297.
348 *The Story of Civilization*, Vol. I, p. 509.
349 "Vishnu" in *Benet's Reader's Encyclopedia.*
350 Deuteronomy 6:5.
351 *The Koran*, 29:46 (p. 199).
352 Matthew 3:17, Matthew 17:5.
353 1 Corinthians 8:6.
354 1 Timothy 2:5.
355 *The Koran* 4:80 (p. 374).
356 *Prophethood in Islam*, p. 3.
357 *What They Say About Muhammad* (PBUH), p. 1.
358 *The Koran*, Introduction, p. 10.
359 *The Koran* 19:88 (p. 37).
360 Id., 43:58 (p. 152).
361 Id., 23:90 (p. 224).
362 *The Koran* 4:157 (p. 382).
363 *The Story of Civilization*, Vol. 1, p. 423.
364 *The Teaching of Buddha*, p. 22.
365 *The Story of Civilization*, Vol. 1, p. 429.
366 *The Religions of Man*, p. 145.
367 Id., p. 187.
368 *The Teaching of Buddha*, p. 4.
369 Id., p. 66.
370 *A Sourcebook in Indian Philosophy*, p. 273.
371 *The Story of Civilization*, Vol. 1, p. 504-05.
372 *The Complete Book of Jewish Observance*, p. 1.
373 p. xli.
374 Numbers 9:8-9.
375 Numbers 24:13.
376 Amos 3:7.
377 *The Living Talmud*, p. 17.
378 *The Complete Book of Jewish Observance*. p. 25.
379 *Book of Prayers*, p. 18.
380 *The Complete Book of Jewish Observance*, p. 64.
381 *The Complete Book of Jewish Observance*, p 217.

[382] *Book of Prayers*, p. 47.

[383] "What is a Jew," in *Religions in America*, p. 106; see also, *Christian Religions: A Comparative Chart*, Vol. 2.

[384] Amidah Morning Prayer, *Book of Prayers*, p. 222.

[385] *Book of Prayers*, p. 209.

[386] *A Sourcebook in Indian Philosophy*, p. 101.

[387] *A Sourcebook in Indian Philosophy*, p. 250.

[388] *Benet's Readers Encyclopedia*, p. 681.

[389] *Eerdmans' Handbook to the World's Religions*, p, 197.

[390] *Pensees*, Section XI, par. 693, *Great Books of the Western World*, Vol. 30.

[391] Mark 14:61-62.

[392] Matthew 21:33-38.

[393] Matthew 11:27; see also, Matthew 24:36.

[394] John 14:6.

[395] Matthew 3:17; Matthew 17:5.

[396] John 4:25-26.

[397] John 5:18.

[398] *Let No Man Deceive You*, p. 59; see also Micah 5:2.

[399] *Pensees*, Section IX, pars. 599-600, *Great Books of the Western World*, Vol. 30.

[400] *The Koran*, 61:6 (p.106).

[401] Ephesians 3:9, Colossians 1:16-17; 1 Corinthians 8:6.; Hebrews 1:2, John 1:3; see also *Catechism of the Catholic Church* par. 291.

[402] *Jesus the Christ*, Index, "Miracles."

[403] Matthew 4:23-24, Matthew 15:29-31, Matthew 21:14.

[404] *A Commentary on the Holy Bible*, p. cix.

[405] John 10:18.

[406] Matthew 16:16-17.

[407] Acts 4:12.

[408] *A Commentary on the Holy Bible*, p. lxxiv.

[409] Id., p. cvi.

[410] Id., p. 714.

[411] Id., p. cxii.

[412] *The Case for Christianity*, p. 45.

[413] *The Book of Mormon*, 2 Nephi 25:26.

[414] Title page, *The Book of Mormon*.

[415] *Christian Religions: A Comparative Chart*, Vols. 1, 2.

[416] Ecclesiastes 12:7.

417 James 2:26.
418 *Eerdman's Handbook to the History of Christianity*, p. 98.
419 1 Corinthians 3:16.
420 *Augsburg Confession*, Article XXVI, quoted in *Creeds of the Churches*, p. 90.
421 *Mere Christianity*, p. 91.
422 *Teachings of the Prophet Joseph Smith*, p. 207; see also *The Doctrine and Covenants* 131:7-8.
423 *The Doctrine and Covenants* 89.
424 *The Religions of Man*, p. 355.
425 *The Teaching of Buddha*, p. 19-20.
426 Id., p. 604.
427 Id., p. 230.
428 Id. p. 404.
429 Id., p. 350.
430 *Tao Te Ching*, Book I, Chapter XIII, 30a (p. 69).
431 *Understanding Islam*, p. 30.
432 *Catechism of the Catholic Church*, par. 1718.
433 *Teachings of the Prophet Joseph Smith*, p. 255-56; *History of the Church of Jesus Christ of Latter-day Saints*, Vol. 5, p. 134-35.
434 *Teachings of the Prophet Joseph Smith*, p. 295.
435 *The Case for Christianity*, p. 43.
436 Alma 41:10.
437 John 6:67-68.
438 Matthew 6:31-33.
439 Mark 8:36.
440 Luke 12:15.
441 Luke 13:12-14.
442 Matthew 26:41.
443 Matthew 10:28.
444 *Catechism of the Catholic Church*, par. 387.
445 Irenaeus, Against Heresies, V, Preface, quoted in, *The Father is Not the Son*, p. 115.
446 *Catechism of the Catholic Church* par. 1850.
447 *Catechism of the Catholic Church*, par. 1803.
448 *Catechism of the Catholic Church*, par. 460.
449 Revelation 3:21.
450 *The Doctrine and Covenants* 93:33, 76:94, 130:1-2.
451 *The Religions of Man*, p. 362.

452 *The Story of Civilization*, Vol. 1, p. 513.
453 *Eerdman's Handbook to the History of Christianity*, p. 7.
454 Alma 34:32.
455 *The Living Talmud*, p. 186.
456 "We, therefore, do not find in Judaism a great preoccupation with the hereafter. The task is here and now." Id., p. 317.
457 *The Living Talmud*, p. 175.
458 *The Religions of Man*, p. 177.
459 *A Sourcebook in Indian Philosophy*, p. xxix.
460 Id., p. xxix-xxx, 99-100.
461 *The Complete Book of Jewish Observance*, p. 217.
462 *Book of Prayers*, p. 89.
463 Mishnah, Bare'hoth 17a, quoted in, *Book of Prayers*, p. 228; see also, the commentary of Rabbi Joseph ben Judah ibn Aknikn, quoted in, *The Living Talmud*, p. 156.
464 *Book of Prayers*, p. 462-63.
465 Ezekiel 37:1-12, Job 14:14, 19:26, Isaiah 26:19.
466 *The Complete Book of Jewish Observance*, p. 328.
467 Id., p. 465.
468 Id., p. 471.
469 Sayings of the Fathers 4:29, quoted in, *Book of Prayers*, p. 251.
470 *The Living Talmud*, p. 117.
471 *The Living Talmud*, p. 158.
472 *The Living Talmud*, p. 179-180
473 Sayings of the Fathers 3:1, quoted in, *Book of Prayers*, p. 242; see also, *The Living Talmud*, p. 118.
474 *The Living Talmud*, p. 143.
475 *The Living Talmud*, p. 146.
476 Id., p. 319.
477 Id.
478 Matthew 22:23-33.
479 *The Complete Book of Jewish Observance*, p. 318.
480 *The Complete Book of Jewish Observance*, p. 336.
481 *A Sourcebook in Indian Philosophy*, p. 31.
482 *The Story of Civilization*, Vol. 1, p. 434-35.
483 *Eerdman's Handbook to the World's Religions*, p. 204.
484 *The Story of Civilization*, Vol. 1, p. 592.
485 *A Sourcebook in Indian Philosophy*, p. xxviii.
486 *Catechism of the Catholic Church*, par. 1013.

487 *Teachings of the Prophet Joseph Smith*, p. 105.
488 *The Analects*, Book XI, par. 12 (p. 107).
489 Par. 366, 997.
490 *Catechism of the Catholic Church*, par. 1681.
491 *Catechism of the Catholic Church*, par. 1690.
492 *Catechism of the Catholic Church*, par. 997.
493 *Catechism of the Catholic Church*, par. 998.
494 *Catechism of the Catholic Church*, par. 999.
495 1 Corinthians 15:20.
496 Luke 24:36-43.
497 Matthew 27:52-53.
498 *A Commentary on the Holy Bible*, p. cxxiv.
499 1 Corinthians 15:3-8.
500 Acts 9:1-11.
501 3 Nephi 11.
502 1 Corinthians 15:21-22; John 5:28-29.
503 *A Commentary on the Holy Bible*, p. cxxvii.
504 *Teachings of the Prophet Joseph Smith*, p. 296.
505 Moses 1:39, *The Pearl of Great Price.*
506 1 Corinthians 15: 21-22.
507 *Catechism of the Catholic Church*, par. 1001; 1 Thessalonians 4:16.
508 Alma 42:9, 2 Nephi 10:25, *The Book of Mormon.*
509 *Life After Death*, p. 1.
510 *The Koran*, 75:2 (p. 55). See also, 45:16 (p. 131); 37:19 (p. 170); 25:69 (p. 213); 23:100 (p. 225).
511 Sura 29:99-104, quoted in, *Life After Death*, p. 3.
512 Suras, 56:15-38 (p. 110-11), 82:17 (p. 16), 12:5 (p. 43), 21:75-76 (p. 213).
513 *Benet's Readers Encylopedia*, “Houris,” p. 462; Suras 56:15-38, 52:20 (p. 110, 117), *The Koran.*
514 *Religions in America*, p. 39, 360.
515 *The Story of Civilization*, Vol. 1, p. 525.
516 Revelations 12:4, *The Doctrine and Covenants* 29:36.
517 *Catechism of the Catholic Church*, pars. 310-11.
518 *Benet's Readers Encyclopedia*, p. 559.
519 *Catechism of the Catholic Church*, pars. 1753, 1756.
520 *The Doctrine and Covenants* 10:28.
521 *Catechism of the Catholic Church*, par. 1933.
522 *Teachings of the Prophet Joseph Smith*, p. 181.

523 *Teachings of the Prophet Joseph Smith*, p. 187.
524 *History of the Church*, Vol. 1, p. 369-70.
525 *Catechism of the Catholic Church*, par. 1792.
526 *The Koran*, 18:50; 14:22; 43:38; 36:59; 20:116; 17:27; 2:36 (p. 95, 102, 151, 177, 232, 235, 336).
527 *A Sourcebook in Indian Philosophy*, p. 354.
528 *The Religions of Man*, p. 89.
529 Id., p. 172.
530 *The Teaching of Buddha*, p. 88.
531 *The Analects*, Introduction, p. 29.
532 Deuteronomy 30:19.
533 *Sayings of the Fathers* 3:19, quoted in, *Book of Prayers*, p. 245.
534 *The Living Talmud*, p. 110.
535 *The Living Talmud*, p. 142.
536 *The Living Talmud*, p. 143.
537 *The Story of Civilization*, Vol. IV, p. 177.
538 *Understanding Islam*, p. 75.
539 Id. p. 76.
540 *How to Think About God*, p. 11.
541 *The Case for Christianity*, p. 55.
542 *The Rites of the Catholic Church*, p. 683; Genesis 14:18-20.
543 *Irenaeus, Against Heresies*, IV, 4, quoted in, *Apostasy from the Divine Church*, p. 47.
544 CXIII, 4, quoted in, *Apostasy from the Divine Church*, p. 48.
545 p. 47.
546 Id. p. 35-38, 47-48.
547 *Pensees*, Section IX, par. 606, *Great Books of the Western World*, Vol. 30.
548 Id., par. 616.
549 Id., Section XII, par. 737.
550 Acts 9:43.
551 Galatians 3:8.
552 *Histoire Generale de l'Eglise* (Paris: Bloud & Gay 1921-1938), Vol. 1, p. 316, quoted in, *Apostasy from the Divine Church*, p. 57.
553 *The History of the Church from Christ to Constantine*, p. 47, fn. 1.
554 *The Westminster Confession of Faith*, Chapter VII, Section V, quoted in, *Creeds of the Churches*, p. 202-03.
555 Id., Chapter VIII, Section VI, p. 204.
556 *A Concise Guide to the Catholic Church*, p. 137.

557 *Catechism of the Catholic Church*, pars. 781-83, 818.
558 *Catechism of the Catholic Church*, pars. 838. 1271.
559 *Catechism of the Catholic Church*, par. 843.
560 *Catechism of the Catholic Church*, par. 846.
561 *Catechism of the Catholic Church*, par. 847.
562 Matthew 28:19; Mark 16:14-16.
563 *Teachings of the Prophet Joseph Smith*, p. 59-61; *History of the Church of Jesus Christ of Latter-day Saints*, Vol. 2, p. 16-17.
564 *Discourses of Brigham Young*, p. 19.
565 *Teachings of the Prophet Joseph Smith*, p. 12.
566 John 5:25.
567 *Catechism of the Catholic Church*, par. 633.
568 *Catechism of the Catholic Church*, par. 634.
569 *A Sourcebook in Indian Philosophy*, p. xxviii-xxix.
570 *The Religions of Man*, p. 85.
571 *A Sourcebook in Indian Philosophy*, p. 167; Santiparva 329.19, 29, 32.
572 Id. p. 168; Santiparva 330.14-16.
573 d. p. 171; Santiparva 174:16-18.
574 *The Teaching of Buddha*, p. 384.
575 *The Teaching of Buddha*, p. 408.
576 *The Story of Civilization*, Vol. I, p. 524.
577 *Tao Te Ching*, Book II, chapter XLVI, verse 105 (p. 107).
578 *The Living Talmud*, p. 86.
579 *The Living Talmud*, p. 109.
580 1 John 4:7.
581 John 13:34-35.
582 1 John 4:19.
583 *Catechism of the Catholic Church*, par. 1970.
584 *A Commentary on the Holy Bible*, p. lxxix.
585 Id., p. lxxx.
586 *Teachings of the Prophet Joseph Smith*, p. 174.
587 Matthew 10:34-38, Luke 14: 25-35.
588 *A Concise Guide to the Catholic Church*, p. 6.
589 *Eerdman's Handbook to the History of Christianity*, p. 208.
590 *The Varieties of Religious Experience*, p. 271-72.
591 Luke 22:32.
592 John 21:15-17.
593 *The Story of Civilization*, Vol. 1, p. 407.
594 *The Story of Civilization*, Vol. 1, p. 410.

595 *The Story of Civilization*, Vol. 1, p. 534.
596 *A Sourcebook in Indian Philosophy*, p. 351.
597 *The Story of Civilization*, Vol. 1, p. 535.
598 Id., p. 351-53, 506.
599 *The Story of Civilization*, Vol. 1, p. 428.
600 p. iv.
601 Id., p. 560.
602 *Eerdman's Handbook to the World's Religions*, p. 201.
603 *The Story of Civilization*, Vol. 1, p. 664-65.
604 Deuteronomy 4:1-2, 6-8.
605 Joshua 1:8-9.
606 *The Living Talmud*, p. 95.
607 *The Living Talmud*, p. 141.
608 *The Living Talmud*, p. 141.
609 *The Living Talmud*, p. 22-23.
610 *The Living Talmud*, p. 23-25.
611 *The Complete Book of Jewish Observance*, p. 237; Rabbi ben Tema, Sayings of the Fathers 5:24, quoted in, *Book of Prayers*, p. 256.
612 *The Complete Book of Jewish Observance*, p. 19.
613 *The Complete Book of Jewish Observance*, p. 18.
614 *The Living Talmud*, p. 71; See also, *The Complete Book of Jewish Observance*, p. 25.
615 *The Complete Book of Jewish Observance*, p. 330.
616 *Prophethood in Islam*, p. 3, 8.
617 *Understanding Islam*, p. 6.
618 *The Koran*, 5:11-14 (p. 388-89).
619 *The Koran*, 41:45; 46:12 (p. 116, 128).
620 *The Story of Civilization*, Vol. IV, p. 184.
621 *The Koran*, 16:102; 2:87; 2:253 (p. 311, 341, 360).
622 Publisher's Note, Sahih Muslim.
623 Id.
624 *A Commentary on the Holy Bible*, p. xcix.
625 Id., p. cxxxvi.
626 *Catechism of the Catholic Church*, par. 1349.
627 *Catechism of the Catholic Church*, par. 1154.
628 John 1:9, *The Doctrine and Covenants* 84: 46, 93:2.
629 Commentary on the Sayings of the Fathers (Pirke Abot) by Rabbi Jonah ben Abraham (d. 1263), quoted in, *The Living Talmud*, p. 45.
630 *The Mishnah*, p. xiv.

631 Id., p. xxviii-xxix.
632 Id., p. xxviii.
633 *The Complete Book of Jewish Observance*, p. 18.
634 *A Commentary on the Holy Bible*, p. 645.
635 *Sayings of the Fathers* 2:18, *Book of Prayers*, p. 241.
636 *The Complete Book of Jewish Observance*, p. 42.
637 Id., p. 250.
638 Id., p. 44-45 (Menahot 43b.)
639 Exodus 20:8-11; Exodus 16:29, Exodus 31:17; Exodus 35:2-3
640 *The Complete Book of Jewish Observance*, p. 70-71.
641 Id.
642 *Book of Prayers*, p. 455.
643 Mark 2:27.
644 Mark 7:5-13.
645 Matthew 5:17-18.
646 Romans 10:4.
647 Acts 15:1-31.
648 3 Nephi 9:17, *The Book of Mormon.*
649 4 Nephi 1:12, *The Book of Mormon.*
650 Jacob 4:14, *The Book of Mormon.*
651 *The Complete Book of Jewish Observance.*, Preface, p. xiii.
652 *Catechism of the Catholic Church*, par. 1113, 1210.
653 *Catechism of the Catholic Church*, par. 1129.
654 *Catechism of the Catholic Church*, par. 1150.
655 *Catechism of the Catholic Church*, par. 1210.
656 *Catechism of the Catholic Church*, par. 1203.
657 *Catechism of the Catholic Church*, pars. 1667, 1672, 1673.
658 *Catechism of the Catholic Church*, pars. 1159-61, 2131.
659 *Catechism of the Catholic Church*, par. 2177.
660 *Understanding Islam*, p. 6-30.
661 *The Story of Civilization*, Vol. 1, p. 402.
662 *The Teaching of Buddha*, p. 204; "Amidism" *Benet's Readers Encyclopedia*, p. 31.
663 *Religions in Japan*, p. 75.
664 *Religions in Japan*, p. 96.
665 *Japanese Things*, p. 76-77.
666 *Eerdman's Handbook to the World's Religions*, p. 198.
667 Id., p. 199, 203.
668 *The Story of Civilization*, Vol. VI, p. 937.

669 *A Sourcebook in Indian Philosophy*, p. xxvii.
670 *The Story of Civilization*, Vol. I, p. 617.
671 *The Story of Civilization*, Vol. I, p. 505-06.
672 *Religions in Japan*, p. 11.
673 *The Analects*, Book IX, par. 4 (p. 96).
674 *The Religions of Man*, p. 235; *The Analects*, Book XIV, par. 34
675 *The Analects*, Book XVII, par. 6.
676 *The Analects*, Appendix I, p. 187.
677 Exodus 22:21, Leviticus 19:33-34, Deuteronomy 10:19, 24:17.
678 Exodus 20:10, Numbers 9:14.
679 "What is a Jew," in *Religions in America*, p. 105.
680 Matthew 5:44.
681 *The Story of Civilization*, Vol. IV, p. 734.
682 Quoted in, *Apostasy from the Divine Church*, p. 750.
683 Works (of Martin Luther) (Erlangen edition, Vol. 32, p. 217-33, quoted in, *The Story of Civilization*, Vol. VI, p. 422.
684 John Knox, History of the Reformation in Scotland (New York1950), Introduction, lxiii, quoted, in *The Story of Civilization*, Vol. VI, p. 610.
685 *The Story of Civilization*, Vol. IV, p. 680.
686 The Brevissima Relacion de la Destruycion de las Indias Occidentales [1554] in History of Scarmentado's Travels, Voltaire: Candide, Zadig and Selected Stories, p. 221.
687 *The Doctrine and Covenants* 121:39.
688 *Catechism of the Catholic Church*, par. 2104.
689 *Teachings of the Prophet Joseph Smith*, p. 313.
690 Article 11.
691 *History of the Church of Jesus Christ of Latter-day Saints*, Vol. 4, p. 306.
692 *The Koran*, 3:19 (p. 409)
693 Id., 3:85 (p. 415).
694 Id., 2:256 (p. 361).
695 Id., 2:192 (p. 352).
696 Id., 48:29 (p. 278).
697 Id. 8:39 (p. 317).
698 Id., 9:5 (p. 321).
699 Id., 9:20 (p. 322).
700 Id., 9:73 (p. 328).
701 Id., 4:104 (p. 377).
702 *The Story of Civilization*, Vol. IV, p. 170.

703 *Understanding Islam*, p. 118.
704 *Understanding Islam*, p.11.
705 *Understanding Islam*, p. x.
706 *The Analects*, Introduction, p. 28.
707 Jeremiah 29:7.
708 Ezra 6:10.
709 Matthew 22:15-22.
710 Matthew 17:24-27.
711 2 Timothy 2:1-2.
712 1 Peter 2:17.
713 Romans 13:1-2.
714 *The Story of Civilization*, Vol. IV, p. 34.
715 *Eerdman's Handbook to the History of Christianity*, p. 192.
716 *Eerdman's Handbook to the History of Christianity*, p. 142.
717 *Eerdman's Handbook to the History of Christianity*, p. 220.
718 Joseph Lortz, History of the Church (Bruce Publishing 1939), p. 174, quoted in, *Apostasy from the Divine Church*, p. 574.
719 *Eerdman's Handbook to the History of Christianity*, p. 311.
720 *Eerdman's Handbook to the History of Christianity*, p. 192, 229, 351.
721 *The Story of Civilization*, Vol. IV, p. 525.
722 *The Story of Civilization*, Vol. IV, p. 762.
723 John 18:36.
724 *A Concise Guide to the Catholic Church*, p. 14, 17.
725 *Eerdman's Handbook to the History of Christianity*, p. 256.
726 *A Concise Guide to the Catholic Church*, p. 18.
727 *Eerdman's Handbook to the History of Christianity*, p. 318.
728 *The Story of Civilization*, Vol. IV, p. 778-79.
729 *The Story of Civilization*, Vol. IV, p. 782.
730 *A Concise Guide to the Catholic Church*, p. 17.
731 A Manual of Church History (The American Baptist Publication Society 1953), p. Vol. 1, p. 464-66, quoted in, *Apostasy from the Divine Church*, p. 590.
732 Quoted in, *Apostasy from the Divine Church*, p. 591.
733 *Apostasy from the Divine Church*, p. 676.
734 Catholic Encyclopedia (New York 1912), Vol. VIII, p. 32b, quoted in, *The Story of Civilization*, Vol. IV, p. 781.
735 *Eerdman's Handbook to the History of Christianity*, p. 416.
736 *Histoire de l'Eglise,* p. 256, quoted in, *Apostasy from the Divine Church*, p. 593.

737 *Second Helvetic Confession*, Article XXX, quoted in, *Creeds of the Churches*, p. 191.

738 *Here I Stand*, p. 207.

739 *Here I Stand*, p. 243.

740 *Here I Stand*, p. 245.

741 *Here I Stand*, p. 295.

742 *Here I Stand*, p. 297.

743 *Here I Stand*, p. 191 .

744 *Eerdman's Handbook to the History of Christianity*, p. 420.

745 *The Story of Civilization*, Vol. VII, p. 551.

746 *Here I Stand*, p. 117.

747 Article XXXVII, quoted in, Creeds of the Church, p. 279.

748 *Historia de la Iglesia*, p. 806-07, quoted in, *Apostasy from the Divine Church*, p. 621.

749 Id.

750 *The Story of Civilization*, Vol. IV, p. 708.

751 *Catechism of the Catholic Church*, par. 2107.

752 *Catechism of the Catholic Church*, par. 2108.

753 *Catechism of the Catholic Church*, pars. 1899, 1903.

754 *Catechism of the Catholic Church*, par. 2148.

755 *Catechism of the Catholic Church*, par. 2298.

756 *An Introduction to Canon Law*, p. 48.

757 Article VI, par. 3.

758 Article 12, *The Pearl of Great Price*, p. 61.

759 *The Doctrine and Covenants* 134:10.

760 Alma 1:17-18, 30:9-10, *The Book of Mormon*.

761 *Religions in America*, p. 227-32.

762 *An Introduction to Canon Law*, p. 150.

763 *A Concise Guide to the Catholic Church*, p. 147.

764 Par. 74.

765 2 Timothy 4:3-4.

766 2 Thessalonians 2:1-4.

767 Isaiah 24:5, Amos 8:11-12, Micah 3:11, Revelation 13:7.

768 *The History of the Church from Christ to Constantine*, p. 9, 143.

769 *The History of the Church from Christ to Constantine*, p. 23.

770 *The History of the Church from Christ to Constantine*, p. 182.

771 *The Story of Civilization*, Vol. III, p. 616.

772 *Eerdman's Handbook to the History of Christianity*, p. 314.

773 *The Story of Civilization*, Vol. VI, p. 354.

774 *Luther and His Times*, p. 509.
775 *Martin Luther: A Biographic Study*, p. 188.
776 *Eerdman's Handbook to the History of Christianity*, p. 346.
777 J.M. Robertson, *A Short History of Freethought*, Vol. 1, p. 12, quoted in, *The Story of Civilization*, Vol. V, p. 558.
778 Ludwig Pastor, *History of the Popes*, Vol, 9, p. 134, quoted in, *The Story of Civilization*, Vol. VI, p. 381.
779 Ludwig Pastor, *History of the Popes*, Vol. 11, p. 134, quoted in, *The Story of Civilization*, Vol. VI, p. 897.
780 E.B. Fox, *Rise and Fall of the Anabaptists*, p. 63, quoted in, McGavin, *Cumorah's Gold Bible*, p. 14, and, *The Father is Not the Son*, p. 11.
781 *Homily* xiv, quoted in, *Jesus the Christ*, p. 699.
782 *Economy of the Restoration of Man*, IV, 205, as quoted in McGavin, *Cumorah's Gold Bible*, p. 13, and, *The Father is Not the Son*, p. 11.
783 Quoted in, *The Story of Civilization*, Vol. 10, p. 316.
784 *Picturesque America*, p. 508, quoted in, *A Marvelous Work and A Wonder*, p. 29.
785 Letter to Timothy Pickering dated February 27, 1821, quoted in, *Jefferson's Complete Works*, Vol. 7, p. 210.
786 Letter to Benjamin Waterhouse dated July 19, 1822, quoted in, *Jefferson's Complete Works*, Vol. 7, p. 257.
787 *Eerdman's Handbook to the History of Christianity*, p. 372-73.
788 Joseph Smith History 1:12, 18, *The Pearl of Great Price.*
789 *Teachings of the Prophet Joseph Smith*, p. 14.
790 Acts 3:19-21.
791 Isaiah 24:5.
792 *The Doctrine and Covenants* 1:14-15.
793 Daniel 2:27-28, 34-35, 44.
794 Isaiah 29:13-14.
795 Joseph Smith History 1:19, *The Pearl of Great Price.*
796 Isaiah 11:11-12; Joseph Smith History 1:40, *The Pearl of Great Price.*
797 *The Doctrine and Covenants* 65:2; see also *Teachings of the Prophet Joseph Smith*, p. 365-66.
798 *Truth in Religion*, p. 29.
799 *A Commentary on the Holy Bible*, p. cxxxii.
800 *The Story of Civilization*, Vol. VI, p. 320.
801 *The Story of Civilization*, Vol. VI, p. 368.
802 *Cambridge Medieval History*, Vol. VII, p. 505, quoted in, *Apostasy from the Divine Church*, p. 680.

803 *The Story of Civilization*, Vol. IV, p. 776.
804 *The Story of Civilization*, Vol. IV, p. 780.
805 *The Story of Civilization*, Vol. VI, p. 571.
806 *Catechism of the Catholic Church*, pars. 133, 2653.
807 *A Commentary on the Holy Bible*, p. liv.
808 *Offenders for a Word*, p. 118-19.
809 *Catechism of the Catholic Church*, par. 120.
810 *Eerdman's Handbook to the History of Christianity*, p. 94-95.
811 *A Concise Guide to the Catholic Church*, p. 6.
812 *A Commentary on the Holy Bible*, p. liv.
813 *Here I Stand*, p. 144.
814 *Here I Stand*, p. 161.
815 2 Corinthians 3:6.
816 *First and Second Propositions, Theses Theologicae of Robert Barclay* (1675), quoted in, *Creeds of the Church*, p. 324.
817 Id., *Third Proposition*, p. 326.
818 *Here I Stand*, p. 202.
819 *Eerdman's Handbook to the History of Christianity*, p. 618.
820 *The Westminster Confession of Faith*, Chapter XXXI, quoted in, *Creeds of the Churches*, p, 228.
821 *Charles Poulet, Histoire de l'Eglise* (Paris: Beauchesne 1943), Vol. 2, p. 112, quoted in, *Apostasy from the Divine Church*, p. 609.
822 *Eerdman's Handbook to the History of Christianity*, p. 14.
823 Par. 82.
824 *The Westminster Confession of Faith*, Chapter I, Section VIII, quoted in, *Creeds of the Churches*, p. 196.
825 *Eerdman's Handbook to the History of Christianity*, p. 544, 598; *The Story of Civilization*, Vol. 10, p. 507, 513-14, Vo. 11, p. 646.
826 Exodus 24:7.
827 Numbers 21:14.
828 Joshua 10:13, 2 Samuel 1:18.
829 1 Kings 11:41.
830 1 Chronicles 29:29.
831 1 Chronicles 29:29, 2 Chronicles 9:29.
832 1 Chronicles 29:29.
833 2 Chronicles 12:15.
834 2 Chronicles 9:29, 12:15, 13:22.
835 2 Chronicles 20:34.
836 2 Chronicles 26:22.

837 Jude 1:14.
838 Matthew 2:23.
839 1 Corinthians 5:9, Ephesians 3:3, Colossians 4:16.
840 *A Commentary on the Holy Bible*, p. xiv.
841 *A Commentary on the Holy Bible*, p. xvi.
842 p. 89, 92.
843 Henri Daniel-Rops, *L'Eglise des Apotres et des Martyrs* (Libraire Artheme Fayard 1948), p. 313, quoted in, *Apostasy from the Divine Church*, p. 14.
844 *The History of the Church from Christ to Constantine*, p. 237.
845 *The Story of Civilization*, Vol. IV, p. 939.
846 Article in the Scotsman, June 5, 1965 (Edinburgh, Scotland), quoted in, *As Translated Correctly*, p. 41.
847 *The Story of Civilization*, Vol. VIII, p. 238-39.
848 *The Works of Josephus*, Book 18, Chapter 3, Section 3, p. 480.
849 Article 8.
850 *Teachings of the Prophet Joseph Smith*, p. 327; *A Comprehensive History of the Church of Jesus Christ of Latter-day Saints*, 6:57.
851 *The Doctrine and Covenants* 91:1-2.
852 2 Nephi 29.
853 *The Doctrine and Covenants* 42:12.
854 *The Book of Mormon*, Frontspiece.
855 Exodus 22:18.
856 Benet's Readers Encylopedia, p. 1071.
857 H.C. Lea, *Inquisition in Spain*, Vol. 4, p. 246; cf. Johannes Janssen, *History of the German People at the Close of the Middle Ages*, Vol 16, p. 506, quoted in, *The Story of Civilization*, Vol. VII, p. 578.
858 *The Story of Civilization*, Vol. VI, p. 233.
859 Philip Hughes, *The Reformation in England*, Vol 2, p, 286n (1952), quoted in, *The Story of Civilization*, Vol. VII, p. 162.
860 1 Corinthians 7.
861 Matthew 5:29-30.
862 Luke 21:32.
863 1 Corinthians 14:34.
864 Genesis 1-2:4 and Genesis 2:4-25.
865 *A Concise Guide to the Catholic Church*, p. 141.
866 Matthew 16:13-19.
867 *Eerdman's Handbook to the History of Christianity*, p. 193.
868 *Eerdman's Handbook to the History of Christianity*, p. 199.

[869] *Here I Stand*, p. 88.
[870] *The Story of Civilization*, Vol. IV, p. 525.
[871] The Book of Pontiffs (Liber Pontificalis), p. 1; cf. *A Commentary on the Holy Bible*, pp, 856-57.
[872] The Book of Pontiffs, p. 93, Romans 15, 16; *A Commentary on the Holy Bible*, p. 856-57.
[873] *Apostasy from the Divine Church*, p. 251-52.
[874] *The Story of Civilization*, Vol. III, p. 617 note.
[875] *The History of the Church from Christ to Constantine*, p. 10-11.
[876] *The Story of Civilization*, Vol. IV, p. 49.
[877] *Eerdman's Handbook to the History of Christianity*, p. 268, 456.
[878] *Catechism of the Catholic Church*, par. 1399.
[879] *An Introduction to Canon Law*, p. 71.
[880] *A Concise Guide to the Catholic Church*, p. 18-19.
[881] Vol V, Part 2, p. 369, quoted in, *Apostasy from the Divine Church*, p. 684.
[882] *An Introduction to Canon Law*, p. 66.
[883] *Second Helvetic Confession*, Article XVII, quoted in, *Creeds of the Churches*, p. 143.
[884] Hippolytus, *Discourse on the Holy Theophany*, quoted in, *Apostasy from the Divine Church*, p. 629.
[885] *De Trinitate*, VI, 37, quoted in, *Apostasy from the Divine Church*, p. 629.
[886] *A Commentary on the Holy Bible*, p. 681.
[887] Id.
[888] *The Story of Civilization*, Vol. IV, p. 537-39.
[889] *Here I Stand*, p. 84.
[890] *The Westminster Confession of Faith*, Chapter XXV, Section VI, quoted in, *Creeds of the Churches*, p. 222.
[891] *Eerdman's Handbook to the History of Christianity*, p. 329-30.
[892] *The Story of Civilization*, Vol. VI, p. 6.
[893] *The Penguin Dictionary of Saints,* p. 27.
[894] *Eerdman's Handbook to the History of Christianity*, p. 333.
[895] *Second Helvetic Confession*, Article XVIII, quoted in, *Creeds of the Churches*, p. 154.
[896] *Here I Stand*, p. 201.
[897] *Augsburg Confession*, Article XIV, quoted in, *Creeds of the Churches*, p. 72.
[898] *Second Helvetic Confession*, Article XVIII, quoted in, *Creeds of the*

Churches, p. 154; *Here I Stand*, p. 212.
899 *The Story of Civilization*, Vol. VI, p. 897.
900 *The Story of Civilization*, Vol. VI, p. 898.
901 *The Story of Civilization*, Vol. VI, p. 899.
902 Hebrews 5:4 (see Exodus 40:13-15).
903 Numbers 27:18-23.
904 Numbers 3:3, 9.
905 Numbers 11:16, 25.
906 Numbers 16, 1 Chronicles 13:10; 1 Samuel 13:5-14; 2 Chronicles 26.
907 Mark 3:14, Matthew 10:1, John 15:16
908 John 15:16.
909 Luke 10:1, 17.
910 Acts 6:2-6.
911 Acts 13:1-3.
912 Acts 14:23; see also Titus 1:5.
913 1 Timothy 4:14.
914 *Eerdman's Handbook to the History of Christianity*, p. 502.
915 *An Introduction to Canon Law*, p. 25; *Eerdman's Handbook to the History of Christianity*, p. 507.
916 *An Introduction to Canon Law*, p. 130 (Canons 1013, 1382).
917 *A Concise Guide to the Catholic Church*, p. 126, 134.
918 Hebrews 5:10; *Catechism of the Catholic Church*, par. 1544.
919 *Catechism of the Catholic Church*, par. 1546.
920 *Catechism of the Catholic Church*, par. 1120; see also 1141.
921 Id. par. 1174.
922 *Catechism of the Catholic Church*, par. 1268.
923 *An Introduction to Canon Law*, p. 121 (Canon 900).
924 *Catechism of the Catholic Church*, par. 1256, *An Introduction to Canon Law*, p. 117 (Canon 861.2, 530); see also *The Rites of the Catholic Church*, p. 8 ("In imminent danger of death and especially at the moment of death, when no priest or deacon is available, any member of the faithful, indeed anyone with the right intention, may and sometimes must administer baptism"); see also p. 432, 887.
925 *Catechism of the Catholic Church*, par. 875.
926 *Catechism of the Catholic Church*, par. 1557.
927 *The Doctrine and Covenants* 13.
928 *The Doctrine and Covenants* 27:12, 128:20.
929 *The Doctrine and Covenants* 132:8.
930 *The Doctrine and Covenants* 42:11.

931 *The Doctrine and Covenants* 110:11-13, 128:21.

932 *Discourses of Brigham Young*, p. 130.

933 *The Doctrine and Covenants* 22.

934 *The Doctrine and Covenants* 63:62.

935 Exodus 20:7.

936 Acts 6:6.

937 The Articles of Faith, No. 5, *The Pearl of Great Price*, p. 60.

938 John 20:22.

939 Mark 13:11; see also Matthew 10:19-20, Luke 21:14-15.

940 Luke 12:11-12.

941 Acts 1:1-2.

942 2 Peter 1:21.

943 *Teachings of the Prophet Joseph Smith*, p. 328.

944 *The Doctrine and Covenants* 68:4.

945 *Apostasy from the Divine Church*, p. 325.

946 *An Outline History of the Church*, p. 72, quoted in *Apostasy of the Divine Church*, p. 499.

947 *The Story of Civilization*, Vol. IV, p. 541.

948 *The Story of Civilization*, Vol. IV, p. 767.

949 *The Story of Civilization*, Vol. IV, p. 541.

950 *The Story of Civilization*, Vol. IX, p. 253.

951 *The Story of Civilization*, Vol. VI, p. 19.

952 Id.

953 *The Story of Civilization*, Vol. VI, p. 21.

954 *The Doctrine and Covenants* 121:36-37.

955 *Teachings of the Prophet Joseph Smith*, p. 274.

956 *The Doctrine and Covenants* 33:11-13.

957 See J.W. Draper, *Intellectual Development of Europe*, Vol. 1, Ch. XII, p. 378-81, quoted in, *The Great Apostasy*, p. 144-47; A *History of the Popes*, particularly chapter 7.

958 *Pensees*, Section VII, No. 434, *Great Books of the Western World*, Vol. 30.

959 *Lehrbuch der Kirchengeschicte* ((Paderborn: Ferdinand Schoningh 1902), p. 294, quoted in, *Apostasy from the Divine Church*, p. 548.

960 *Histoire Abregee de l'Eglise*, p. 155, quoted in, *Apostasy from the Divine Church*, p. 549.

961 *The Story of Civilization*, Vol. IV, p. 587.

962 Charles Philip Steward Clarke, *Short History of the Christian Church* (London: Longmans, Green 1882), p. 507-08 Appendix, quoted in,

Apostasy from the Divine Church, p. 551.
963 *Here I Stand*, p. 54, 60..
964 *Here I Stand*, p. 58.
965 *Here I Stand*, p. 192.
966 *The Story of Civilization*, Vol. VI, p. 24.
967 *The Story of Civilization*, Vol. VI, p. 115.
968 *Here I Stand*, p. 62.
969 *The Story of Civilization*, Vol. IV, p. 736.
970 *Here I Stand*, p. 67. (See also Luke 13:3).
971 *The Westminster Confession of Faith*, Chapter XVI, Sections IV, V, quoted in, *Creeds of the Churches*, p. 211.
972 *Religions in America*, p. 84.
973 *Short History of the Christian Church*, p. 307, quoted in, *Apostasy from the Divine Church*, p. 701.
974 Par. 431.
975 Par. 1441.
976 Par. 1442.
977 Par. 1461.
978 *Catechism of the Catholic Church*, par. 1424.
979 *Catechism of the Catholic Church*, par. 982.
980 *Catechism of the Catholic Church*, par. 979.
981 *Catechism of the Catholic Church*, pars. 1459-60.
982 *Catechism of the Catholic Church*, pars. 1471, 1472.
983 *Catechism of the Catholic Church*, pars. 1476, 1477.
984 Par. 958.
985 2 Maccabees 12:46.
986 *Catechism of the Catholic Church*, par. 1032.
987 Par. 1498.
988 *An Introduction to Canon Law*, p. 125-26 (Canon 959).
989 *An Introduction to Canon Law*, p. 176 (Canons 1312, 1340); see also *The Rites of the Catholic Church*, p. 535.
990 *Catechism of the Catholic Church*, par. 1460.
991 *The Rites of the Catholic Church*, p. 535.
992 *Catechism of the Catholic Church*, par. 2042.
993 *The Rites of the Catholic Church*, p. 856.
994 *Apostasy from the Divine Church*, p. 555-56.
995 *Religions in America*, p. 371-73.
996 Mosiah 3:18, *The Book of Mormon*.
997 Mosiah 3:16, 27:25, *The Book of Mormon*.

998 Moses 6:54, *The Pearl of Great Price.*

999 *The Pearl of Great Price*, p. 61.

1000 *The Doctrine and Covenants* 76:31-39, 98-112.

1001 *History of the Church of Jesus Christ of Latter-day Saints*, Vol 4, p. 555.

1002 *The Doctrine and Covenants* 19:16-18.

1003 *The Doctrine and Covenants* 58:43.

1004 *Teachings of the Prophet Joseph Smith*, p. 148.

1005 *Eerdman's Handbook to the History of Christianity*, p. 257.

1006 *Catechism of the Catholic Church*, par. 1257.

1007 *Catechism of the Catholic Church*, par. 1263.

1008 *Catechism of the Catholic Church*, par. 1225.

1009 *Here I Stand*, p. 200, 207.

1010 *A Concise Guide to the Catholic Church*, p. 6.

1011 *The Story of Civilization*, Vol. IV, p. 738.

1012 Auguste Boulenger, *Histoire Generale de l'Eglise*, Vol. III, p. 150, quoted in, *Apostasy of the Divine Church*, p. 454.

1013 Histoire General de l'Eglise, Vol, III, p. 146, quoted in, *Apostasy from the Divine Church*, p. 482.

1014 *The Story of Civilization*, Vol. IV, p. 734.

1015 Hell, Canto IV, Lines 31-42, *Great Books of the Western World*, Vol. 19.

1016 *Apostasy from the Divine Church*, p. 181.

1017 *Offenders for a Word*, p. 134.

1018 *Augsburg Confession*, Articles II, IX, quoted in, *Creeds of the Churches*, p. 68, 70-71.

1019 *Eerdman's Handbook to the History of Christianity*, p. 374.

1020 *Second Helvetic Confession*, Article XIX, quoted in, *Creeds of the Churches*, p. 162.

1021 *Second Helvetic Confession*, Article XX, quoted in, *Creeds of the Churches*, p. 168-69; *The Westminster Confession of Faith*, Chapter VI, Section III, Chapter XXVIII, Sections III, IV, V, Id., p. 201, 224.

1022 *The Westminster Confession of Faith*, Chapter XXVIII, Section V, quoted in, *Creeds of the Churches*, p. 224.

1023 *The Westminster Confession of Faith*, Chapter X, Section III, quoted in, *Creeds of the Churches*, p. 206.

1024 *Augustine, Admonition and Grace*, Chapter, VI, as quoted in, *Apostasy from the Divine Church*, p. 440.

1025 *Histoire Generale de l'Eglise* Vol. III, p. 146, quoted in, *Apostasy from the Divine Church*, p. 482.

[1026] Romans 3:23.

[1027] *Apostasy from the Divine Church*, p. 179, 440.

[1028] Auguste Boulenger, *Histoire Generale de l'Eglise* (Paris: Libraire Catholique 1031-1947), p. 271, quoted in, *Apostasy from the Divine Church*, p. 185.

[1029] *Catechism of the Catholic Church*, pars. 1230-32.

[1030] *Catechism of the Catholic Church*, par. 1250.

[1031] *Catechism of the Catholic Church*, par. 1261.

[1032] *Catechism of the Catholic Church*, par. 847.

[1033] *Catechism of the Catholic Church*, par. 1260.

[1034] *Catechism of the Catholic Church*, par. 1258-59.

[1035] *Catechism of the Catholic Church*, par. 403.

[1036] *Catechism of the Catholic Church*, par. 405.

[1037] *Catechism of the Catholic Church*, par. 405.

[1038] *An Introduction to Canon Law*, p. 118-19 (Canons 867, 868); *The Rites of the Catholic Church*, p. 368-69.

[1039] *An Introduction to Canon Law*, p. 119 (Canon 872).

[1040] *The Rites of the Catholic Church*, p. 381.

[1041] *Catechism of the Catholic Church*, par. 1214.

[1042] *The Rites of the Catholic Church*, p. 9, 159, 344.

[1043] *Catechism of the Catholic Church*, par. 1239.

[1044] *The Rites of the Catholic Church*, p. 365.

[1045] *Catechism of the Catholic Church*, pars. 1288, 1315; Acts 8:14-17.

[1046] *Catechism of the Catholic Church*, par. 1289

[1047] *The Rites of the Catholic Church*, p. 482.

[1048] *Catechism of the Catholic Church*, par. 1241.

[1049] *Catechism of the Catholic Church*, par. 1290.

[1050] *The Rites of the Catholic Church*, p. 164, 280-81.

[1051] *The Rites of the Catholic Church*, p. 371.

[1052] *Catechism of the Catholic Church*, par. 1310.

[1053] *Catechism of the Catholic Church*, par. 1311.

[1054] *Catechism of the Catholic Church*, par. 1087.

[1055] *The Rites of the Catholic Church*, p. 929, 1005.

[1056] *Religions in America*, p. 346-47.

[1057] *Christian Religions: A Comparative Chart*, Vol. 1.

[1058] Moses 6:64-66, 7:11, *The Pearl of Great Price*; Mosiah 18:12-16, Helaman 5:19, *The Book of Mormon*.

[1059] Moroni Chapter 8, *The Book of Mormon*.

[1060] John 3:3-5.

[1061] Romans 6:3-5.

[1062] *Teachings of the Prophet Joseph Smith*, p. 148.

[1063] *An Introduction to Canon Law*, p. 121; see also *Catechism of the Catholic Church*, par. 1211.

[1064] *Catechism of the Catholic Church*, par. 1324.

[1065] *The Rites of the Catholic Church*, p. 212.

[1066] *The Rites of the Catholic Church*, p. 353.

[1067] *Eerdman's Handbook to the History of Christianity*, p. 9.

[1068] Boulenger, Histoire Abrege de l'Eglise (Paris: Emmanuel Vitte 1943), pp, 119, 155, quoted in, *Apostasy from the Divine Church*, p. 536; see also, *Catechism of the Catholic Church*, par. 1244.

[1069] *Catechism of the Catholic Church*, par. 1244.

[1070] *Catechism of the Catholic Church*, par. 1390.

[1071] The Catholic Church had stopped offering the wine to the laity "out of fear that the laity in clumsiness might spill some of the blood of God." *Here I Stand*, p. 108.

[1072] John 6: 51-58.

[1073] *The Story of Civilization*, Vol. IV, p. 740-41; *Medieval Church Treasuries*, p. 11.

[1074] *The Story of Civilization*, Vol. IV, p. 741.

[1075] *Eerdman's Handbook to the History of Christianity*, p. 231.

[1076] *Eerdman's Handbook to the History of Christianity*, p. 257-58.

[1077] *Eerdman's Handbook to the History of Christianity*, p. 274.

[1078] *A Concise Guide to the Catholic Church*, p. 12, 14.

[1079] *A Concise Guide to the Catholic Church*, p. 106.

[1080] *Augsburg Confession*, Article XXIV, quoted in, *Creeds of the Churches*, p. 84-85.

[1081] *Second Helvetic Confession*, Article XXI, quoted in, *Creeds of the Churches*, p. 171.

[1082] *The Westminster Confession of Faith*, Chapter XXIX, Section II, quoted in, *Creeds of the Churches*, p. 225.

[1083] Second Helvetic Confesssion, Article XXI, quoted in, *Creeds of the Churches*, p. 172.

[1084] Matthew 26:26, Mark 14:22.

[1085] Luke 22:19, 1 Corinthians 11:24.

[1086] *Here I Stand*, p. 249.

[1087] *Here I Stand*, p. 200.

[1088] *The Westminster Confession of Faith*, Chapter XXIX, Section IV,

quoted in, *Creeds of the Churches*, p. 225-26.
[1089] Hebrews 10:10.
[1090] *The Westminster Confession of Faith*, Chapter XXIX, Section VI, quoted in, *Creeds of the Churches*, p. 226.
[1091] *Augsburg Confession*, Article X, quoted in, *Creeds of the Churches*, p. 71; *Eerdman's Handbook to the History of Christianity*, p. 374.
[1092] *A Concise Guide to the Catholic Church*, p. 122.
[1093] *The Story of Civilization*, Vol. VI, p. 354.
[1094] *Here I Stand*, p. 156.
[1095] *The Rites of the Catholic Church*, p. 637.
[1096] *The Rites of the Catholic Church*, p. 639.
[1097] *Catechism of the Catholic Church*, par. 1333.
[1098] *Catechism of the Catholic Church*, par. 1373.
[1099] *Catechism of the Catholic Church*, par. 1364.
[1100] *Catechism of the Catholic Church*, par. 1377.
[1101] *Catechism of the Catholic Church*, par. 1378.
[1102] Par. 1106.
[1103] Par. 1381.
[1104] *Catechism of the Catholic Church*, par. 1371.
[1105] *Catechism of the Catholic Church*, pars. 1394, 1395.
[1106] *Catechism of the Catholic Church*, par. 1457.
[1107] *The Rites of the Catholic Church*, p. 641.
[1108] Id.
[1109] *The Rites of the Catholic Church*, p. 651.
[1110] *An Introduction to Canon Law*, p. 121 (Canon 900).
[1111] *An Introduction to Canon Law*, p. 124 (Canon 945).
[1112] *The Rites of the Catholic Church*, p. 721.
[1113] *The Rites of the Catholic Church*, p. 848.
[1114] *The Rites of the Catholic Church*, Preface, p. xiii.
[1115] *The Rites of the Catholic Church*, p. 65.
[1116] *Catechism of the Catholic Church*, par. 2042.
[1117] *Religions in America*, p. 356-57.
[1118] 1 Corinthians 10:1-4.
[1119] 3 Nephi 20:8.
[1120] 3 Nephi 18:7, 11-12, *The Book of Mormon*.
[1121] *The Doctrine and Covenants* 27:2.
[1122] Moroni Chapters 4-5, *The Book of Mormon*; *The Doctrine and Covenants* 20:76-79.
[1123] 3 Nephi 18:28-29, *The Book of Mormon*; *The Doctrine and Covenants*

46:4.

1124 2 Corinthians 5:10.

1125 James 2:20.

1126 *Augsburg Confession*, Article XXVI, quoted in,*Creeds of the Churches*, p. 88.

1127 Ephesians 2:8-9.

1128 Romans 1:17.

1129 *Augsburg Confession*, Article IV, quoted in, *Creeds of the Churches*, p. 69.

1130 *Augsburg Confession*, Article VI, quoted in, *Creeds of the Churches*, p. 69-70.

1131 *Augsburg Confession*, Article VI, quoted in, *Creeds of the Churches*, p. 70.

1132 James 2:20.

1133 *Here I Stand*, p. 258.

1134 *Here I Stand*, p. 258.

1135 *Table Talk*, p. 283, quoted in, *The Story of Civilization*, Vol. VI, p. 373.

1136 *Offenders for a Word*, p. 126.

1137 *Augsburg Confession*, Article XX, quoted in, *Creeds of the Churches*, p. 75.

1138 Romans 3:23.

1139 *Second Helvetic Confession*, Article XXVII, quoted in, *Creeds of the Churches*, p. 186.

1140 Matthew 7:21.

1141 Matthew 16:27.

1142 Luke 6:46.

1143 Romans 2:6.

1144 Galatians 6:7.

1145 1 John 3:7; see also Matthew 25:35, 1 Corinthians 3:8, 1 Peter 1:17, Revelations 2:23, 22:12.

1146 Matthew 5:48.

1147 *Here I Stand*, p. 178.

1148 *Here I Stand*, p. 259.

1149 *A Concise Guide to the Catholic Church*, p. 132.

1150 2 Nephi 25:23, *The Book of Mormon*.

1151 *The Pearl of Great Price*, p. 60.

1152 *The Doctrine and Covenants* 52:15-16.

1153 *Mere Christianity*, p. 129-30.

[1154] Titus 3:1-8.

[1155] *Offenders for a Word*, p. 142.

[1156] *Eerdman's Handbook to the History of Christianity*, p. 199.

[1157] *Augustine, Admonition and Grace*, Chapter XIII, quoted in, *Apostasy from the Divine Church*, p. 452.

[1158] Quoted in, *Apostasy from the Divine Church*, p. 453-55.

[1159] *Histoire Generale de l'Eglise*, Vol. III, p. 163-64, quoted in, *Apostasy from the Divine Church*, p. 493.

[1160] *The Divine Comedy, Paradise*, Canto V, Lines 16-33, *Great Books of the Western World*, Vol. 19.

[1161] *Augsburg Confession*, Article XVIII, quoted in, *Creeds of the Churches*, p. 73-74.

[1162] *Here I Stand*, p. 196-97.

[1163] *Eerdman's Handbook to the History of Christianity*, p. 381.

[1164] Article X, quoted in, *Creeds of the Churches*, p. 137.

[1165] Chapter III, Section III, quoted in, *Creeds of the Churches*, p. 198.

[1166] *The Westminster Confession of Faith*, Chapter III, Section V, VII, Chapter XI, Section V, quoted in, *Creeds of the Churches*, p. 198-99, 207.

[1167] *The Westminster Confession of Faith*, Chapter XVII, Section I, II, quoted in, *Creeds of the Churches*, p. 212.

[1168] Romans 2:6-11.

[1169] Hebrews 5:9.

[1170] 1 Timothy 2:3-4.

[1171] Joseph McSorley, *An Outline History of the Church by Centuries* (B.Herder 1957), p. 124, quoted in, *Apostasy from the Divine Church*, p. 495.

[1172] *Catechism of the Catholic Church*, pars. 1730-31.

[1173] *Catechism of the Catholic Church*, pars. 1733-34.

[1174] Par. 1037.

[1175] *Catechism of the Catholic Church*, par. 1704.

[1176] *Mere Christianity*, p. 149.

[1177] *The Rites of the Catholic Church*, p. 90.

[1178] *The Rites of the Catholic Church*, p. 94, 314.

[1179] *Religions in America*, p. 144.

[1180] Alma 31:16-17.

[1181] Alma 31:30.

[1182] *Teachings of the Prophet Joseph Smith*, p. 189.

[1183] 2 Peter 1:10.

1184 *History of the Church of Jesus Christ of Latter-day Saints*, Vol. 3, p. 379-80.
1185 *The Doctrine and Covenants* 84:33-34.
1186 *Here I Stand*, p. 24.
1187 1 Timothy 4:1-3.
1188 1 Timothy 3:2
1189 Titus 1:5-6.
1190 1 Corinthians 11:11.
1191 Genesis 2:18.
1192 Genesis 2:24.
1193 Genesis 1:28.
1194 *The History of the Church from Christ to Constantine*, p. 140; Matthew 8:14, Luke 4:38, 1 Corinthians 9:5.
1195 *A Concise Guide to the Catholic Church*, p. 5.
1196 *A Concise Guide to the Catholic Church*, p. 118.
1197 *The Story of Civilization*, Vol. III, p. 662 note.
1198 *Catechism of the Catholic Church*, par. 1580.
1199 *The Story of Civilization*, Vol. IV, p. 541-42.
1200 *Eerdman's Handbook to the History of Christianity*, p. 216.
1201 Philip Schaff, *History of the Christian Church*, p. 53, quoted in, *The Story of Civilization*, Vol. VI, p. 407.
1202 *Here I Stand*, p. 234.
1203 *Here I Stand*, p. 264.
1204 Article XXIII, quoted in, *Creeds of the Churches*, p. 81.
1205 *Augsburg Confession*, Article XXVII, quoted in, *Creeds of the Churches*, p. 92.
1206 *Here I Stand*, p. 156.
1207 *Second Helvetic Confession*, Article XXIX, quoted in, *Creeds of the Churches*, p. 188.
1208 *Second Helvetic Confession*, Article XVIII, quoted in, *Creeds of the Churches*, p. 153.
1209 *The Westminster Confession of Faith*, Chapter XXII, Section VII, quoted in, *Creeds of the Churches*, p. 219.
1210 The *Augsburg Confession*, Article XVI, quoted in, *Creeds of the Churches*, p. 73.
1211 *An Introduction to Canon Law*, p. 63 (Canon 277); p. 95
1212 *The Rites of the Catholic Church*, p. 730.
1213 *The Rites of the Catholic Church*, p. 727-28.
1214 *The Christian Faith in the Doctrinal Documents of the Catholic*

Church, p. 691.

1215 *Catechism of the Catholic Church*, par. 2231.

1216 *Catechism of the Catholic Church*, par. 2233.

1217 *An Introduction to Canon Law*, p. 133 (Canons 1061, 1141); *Catechism of the Catholic Church*, par. 1640, 2382.

1218 Matthew 19:6; *Catechism of the Catholic Church*, par. 1614.

1219 *Catechism of the Catholic Church*, par. 2388

1220 *Catechism of the Catholic Church*, pars. 2384, 1650.

1221 *An Introduction to Canon Law*, p. 140.

1222 *Catechism of the Catholic Church*, par. 1638.

1223 Mark 12:25, 1 Corinthians 7:31; *Catechism of the Catholic Church*, par. 1619.

1224 *Catechism of the Catholic Church*, pars. 2366, 2370.

1225 *Catechism of the Catholic Church*, par. 2272.

1226 *Religions in America*, p. 84; *A Commentary on the Holy Bible*, p. 643.

1227 Article on Marriage, *History of the Church of Jesus Christ of Latter-day Saints*, Vol. 2, p. 247.

1228 *Teachings of the Prophet Joseph Smith*, p. 300-01.

1229 Matthew 22:30 (22:23-33), *The Doctrine and Covenants* 132:15-16.

1230 *Catechism of the Catholic Church*, pars. 2665, 2670.

1231 *The Rites of the Catholic Church*, p. 459, 461, 580.

1232 *Catechism of the Catholic Church*, par. 2616, 2621; see also 2665, 2668.

1233 *Catechism of the Catholic Church*, par. 2670.

1234 *Catechism of the Catholic Church*, par. 2676.

1235 *The Penguin Dictionary of Saints*, p. 9.

1236 *The Penguin Dictionary of Saints*, p. 23.

1237 *A Concise Guide to the Catholic Church*, p. 127.

1238 *Philosophical Dictionary*, p. 152, fn. 1.

1239 *Eerdman's Handbook to the History of Christianity*, p. 80.

1240 *A Concise Guide to the Catholic Church*, p. 13.

1241 *The Penguin Dictionary of Saints*, p. 10.

1242 *The Story of Civilization*, Vol. IV, p. 743.

1243 *The Penguin Dictionary of Saints*, p. 12, 25.

1244 *The Penguin Dictionary of Saints*, p. 22.

1245 *The Penguin Dictionary of Saints*, p. 12-13, 24.

1246 *Eerdman's Handbook to the History of Christianity*, p. 296.

1247 *Eerdman's Handbook to the History of Christianity*, p. 342.

1248 *Apostasy from the Divine Church*, p. 534-35.

1249 *The Penguin Dictionary of Saints*, p. 236.
1250 *A Concise Guide to the Catholic Church*, p. 58.
1251 *True Devotion to Mary*, p. ix, x.
1252 Id. p. 70-71.
1253 Id. p. 210.
1254 Id. p. v, xx.
1255 *Religions in America*, p. 25.
1256 *The Rites of the Catholic Church*, p. 149-50, 459-61.
1257 *The Rites of the Catholic Church*, p. 393.
1258 *The Rites of the Catholic Church*, p. 553.
1259 *Second Helvetic Confession*, Article XXIII, quoted in, *Creeds of the Churches*, p. 177-78.
1260 Luke 2:7.
1261 Matthew 1:18-25.
1262 Matthew 12:46, 13:55, Mark 6:3, John 2:12, Acts 1:14, Galatians 1:19.
1263 *A Commentary on the Holy Bible*, p. 670-71,
1264 *The Father is Not the Son*, Preface, p. viii.
1265 *Eerdman's Handbook to the History of Christianity*, p. 132.
1266 *Augsburg Confession*, Article XXI, quoted in, *Creeds of the Churches*, p. 78.
1267 *The Westminster Confession of Faith*, Chapter XXI, Section II, quoted in, *Creeds of the Churches*, p. 217.
1268 *Eerdman's Handbook to the History of Christianity*, p. 505.
1269 Ineffabilis Deus, *Histoire Generale de l'Eglise*, Vol. ix p. 407, quoted in, *Apostasy from the Divine Church*, p. 618-19.
1270 Pars. 411, 491.
1271 Par. 493.
1272 *A Concise Guide to the Catholic Church*, p. 26, 29.
1273 *A Concise Guide to the Catholic Church*, p. 58.
1274 *Catechism of the Catholic Church*, par. 966.
1275 *Catechism of the Catholic Church*, par. 969.
1276 *Catechism of the Catholic Church*, par. 971.
1277 *Catechism of the Catholic Church*, par. 2030.
1278 *Religions in America*, pp, 83, 87.
1279 *The Penguin Dictionary of Saints*, p. 17.
1280 *An Introduction to Canon Law*, p. 142 (Canon 1186).
1281 *Catechism of the Catholic Church*, par. 828.
1282 *Catechism of the Catholic Church*, par. 2683.
1283 *A Manual of Church History*, Vol. 1, p. 297-98, quoted in, *Apostasy*

from the Divine Church, p. 543.
[1284] *Apostasy from the Divine Church*, p. 694.
[1285] *A Concise Guide to the Catholic Church*, p. 6.
[1286] *Here I Stand*, p. 53.
[1287] Vol. 1, p. 390, quoted in, *Apostasy from the Divine Church*, p. 694.
[1288] *Here I Stand*, p. 35-36.
[1289] *Medieval Church Treasuries*, p. 45.
[1290] *The Story of Civilization*, Vol. IV, p. 743-44.
[1291] *Here I Stand*, p. 231.
[1292] *An Introduction to Canon Law*, p. 144 (Canons 1237, 1239).
[1293] *A Concise Guide to the Catholic Church*, p. 146.
[1294] *Creeds of the Churches*, p. 22, 24.
[1295] John 10:30.
[1296] John 10:38.
[1297] John 14:9.
[1298] *Creeds of the Churches*, p. 3, 28.
[1299] *Eerdman's Handbook to the History of Christianity*, p. 162.
[1300] *A Commentary on the Holy Bible*, p. cxiii.
[1301] *Syntopicon*, "Theology," Vol. 2, p. 698.
[1302] Id.
[1303] Par. 237.
[1304] *Catechism of the Catholic Church*, par. 251.
[1305] *The Story of Civilization*, Vol. III, p. 607-11.
[1306] *The Story of Civilization*, Vol. III, p. 501-02.
[1307] *Syntopicon*, "Theology," Vol. 2, p. 700, *Great Books of the Western World.*
[1308] *Offenders for a Word*, p. 69.
[1309] *Eerdman's Handbook to the History of Christianity*, p. 496.
[1310] *Eerdman's Handbook to the History of Christianity*, p. 494.
[1311] *The Story of Civilization*, Vol. VIII, p. 239, 543.
[1312] Matthew 5-7.
[1313] Matthew 3:13-17, Matthew 17:5.
[1314] John 17:11, 21.
[1315] Deuternonomy 17:6, 19:5, Matthew 18:16, 2 Corinthians 13:1.
[1316] John 8:16-18.
[1317] *Catechism of the Catholic Church*, pars. 202, 230, 237.
[1318] Acts 17:55-56.
[1319] Romans 8:34; see also Hebrews 7:25; 9:24; 1 Timothy 2:5; 1 John 2:1; John 14:6.

1320 Matthew 6:9.

1321 Mark 10:18.

1322 Mark 13: 32.

1323 Mark 14:36.

1324 John 5:19 (17-47).

1325 John 17:3; see also John 7:16-17, 28-29, 33, 8:16, 26-27, 29, 38.

1326 Quoted in, *The Father is Not the Son*, p. 33.

1327 Against the Heresy of Noetus, pp, 7, 11, quoted in, *Apostasy from the Divine Church*, p. 43-44. Accord, Novatian, Concerning the Trinity, XXVI and Origen, Id.

1328 John 15:26.

1329 *Catechism of the Catholic Church*, pars. 202, 446.

1330 John 8:52-58 (compare Exodus 3:14); Matthew 22:41-46, Mark 12:35-37, *Catechism of the Catholic Church*, par. 202.

1331 Colossians 1:15, Psalms 89:27, Romans 8:29, Revelation 3:14.

1332 Ephesians 3:9, Colossians 1:16-17, 1 Corinthians 8:6, John 1:3.

1333 Genesis 1:26.

1334 Genesis 3:5.

1335 Genesis 3:22.

1336 Ether 3:6-17, *The Book of Mormon.*

1337 *A Commentary on the Holy Bible*, p. xxxvi-xxxvii.

1338 Genesis 2:5, Moses 3:5, Abraham 4, 5:1-3, *The Pearl of Great Price.*

1339 Jeremiah 1:4-5.

1338 8:19-20.

1339 Jude 1:6.

1342 *The Rites of the Catholic Church*, p. 1098.

1343 *Christian Religions: A Comparative Chart*, Vol. 1.

1344 John 1:1-2, 6:62, 17:5.

1345 Job 38:4-7.

1346 Acts 11:26.

1347 Alma 46:13-15.

1348 3 Nephi 27:3-11, *The Book of Mormon.*

1349 *The Doctrine and Covenants* 115:4.

1350 *Second Helvetic Confession*, Article XVII, quoted in, *Creeds of the Churches*, p. 141.

1351 p. 7.

1352 *A Commentary on the Holy Bible*, p. xcvi; cxliii.

1353 *Catechism of the Catholic Church*, par. 946.

1354 *Catechism of the Catholic Church*, par. 1309.

1355 *Catechism of the Catholic Church*, par. 823.
1356 Par. 66.
1357 Par. 65.
1358 Par. 523.
1359 Par. 719.
1360 *The Westminster Confession of Faith* (1646), Chapter 1, Section 1, quoted in, *Creeds of the Churches*, p. 193.
1361 *The Westminster Confession of Faith* (1646), Chapter 1, Section VI, quoted in, *Creeds of the Churches*, p. 195.
1362 *A Concise Guide to the Catholic Church*, p. 145.
1363 Joseph McSorley, *An Outline History of the Church by Centuries* (B. Herder 1957), note, p. xiii, quoted in, *Apostasy from the Divine Church*, note, p. 5.
1364 *A Commentary on the Holy Bible*, p. liii.
1365 Quoted in, *Apostasy from the Divine Church*, p. 41.
1366 *The Westminster Confession of Faith* (1646), Chapter 1, Section III, quoted in, *Creeds of the Churches*, p. 195.
1367 Revelation 22:18-19.
1368 Deuteronomy 4:2.
1369 Acts 13:1.
1370 Acts 15:32.
1371 Amos 3:7.
1372 *History of the Church of Jesus Christ of Latter-day Saints*, Vol. 3, p. 28.
1373 *History of the Church of Jesus Christ of Latter-day Saints*, Vol. 1, p. 278.
1374 The Articles of Faith, *The Pearl of Great Price*, p. 61
1375 *History of the Church of Jesus Christ of Latter-day Saints*, Vol. 5, p. 135.
1376 Hugh B. Brown, He Does Speak, in *Best Loved Stories of the LDS People*, Vol. 1, p. 279-82.
1377 *A Concise Guide to the Catholic Church*, p. 120.
1378 *Catechism of the Catholic Church*, par. 2116.
1379 p. 61-63.
1380 *A Concise Guide to the Catholic Church*, p. 147.
1381 *Signs and Symbols in Christian Art*, p. 49.
1382 *Signs and Symbols in Christian Art*, p. 96.
1383 Vol. XIII, Article "Revelation," p. 4, quoted in, *Apostasy from the Divine Church*, p. 654.

1384 See 1 Corinthians 12:1-12, *The Doctrine and Covenants* 46:10-26.
1385 *Religions in America*, p. 164-66.
1386 *Christian Religions: A Comparative Chart*, Vol 1.
1387 *Christian Religions: A Comparative Chart*, Vol 2.
1388 Luke 16:19-31.
1389 *Second Helvetic Confession*, Article XXVI, quoted in, *Creeds of the Churches*, p. 184.
1390 *Apostasy from the Divine Church*, p. 493.
1391 *Apostasy from the Divine Church*, p. 493.
1392 *Catechism of the Catholic Church*, pars. 1031, 1032.
1393 *A Concise Guide to the Catholic Church*, p. 132.
1394 *Syntopicon*, "Immortality," p. 610, *Great Books of the Western World.*
1395 *Catechism of the Catholic Church*, par. 1022.
1396 *A Concise Guide to the Catholic Church*, p. 135.
1397 Matthew 7:14.
1398 Matthew 22:14.
1399 Mark 16:16.
1400 *The Story of Civilization*, Vol. IV, p. 734.
1401 *A Concise Guide to the Catholic Church*, p. 138.
1402 Introduction, Section 76, *The Doctrine and Covenants.*
1403 John 14:2.
1404 Luke 16:19-31; Alma 40:11-14, *The Book of Mormon.*
1405 1 Peter 3:18-19, 4:6.
1406 *The Doctrine and Covenants* 138.
1407 *The Doctrine and Covenants* 76:51-53.
1408 *The Doctrine and Covenants* 137.
1409 *The Doctrine and Covenants* 76:62.
1410 *The Doctrine and Covenants* 88:97-98.
1411 *The Doctrine and Covenants* 132:22; Matthew 7:13-14.
1412 *The Doctrine and Covenants* 131:1-2, 132:19; *Teachings of the Prophet Joseph Smith*, p. 300-01.
1413 *The Doctrine and Covenants* 76:72-79.
1414 *The Doctrine and Covenants* 88:99.
1415 *The Doctrine and Covenants* 76: 82-85, 112; 88:101.
1416 *The Doctrine and Covenants* 76: 25-39; see Matthew 12:31-33, Alma 39:6, *The Book of Mormon*; see also *The Doctrine and Covenants* 42:18, 84:40-41.
1417 *The Doctrine and Covenants* 138:30, 57.
1418 Acts 10:35; *The Doctrine and Covenants* 76:38, 42-44.

[1419] 2 Chronicles Chapters 5-7.
[1420] Ezra Chapters 1-6.
[1421] Exodus 26, 27.
[1422] Luke 2:22-39.
[1423] Luke 2:41-49.
[1424] Matthew 21:12; Mark 11:15; Luke 19:45; John 2:14.
[1425] John 8:20; Mark 12:41-44.
[1426] *Book of Prayers*, p. 10.
[1427] Zechariah 1:16.
[1428] *Catechism of the Catholic Church*, par. 593.
[1429] 2 Nephi 5:16, Jacob 1:17, 2:2, 11, Mosiah 1:18, Alma 10:2, 16:13, 3 Nephi 11:1.
[1430] *The Doctrine and Covenants* 88:119, 95:8.
[1431] *The Doctrine and Covenants* 110:7-8.
[1432] *The Doctrine and Covenants* 95:8, 110:9.
[1433] 1 Peter 3:18-19, *The Doctrine and Covenants* 138.
[1434] 1 Corinthians 15:29.
[1435] *Teachings of the Prophet Joseph Smith*, p. 331.
[1436] *Teachings of the Prophet Joseph Smith*, p. 224.
[1437] Revelations 21:22.
[1438] Amos 3:7.
[1439] Mark 3:14, Luke 6:13, John 15:16.
[1438] Luke 10:1, 17.
[1439] Philippians 1:1, 1 Timothy 3:15, Titus 1:7, Ephesians 4:11.
[1442] Acts 14:23, Titus 1:5, James 5:14.
[1443] Ephesians 4:11, Acts 21:8, 2 Timothy 4:5.
[1444] 1 Corinthians 12:28, Ephesians 4:11.
[1445] Philippians 1:1, 1 Timothy 3:8.
[1446] Ephesians 2:19-20.
[1447] John 17:11, 21.
[1448] Ephesians 4:5.
[1449] *Religions in America*, pp 255-56.
[1448] *Religions in America*, p. 255-57.
[1449] Id.
[1452] Id.
[1453] *The Doctrine and Covenants* 21:1.
[1454] *The Doctrine and Covenants* 21:4-6.
[1455] *The Doctrine and Covenants* 81:1-2, 90:6, 107:22.
[1456] Matthew 17:1, Mark 9:2.

[1457] Mark 5:37.
[1458] Matthew 26:37, Mark 14:33.
[1459] *The Doctrine and Covenants* 18:26-32, 107:33.
[1458] *The Doctrine and Covenants* 107:25, 34, 93-97.
[1459] The Articles of Faith, No. 6, *The Pearl of Great Price*, p. 60.
[1462] *Teachings of the Prophet Joseph Smith*, p. 111.
[1463] *Teachings of the Prophet Joseph Smith*, p. 21.
[1464] *The Doctrine and Covenants* 124:126.
[1465] *The Doctrine and Covenants* 20:63, 65-66, 26:2, 28:13, 38:4, 41:9, 124:144; cf. 1 Samuel 8:4-22.
[1466] *An Introduction to Canon Law*, p. 166 (Canon 1262); see also, *Catechism of the Catholic Church*, par. 1351.
[1467] *Eerdman's Handbook to the History of Christianity*, p. 190.
[1468] *The Story of Civilization*, Vol. IV, p. 765-67.
[1469] *An Introduction to Canon Law*, p. 20.
[1470] *An Introduction to Canon Law*, p. 88.
[1471] *Apostasy from the Divine Church*, p. 726.
[1472] *Here I Stand*, p. 201.
[1473] *An Introduction to Canon Law*, p. 25.
[1474] *Eerdman's Handbook to the History of Christianity*, p. 340-42.
[1475] *Catechism of the Catholic Church*, par. 2042.
[1476] *An Introduction to Canon Law*, p. 63 (Canon 281).
[1477] *An Introduction to Canon Law*, p. 118(Canons 952, 1264); p. 142 (Canon 1181); *A Concise Guide to the Catholic Church*, p. 152.
[1478] *Catechism of the Catholic Church*, par. 2122.
[1479] *An Introduction to Canon Law*, p. 124 (Canon 945); *A Concise Guide to the Catholic Church*, p. 152.
[1480] *A Concise Guide to the Catholic Church*, p. 154.
[1481] Article, "So You're Going to Live in Europe? Say Hello to the Church Tax," Journal of Commerce, August 13, 1997, p. 28C.
[1482] *Understanding Islam*, p. 18-19.
[1483] Genesis 14:20, Genesis 28:22, Leviticus 27:30, Numbers 18:26,Deuteronomy 14:22, 2 Chronicles 31:5, Malachi 3:8; Luke 18:12, *The Doctrine and Covenants* 64:23, 85:3, 97:12, 119:4.
[1484] *The Doctrine and Covenants* 56:16-17.
[1485] Moroni 7:16, *The Book of Mormon*; *The Doctrine and Covenants* 84:46.
[1486] *The Doctrine and Covenants* 123:12.
[1487] John 7:16-17.

[1488] Moroni 10:3-5.

[1489] Matthew 13:45-46.

[1490] *Teachings of the Prophet Joseph Smith*, p. 275.

[1491] *History of the Church of Jesus Christ of Latter-day Saints*, Vol. 5, p. 499.

[1492] *Discourses of Brigham Young*, p. 3.

[1493] *The Philosophical Basis of Mormonism*, p. 42.

[1494] *Teachings of the Prophet Joseph Smith*, p. 139.

[1495] John 3:7.

[1496] John 3:11, cf. 1 John 1:6.

[1497] *Discourses of Brigham Young*, p. 220.

[1498] Philippians 4:7.

[1499] Alma 5:45-46, *The Book of Mormon.*

[1500] 1 Peter 3:15.

Index

ABOUT THE AUTHOR

Thomas E. Johnson is an attorney, originally from Nephi, Utah, who has been living in Chicago for the past 30 years. He attended Snow College, the University of Utah and Northwestern University. He served a mission for The Church of Jesus Christ of Latter-day Saints in Japan. He is a former bishop and stake president in The Church of Jesus Christ of Latter-day Saints. He is married to Norma Lee Christensen and they have five children—Mary Melinda, Elisabeth, Eve, Susanna and Heidi.